"In this debut Chicago-set crime novel, police nickname a brutal serial killer Slugger because he beats his victims with a "bat-like weapon" and leaves a folded, collectible baseball card.

...fans of gritty crime stories and methodical police work will find the book a page-turner, complete with notable characters, dialogue, and descriptions ("He guessed her at six foot two and skinny as a Ball Park frank"). Names and depictions of Chicago attractions and streets are accurate, with the exception that Canarytown is most likely a stand-in for Canaryville, a community on the city's South Side that was originally a largely Irish neighborhood.

The authors hit this one out of the park; a highly recommended mystery."

—Kirkus Indie

CANARYTOWN

City of Grief

A NOVEL

M. BROOKE MCCULLOUGH
and J.E. BOYDSTON

PAGE PUBLISHING, INC.
Conneaut Lake, PA

First originally published by Page Publishing 2020

ISBN 978-1-6624-0538-9 (pbk)
ISBN 978-1-6624-0539-6 (digital)

Printed in the United States of America

Acknowledgments

There is no limit to my gratitude for the love of my family and friends who believed in me and this journey I began. With deepest thanks to my daughter, Shannon, who, due to her interest for Victorian romance, helped me create the perfect love scene, and my son, Tim, for his invaluable assistance in advising me on Chicago police protocol and all the nuances of investigative work, which all became part of the exciting memorable chapters throughout the story. I could never have started or continued on with my project without the involvement of my friends checking the pages to ensure I dotted my *Is* and crossed my *Ts*, in addition to the helpful suggestions, all the love, and promptings from myriad family and friends that in some way all contributed to the success of the story. I am deeply grateful, and I love you all.

And last but never the least, I will be forever grateful to my brother, Joel, for his patience and unwavering belief in me and trust that I would finish my story. With his assistance and an uncanny knack for details and edits, we were able to blow the dust off my original characters and breathe new life into my story, and that's when my story became our story. Thank you, brother.

M. Brooke McCullough

* * *

I owe an everlasting debt of gratitude to my family and friends for their support, advice, and encouragement over the many years it took to complete this work. My foremost bow is to my dear sister, Brooke, whose inspiration and creativity gave birth to this work. This is your baby, sis, and I'm proud to say we raised it together. My love to you all.

I would be remiss if I neglected to also acknowledge those others who contributed directly and indirectly to our efforts: William (my bro) Boydston, Ron and Linda Ludwin, Gary Winokur and Liz Lafalce, John Chaplick, Barbara Dandro, Wendy Samford, C. J. (the one with a song in her heart), Pat O'Shea, and Joe Collier, photo contributor for the Graceland Cemetery and valuable story resource.

J. E. Boydston

Through me lies the road to the city of grief.
Through me lies the pathway of woe everlasting.
Through me lies the road to the souls that are lost.
—Dante Alighieri

CHAPTER 1

A gauzy mist crept along the deserted street, drifting in and out of the darkened doorways of late-night Canarytown. Moved by the night breeze, it enveloped everything in its icy embrace. The muffled sound of a lone walker's footsteps came to a halt outside a pub door. The squeaking complaint of the door heralded a dark stranger's entrance into the quiet solitude of the interior.

The droopy-eyed bartender glanced at his watch with a shrug of his shoulders as Sade softly sang "Your Love Is King" from the jukebox. Four men seated at separate tables along the far wall of the room, all on their last hollow leg, bobbed their heads over cocktails, all dreading the inevitable last call.

The visitor, wearing a dark fedora, opened the top of his high-collared trench coat, approached the bar, and ordered a brandy.

From a distant corner of the room, two women studied the mysterious newcomer with narrowed eyes, vultures hovering over newfound carrion. They exchanged glances, confirming territorial rights, taking a quick measure of the new visitor while he twisted the glass in his gloved hand, in no hurry to taste the liquid. The dark corner of the bar where he stood made him look even more mysterious to the hungry women. They exchanged a few words before the shorter and heavier of the two rose from her chair. She wriggled to straighten her clinging knit miniskirt and patted her teased hair before she ambled across to where he stood.

The man guessed she could be Spanish or mulatto but couldn't tell in the dim light. She slid onto the adjacent barstool and leaned in toward him, allowing her melon-sized breasts to brush against his arm. Her cheap perfume did not mask the smell of stale tobacco that clung to her hair.

"Hello, mister. You look to be the sort of gentleman who'd buy a lady a drink before this hop house closes," she purred as she rubbed her hand up and down the length of her fleshy thigh. The stranger nodded to the bartender without raising his eyes from the rock glass in his hand.

"My, aren't you the quiet one," she teased as she accepted the fresh drink. "That's okay. I like the strong, silent type. Are you lonely, sugar? Maybe new to this part of town? We don't see many suits this side of Halsted."

"What's your name?" the man whispered.

"Whatever you want it to be, honey. Names ain't important in my line of work."

"What's your name?" he repeated in a raised voice.

The young woman fidgeted in her seat, alarmed by his abruptness, "Ruby. The name's Ruby, 'cause of my red hair and all." She tilted her head closer to the man and pointed. "Look. You might think it's dark brown at first, but it's red. Got it from my old lady. She's Irish, don't cha know, though she always said my old man was Jamaican."

"There someplace we can be alone?"

"Sure, sure. You wanna go now? Without even knowin' my charge?"

"I'll give you whatever you ask. Name your price. I'll make sure you get what you've earned."

"Say, you ain't a cop or somethin', are ya? I can smell 'em a mile away," she said, edging back a little on her stool.

His hand reached out for her so swiftly she didn't see it before he locked it around her wrist. "No, I'm not a cop."

The woman smacked her chewing gum and giggled, glancing around the room. Only two other people were in the bar now— both passed out at their tables. Her intuition screamed at her to walk away from this cold stranger, to give him to her friend if she wanted him. She preferred the rough ones anyway. For several indecisive moments, she sat motionless and mute. She reasoned that she needed the money and convinced herself she could handle almost anything for half an hour. She turned to give a nod to her girlfriend and noticed she'd left. The bitch had split after losing her shot.

"So are we on?" he prodded.

"Sure, sure, mister, I gotcha. It's just you worried me there for a minute. A lady has to be careful, ya know. I can't afford another pinch by vice again this month. I'm a working gal, and my rent don't get paid if I'm locked up."

"Then let's go." He reached into his pocket and threw several folded bills on the bar. She held her faux fur coat out to him, but when he ignored her, she threw it around her shoulders herself. As the door closed behind them, a cold chill flooded the room, and the dim ceiling lights stirred on their brass chains. The weary bartender put the bills in his pocket and drank the untouched brandy left on the bar.

* * *

The shadowy, cloaked figure retreated unobserved from an alleyway that ran between two weathered brick buildings a few blocks from the Pour House Tavern. Gusts of wind whistled through the street. The vengeful blasts blew with a force that fought the stranger's progress down the deserted street. Flashes of lightning tore across the sky, accompanied by muffled thunder. The streetlight blinked twice and went dark, signaling an approaching storm. He leaned into the wind and moved swiftly now. When he reached the corner, he darted across the street, clutching a pair of pink silk panties tucked in his coat pocket. He turned the corner and vanished.

CHAPTER 2

It was reported as one of the wettest springs on record, and an early morning mist graduated to a persistent drizzle and finally a steady, pelting rain when Detectives Kyle McNally and Sam Weller arrived. Another hooker had turned up mauled and murdered in Canarytown sometime the night before. There were now three murders with nearly identical signatures. It looked to be the Canarytown Slugger's signature. The name was pinned on him by cops after the second one. It was done in the tavern district of south-central Chicago, late at night. With no identification found on her, she'd ended up wearing a Jane Doe toe tag.

In the first officer's report, a patrol car arrived to investigate a victim found lying on the pavement in an alleyway with her legs splayed wide, underpants missing. She'd been bludgeoned to death and left with a folded Chicago White Sox baseball card inserted in her vagina. Visible signs of the brutality included blunt-force contusions; blood splatters and viscera around the head, shoulders, trunk; and mutilated flesh in and around the labia and vulva. The battering left the victim's face caved-in and featureless—nose crushed, eye sockets pulverized and flattened against what remained of formless indentations that once were the victim's cheeks.

By the time the duty medical examiner (or ME) arrived, they had cordoned off, photographed, and begun an initial site survey. Kyle identified himself and Sam as lead investigators. The two previous victims had signature collector cards of Tommy John and Eddie Fisher, both members of the 1965 team. The ME took the body temperature, made an initial estimation of the time of death, and prepared the body for transport to the morgue. After McNally informed him that two prior victims had ketamine residue in their blood, he agreed to order toxicology labs STAT. They believed the attacker first choked his victims to disable them before injecting them with a low dose of ketamine, called Special-K on the street. That gave him time to relocate his victims before they regained consciousness when he began his "artwork." The approximate time of death was estimated between 2:00 and 4:00 a.m.

While Sam did a walk around of the immediate area to verify security and search for evidence, Kyle made notes documenting the scene and the overall condition, placement, and appearance of the body. He assigned a member of his team, Detective Tony Petrocelli, to canvas the nearby neighborhood for leads.

Petrocelli found one interesting lead on a witness. A Mrs. Ziomecki, who lived nearby, heard something unusual earlier the previous night. Kyle would let him conduct the initial interview, and then, if it looked promising, he'd follow up.

Shortly after the photographer finished and left the scene, McNally, rain-soaked and feeling frustrated at the lack of physical evidence found, was ready to return to headquarters.

"Hey, Sam, we're wrapped here. What say we get back to the department and take care of the paperwork. I need to dry off and get more java in my veins," McNally said.

"I'm all in, amigo, but how about we stop for a burger on the way. Okay?"

"You feeling a need for one of your heart attack specials? Add in cheese, a slice of tomato, a lettuce leaf with an order of fries, and you've covered four of the five major food groups, right? All we need to do now is drive by an apple tree, and you'll have covered them all." Kyle smiled with one eyebrow raised.

"I'm gonna keep eating 'em as long as you insist on playing that crapical music on the radio when I'm ridin' with you, Streetoven. Yeah, so doubt me all you want, partner, but bet I'll still beat you in a forty-yard dash."

Kyle laughed out loud as he drove away. "Right. Maybe if I gave you a twenty-yard head start."

CHAPTER 3

McNally loathed this nasty weather, especially the icy wind, loud and persistent, screaming like hordes of tortured souls from the seventh circle of hell. He smelled the rain coming, again. Already late March, and it hadn't made up its mind whether it was still winter or just stumbling around, trying to find spring. Though they called Chicago the Windy City, named after a handful of blustering politicians in the thirties, he believed the name was derived from the incessant winds that tried to blow the city off the map. As a boy, he'd loved thunderstorms; their persistent violence fascinated him. Nature had inspired him then. Now it was only one more thing to irritate the hell out of him.

He had come to meet his informant, Ezekiel Love, who went by EZ Love in the neighborhood, to see if he'd caught anything in the wind about the Slugger. The three recent hooker vics were murdered there—the latest one, yesterday.

He rubbed his eyes and frowned at the grim reflection in the rearview mirror of his wet hair curled close to his scalp. The circles under his eyes combined with his unshaven face gave him a sinister look. Why did it seem like every time he met with EZ, it was during one of these hateful storms?

Fate, fortune, or an omen?

McNally cracked the window, started the car, and popped the defrost fan to full blast. As the warm air settled around the close confines of the car, he watched with detached fascination as the first raindrops exploded against the windshield. The invading mist cooled his face. He watched as the wind gusts trapped themselves between buildings, twisting in search of escape. The wind lifted the rain upward in long shiny tentacles that reached through the broken tenement windows, whipping the torn, wet curtains in and out of the skeletal openings in the dozens of long-abandoned apartments.

He compared the city to a leviathan, with this place smack in the center of its bowels. Kyle found both this neighborhood and EZ equally oppressive and offensive. EZ called this place home. He chose it because of how easily he could disappear into the empty buildings.

These days, Kyle flirted with the notion of dropping out of the rat race and finding a nice little sheriff's job in Podunk, USA, a place where crime meant the local high school boys drinking too much on Saturday night and "tipping" Farmer Jones's cows for fun. A wry smile crossed his lips.

Even his longtime partner, Sam Weller, told him he'd been working the streets too long. Maybe he was right. He viewed it all as a man-made shit pile camouflaged by a forest of steel girders and copper-tinted glass. Its beauty fooled so many here. Most of them hadn't a clue they lived in a city where architectural works of art disguised a monster in its belly.

He needed a break in this case soon. The press hadn't connected the dots that the three gruesome murders were serial crimes yet. When McNally came across the earlier site reports, he recognized the connections. The initial reports from the coroner only identified them as Jane Does. Given the neighborhoods they were found in, he'd pegged them as hookers. The thinking went that they'd either strayed onto the wrong streets or were victims of unhappy Johns— toe tags on unclaimed bodies. There'd also been little initial interest in the department as there were no missing persons reports filed. The media overlooked them as just more violent crimes against prostitutes. That was not uncommon in a city of millions. But an important piece of the story never made the police reports; in a well-intentioned effort to discourage copycats, the baseball cards were omitted from the report.

It had only been a few weeks since the first body turned up under the Halsted El station. The second body was discovered near Sherman Park and the third near the Thirty-Fifth Street station and Comiskey Park on Wentworth. All bodies found were missing their underwear and had no identification. They'd been hideously beaten with a club and raped after the assault with the same weapon. With faceless masks of torn flesh, their bodies were left with few unbroken bones. All had collector cards from the midsixties inserted in their vaginas.

The killer had been cunning so far—no finger or footprints, no bite marks, no blood or other DNA of any kind found, nothing at all for the CSI team.

Kyle ordered his team to keep the collector cards out of the police reports. His supervisor, Commander Rouse, opposed it until Kyle reminded him it reflected on his management image and would draw bad publicity. The superintendent would appreciate his discretion until they delivered solid leads.

The victims worked the New City area in a district known as the Back of the Yards, a neighborhood that had seen its share of changes since the mid-nineteenth century. About then, the first skilled German and Irish butchers began arriving to work in what would become the Union Stock Yards, made infamous in Upton Sinclair's book *The Jungle*. A coalition of the biggest railroads constructed the stockyards during the explosive growth of the national railway system and major improvements to refrigeration methods. Those two factors turned Chicago into the perfect midcontinent staging area for meat processing and distribution. The ethnic makeup of the area changed with time, becoming variously Polish, Czech, Lithuanian, Slovak, Chicano, and now mostly black enclaves. The death of the meat-packing industry in the sixties signaled the end of the middle class in this district.

Thinking the decades-old Chicago history only reminded Kyle of how much he hated change, whether in people, in partners, or in neighborhoods.

It's hard to give a damn when the carpet's always shifting under you.

CHAPTER 4

Restless and uncomfortable in his car, McNally sniffed the air, then himself. A high school locker room came to mind.

I'd pay a hundred bucks for a can of Mitchum deodorant, a change of shirt, and a bottle of Maker's Mark. Anything to burn away the scum. C'mon, let's move it, EZ!

As he waited in the dark, he questioned his reasons for calling the meeting. Could he trust anything EZ told him? EZ became his CI after Billie Fong floated to the surface in the Chicago River with a bullet in his brain during the Chinatown fiasco. McNally still blamed himself for loaning Billie to Drug Enforcement. Good informants like Billie came around only once or twice in a cop's career, while EZ had the endearing attributes of the ugly kid at an Arthur Murray dance class—always picked last.

McNally sank back into the car seat and scowled at the darkness through the window. Even Vivaldi's second movement of the "Spring" season symphony playing on the radio did little to relieve the edge from his impatience. He attempted to stretch his long cramped legs across the width of the seat.

I'd better get a break in this case soon before the media pieces together that Chicago has a serial killer.

EZ's distorted shadow snaked across the lot toward the car. EZ and Billie were as different as stink and scent. The best informants cleared good money between the feds and the city cops, but after the murder of Billie, EZ got skittish and greedy. He wanted both the money and the respect Billie had earned. But if he didn't stop talkin' shit, he'd end up like Billie. He claimed a bad cop put the .22 in Billie's head.

To this day, EZ would swear he knew the truth but refused to say any more without a big payday. And if he disappeared, he promised a recording he stashed would be delivered to *Eyewitness News*. McNally warned EZ he could be confirming his reservation in the cab of a hell-bound train. The DEA's field office believed he was a lying sack of shit and suggested he'd better watch his back. There were cops in the city who took that kind of talk personally. He was lucky to only catch a beating from CPD.

"Stupid son of a bitch," McNally mumbled. The commander would own his nuts if he found out about EZ, even though he paid him out of his own pocket. But McNally hadn't cut him loose, not yet anyway. Besides, EZ owed him a favor for taking him back in when everyone else treated him like he had AIDS. Kyle made him work a little harder for paydays now. EZ had no conscience but an eager eye for a Jefferson twenty, and that worked in the detective's favor.

"Where the fuck have you been, dickhead?" McNally snapped. He left him standing in the rain and watched EZ fidget and dance as he pulled his oversized army jacket closer around his head. EZ, a tall, skinny black guy with protruding lips and a lizard-like skull, reminded Kyle of the monster in the *Predator* movies. That head sat just beneath nasty, knotty dreads and a black leather baseball cap with a Sox logo. His dirty jacket partially hid a Marvel comic hero T-shirt. Even in the dark rain-soaked night, EZ wore mirrored sunglasses. He thought they made him invisible.

Out of breath and gasping for air from sprinting across the parking lot, EZ croaked, "You got my money, man? I'm gonna need plenty fo' dis. Yo! An' what's 'at tell you? You ain't paying me shit."

McNally snarled and lowered his window and reached his arm through to pat EZ's jacket pockets.

EZ jumped back. "Yo! What the shit? I ain't totin'. You got my money?"

"You know the routine, EZ. You better not be carrying around me. And it'd be a favor if I threw away that shit you've been drinking. It'll fry your brain and rot your liver. And I've already lost one informant."

Since Billie's murder, EZ had grown nervous. He bought a .22 and carried it with him almost everywhere. He'd close faster than a bear trap if he thought McNally didn't trust him.

The CI licked his thick lips, dancing in front of the window. "Jeeez-zus," he screeched. "Henry finds out I'm talkin' to 5-0, this nigga' gonna need to run hard. I been a fool telling you shit, man. C'mon, gimme a break, Mister Dick-tective. Yo gonna get me in some deep shit."

McNally had to resist the temptation to pull EZ through the window and beat the crap out of him. Even in the near darkness, McNally saw EZ Love's body fidgeting and rocking from side to side.

"Calm down, EZ. Take off those stupid sunglasses, and get in. I want to see your eyes when I'm talking to you." He nodded toward the front seat passenger side. "Just give me what you got, and I'll pay you. After that, you can go. Just don't leave the city. Last thing you want is to piss off me *and* your parole officer."

In the car now, EZ stared into cold green eyes that didn't say "Good to see you again." A chill shook his skinny frame. He understood the threat and remembered the last time he gave the cops bogus information to get a payoff. He received a beat-down he wouldn't soon forget.

EZ knew the Chinatown bust was bad from the start. Too bad for Billie The Triads found out. Then Billie said the wrong things to the wrong people. He'd tried to tell them a dirty cop steered the deal wrong. But those were Billie's last words before he took a bullet to the head. EZ saw him go in the river. He swore he'd never buy it the same way. He'd seen the cop who offed him, but didn't recognize him. So for now, he'd stopped talking about it. It was a pig problem, and EZ knew better than to mess with pig problems. Nothing but bad mojo there. But McNally treated him different. He came across righteous.

McNally smelled the thick fruity scent of cheap wine on EZ's breath. "I see you're still getting twisted on Mad Dog these days, right? I'm thinking with what you make off me, you can afford something that wouldn't make your breath stink like a dog's asshole. And who's this Henry you've been telling me about? Where can I find him?"

EZ showed excitement for the first time since he'd gotten into McNally's car. He turned and leaned toward McNally, his face and breath close enough to make Kyle's eyes water. "Yo, word is some cracker's beatin' Henry's hos. It ain't Henry. Heard this guy was tore up on crack or something. Henry's real mad and says it's some whitey who likes beatin' his trim, not fuckin' 'em." EZ leaned closer to McNally's ear. "Henry beats his hos too. Some thinkin' it be Henry doin' the beatin' and sayin' it's the cracker. Word is that one got beat by the cracker an' got away."

By now, EZ's hot, foul-smelling breath had created a dense cloud of suffocating noxious air. McNally saw the bulging whites of his eyes in the dark and sneered when EZ sprayed spittle against his dashboard as he described the fear among the prostitutes in the neighborhood.

"So where do I find Henry?"

EZ began hugging himself and rocking back and forth. "Don't know, man. Dat nigga ain't been seen fo' days."

"Where does he lay his head?"

"He be movin' lots lately."

"So what's Henry look like?"

"He's a big mothafucka. Maybe seven foot big!"

McNally's irritation at EZ's answers was rising like a boil on his ass. "Is he moving drugs? How many whores?"

"Crack. Yeah. An' more. Seven, ten hos."

"Does Henry carry a piece?"

"Nah, he don't. Just a big-ass walking stick."

Done asking questions and getting useless information, McNally sighed and said, "Enough! Sorry, EZ, but if that's the best you've got for me…" He handed EZ a twenty and a ten. "That's sad. Catch you later. Stay in touch."

"What! This all?" EZ whined, staring at the bills in his hand. "How you expect me to eat?"

"Get a job."

"I ain't fooling wit you, cop! This all I got. Why you trippin' on me, man? You don't fuck with dat nigga. His boys smoke anybody gets in his face. Yo! Henry got his own law. You don't cross him, not if you like breathin' in and out. Man, every ho in the hood freakin'. They ain't workin'. Dey ain't doing nothin'. Ole Henry making no snap, and he mothafuckin' mad—bad like nobody remembers. He crazy fucked up. Dat all I got. Why you dissin' me now?"

McNally pointed a threatening finger at EZ's face. "Now listen up, asshole. I don't give a shit about *your* personal problems. The number of dead women around this town is piling up, and you're giving me jack shit to work with. Do you think I'm stupid? You tell me some giant black guy who carries a big stick might be doing it, but that same black guy may know about a white guy that gets high who might be the perp. And there's a whore that got beat up by a white guy, but she got away, and you can't tell me who she is or where she went. She's mysteriously vanished. Nice try, EZ. Most pimps in this city beat their whores. You can't sell me that bullshit!" McNally reached across EZ and opened the door. "Now get the fuck out of my car."

"Yo, man. Why you trippin'? Henry don't need no piece. He got a big fuckin' stick. He takes it everywhere," EZ pleaded. "I seen it, man. You gotta believe I seen it. He'd soon as twist my cap off he hears 'bout me talkin' to you."

McNally grabbed EZ by the collar. "You find me Henry, and don't stop until you do. If another woman dies, EZ, you'll beg for Henry's stick before I'm done with you. Now take you and your shitty Mad Dog breath out of my car!"

EZ started to leave. "Aight, aight, I hear something, I do dat, man."

"Keep the money and consider yourself lucky," McNally said. "I want you to get word on the street that I need to talk to Henry. Say there's a lot of money in it for the person who finds him. There's a C-Note on the other side of that news. So say anything, EZ, but find him. You've got my pager number. Use it."

EZ slid out of the car, never taking his eyes off the detective. He stuffed the money into his pocket and, under his breath, muttered, "Yeah, an' fuck you too."

Then he was gone. McNally considered what he'd learned from EZ. Henry couldn't hide for long. He didn't get much, but at least he had a name, and his CI craved that C-Note.

McNally's thoughts drifted back to Chinatown. He'd spent a year's worth of grinding setup while working in cooperation with the Organized Crime Unit (OCD), painstaking time spent trying to catch up with the Chinatown drug operators. Rival gangs were blowing each other's brains out all over the area, and most of their coke, crack, and smack came from somewhere around Archer Avenue—so far, from an unknown source. There'd been no solid leads, though they were getting close. The mob blamed the Triads for the blood spilling, the Chinese blamed the black gangs, and the blacks blamed the Mexicans. Who blamed the mob? The US attorney, naturally.

The hit on Billie was professional—a .22-caliber bullet to the head, typically the mob's way of marking their kills. Love's claim of it being "in house" held no credibility in the squad room. McNally couldn't confirm or deny it.

The department took a lot of heat for the bad bust. After all their background work, the Organized Crime Division, aka OCD, made it clear they were there as backup only. It was funny, though, that when the deal went south, the Chicago PD took almost all the heat. When heads started to roll, Detective Liz Dumont and McNally topped the list. She'd been temporarily assigned to McNally, while his usual partner and best friend, Sam Weller, was out of pocket with a long-delayed court testimony commitment. OCD blamed Mac and Liz, and his commander unjustly pulled them off the case.

EZ just might make good for all the problems he caused if he delivered Henry.

I'll kiss EZ's twitchy black ass on the fifty-yard line at Soldier Field during a Bears game if Henry turns out to be the Slugger.

The howling wind and relentless rain were growing in ferocity, becoming deafening. McNally cursed the dark, knowing the storm was only beginning.

CHAPTER 5

On the morning after they found victim number four, Detective Liz Dumont lifted her large brown eyes and smiled at McNally when he entered the squad room. Liz—a five-foot-four-inch dynamo, eager to please, dedicated, and easy on the eyes—was a breath of fresh air in an office filled with overworked, pasty-faced investigators and their underlings.

To her credit, at thirty-two, she was the youngest of the seventy detectives in the division. There were just five females assigned to the Violent Crimes Unit, along with four male Hispanics and nine African Americans. The men and women who made up the unit were family to one another. They worked together and hung out together, and if they were lucky enough to have a good watch commander and a few capable lieutenants, life wasn't bad.

Liz grew up on the streets of Chicago, the daughter of a retired North Shore commander who some mistakenly believed pulled strings to get her assigned to Area 1 on the south side. It was a damned lie, and anyone with an ounce of sense should have known her accomplishments were based on both merit and having finished in the top 10 percent of a competitive cadet class. Desire and deter-mination to excel helped Detective Dumont break through the glass ceiling of the male promotional ladder, and in a couple more years, her well-earned reputation for hard work would make her eligible for a much-deserved increase in rank and pay.

"Hey, McNally, I didn't expect to see you today."

"I'm in and out. I wanted to pick up my messages and check on the progress of the interviews I assigned to the team. After that, I've got one of my own to conduct."

"Messages are on your desk. All forty of them. I think one of them is from your CI. The teams are out interviewing. No word back from them yet." Then she moved closer and spoke more quietly, "Is he still banging that drum on how he believes the department is covering for a bad cop on Billie's hit?"

"Yep. He's still certain one of us is on the take and put a bullet through his buddy's head."

Liz raised a questioning brow. "And you believe him? Sounds like a can of worms no one wants to see opened."

McNally grinned. "Don't worry, Lizzie. All we know is it's not you or me, right?"

"What's that supposed to mean?" Liz said, feigning indignation.

"Chill out, girl. EZ wouldn't be talking if he was suspicious. You and I took a hell of a lot of heat for that failed bust."

She grumbled, "And I won't be forgetting that soon. I've gotten shit cases ever since. I'm only assigned back with you until Sam's back from jury duty. But you're not hurting so bad. You got the Slugger assignment."

"Just a walk in the park, huh, Liz?"

Roy Ramirez overheard them and grumbled, "Yeah, and since she's back on temp assignment to you, I got no partner. But she's been helping me out a little." He patted his Selectric typewriter and grinned. "Some of us still have other things to work on."

"Meaning?" McNally asked.

"Meaning you never seem to catch any heat for your backlog like the rest of us."

"It must suck to be you, Romeo."

Ramirez laughed. "Yeah, story of my life. Shit storms and collateral damage all day every day."

Liz shrugged. "Just because I'm not assigned to the case doesn't mean I haven't been following it, especially with the Slugger. This one intrigues me."

"*Intrigues* you? You've got to be kidding me," McNally said, one eyebrow rising sharply.

"Doesn't Slugger make you wonder what he's thinking or feeling?"

"If I knew what he thought, I'd have him in custody, and we wouldn't be looking at his latest piece of artwork. And I don't give three shits what he's feeling. I'll leave that to the shrinks, thank you."

McNally lowered his voice in a warning. "Serious word of caution, girl. Don't get caught up any deeper than you are in this one, Liz. Just because you have a gun doesn't make you safe. No one is. And no one will be until I get this twisted knot off the streets."

She laughed. "Okay, *Dad*. I promise I'll be careful."

He nodded his head. He knew she was teasing, but he was dead serious. Until they captured and arrested the Slugger, even a woman like Liz, who was cleverer and stronger than most men, could be a target.

McNally stood in front of the blue and white area map hanging on the wall behind his desk. He stuck a small red pushpin in the location where the latest vic's body had turned up. He frowned and studied the growing pattern of pushpins—they were like drops of blood—on the map.

"Oh, Kyle," Liz interrupted. "I almost forgot. Uh, the commander wants to see you."

McNally's expression changed from focused to resigned. "So you saved the best for last?"

Liz Dumont understood the strain these murders put on him. His downcast eyes revealed an uncommon weariness. Even when they had worked around the clock on the Chinatown murders together, it always seemed to stir a kind of rush or high in him. The commander rode him hard, pushing him to work faster; he looked exhausted. Everyone in the unit knew Rouse was desperate to save his own ass from getting flushed down the shitter by the superintendent. And Kyle landed right in the middle of it all.

Anyone could see what made Rouse tick, but it was not so easy to read Mac. He solved cases involving the worst this city threw at him. Liz admired the way he always found a parking place inside a killer's head and studied their emotional backyard. He was one of a kind.

"Roger that." He turned toward Rouse's office. "If I'm still in there in ten minutes, think up something and come get me. Any longer, and you'll find his body two stories down, on the sidewalk… I've got to get to my interview with Mrs. Ziomecki today."

"Okay, Mac. Good luck. I'll catch up with you later."

CHAPTER 6

McNally knocked on the window to Commander Alfred "Al" Rouse's office and opened the door. "You wanted to see me?"

"Yeah, come on in and sit down, Kyle."

He hated it whenever Rouse called him Kyle; it made his sphincter tighten involuntarily—a bad sign from him. He eased into the chair and took a good look at his boss. Rouse was a short balding man, five feet, six inches tall. He had his Monte Rosso shoes on. He sported a well-tended potbelly. A jowly chin hung beneath a red splotchy face marred by many years of extra-dry gin martinis, and he had a voice that had that droning, nasally resonance you only heard from people raised in the inner city. The tip of his broad nose bore a small vertical cleft, which reminded Kyle of a miniature ass. The overall effect gave him the look of someone begging for a punch in the face. He fancied himself to be a sharp dresser with his knockoff Armani suits, even though they always looked like he'd worn them once too often before a return to the cleaners.

McNally didn't want to hear any of the commander's bullshit today. He watched, bemused, as Rouse's expression transformed from dull confusion, trying to remember why he summoned McNally, to something sharp and weasel-like, more akin to his ordinary expression. With that change, McNally could see the hammer coming down.

The detective appeared relaxed, even bored, to Rouse, but he missed the glint of resentment reflected in his green eyes. Anyone who knew even a little about Kyle McNally recognized that red flag. Al missed it.

McNally tried to ignore people who annoyed him. He reported to the area commander daily, but most days, he found ways to avoid him. Because he didn't trust him, the best way to make sure he didn't muddy the waters during an investigation was to make these occasional pointless visits to his shuttered office.

"I put you in charge of this team, McNally, because of your experience. I'm growing concerned this case will blow up and become a circus sideshow unless we can solve it. The FBI is sniffing around, and the superintendent has been hammering me to turn this case over to them. So tell me, what the fuck have you got? I need a trail of evidence. I need a suspect. Goddamnit, I need some indication from you that you've got this case under control!"

He recognized the flaw in Rouse's attack and responded, "Do you know something about the feds that I don't? It's too early in our investigation to turn it over to them. We'll get the Slugger, Al. Besides, so far, there's been no federal violation here. If we call in the FBI now, it would do more harm than good." McNally saw Rouse churning these ideas around in his now more red-faced, swollen head. "But this is not under their authority yet, and any interest they are showing is likely rooted in a desire to showboat. So far, our newest vic is another Jane Doe. We don't have any conclusive results back from either Forensics or the ME's office yet, but there are two important facts that link this to the two earlier Canarytown murders—the use of a bat and the collector's baseball cards. No disrespect here, Commander, but after the first two murders, you were the one who decided to fence the FBI out of this case." McNally continued, his tone patronizing, "Let me confirm that the Slugger murdered this victim and not a copycat. Wouldn't you agree that it'd be a mistake to do anything else too soon?"

Rouse fidgeted in his chair. His eyes were blinking, and he tugged on the collar of his shirt.

McNally held the upper hand, and he continued, "If this is the Slugger, Al, give me a little more time to track him down. We may have an eyewitness on this one. And I'm close to locating a local pimp, a real bad guy, who might be our perp. But we're gonna need more time. This case is only weeks old, and without the vics' identification, we have a limited firsthand evidence trail to follow. You understand that, Al. We'll get this guy. I promised you I would. We're moving step-by-step, following every lead, the way you like it. You've built your reputation on discipline and investigative thoroughness, right?

"Well, yes."

Gotcha! McNally thought. He continued, "Commander, we are doing this investigation your way, by the book. No mistakes." His own false-hearted words made McNally cringe. He knew this was a dance he knew better than Rouse, and if it meant mollifying him, then he'd put on a kilt and play bagpipes—at least for now. "When we collar Slugger, it's gonna make you look like a superstar, Al. I'm asking you to stay the course on this one."

Rouse's expression became contemplative. Although he had a vague sense of being handled, the idea Kyle suggested sounded good. Still he spat back, "I'm not just talking about the latest murder, goddamnit! This city's seen over seven hundred murders in the past year. The media and public are questioning our ability to perform. That, and now our area has three successive murders all by the same puke-faced, mother-hating son of a bitch! I set this team up, remember? I decided to assign you as team leader. But you haven't given me shit to give to the superintendent's office. You tell me what the hell is going on."

McNally held his hands up in front of him, trying to calm the hurricane he saw brewing. "I told you we have some leads and I've got every man on our team working them. We've requested increased patrols in the Canarytown district, and we're pursuing all witness leads. We're closing the loop on this miscreant. You understand that we can't afford to have the superintendent spill too much to the media. We can't afford to jeopardize this case and open the door to copycats and ambulance chasers. We need to keep the press and brass off our backs a little longer. I'm not trying to blow smoke up your ass here, Commander, but you don't want to play this like we did with the zoo murder, do you?"

His cheeks now glowing red, Rouse felt the full sting of McNally's contempt. He loathed his cockiness and resented the suggestion that he'd mishandled that mess. He'd let this one go for now, admitting to himself that McNally could be the most critical chess piece on the board. As a man, Rouse didn't like him, but he made the department look good. That mattered right now.

"All right, McNally, I'm gonna give you a little more rope, but I expect you to keep me informed. You don't work alone here. There are six other detectives on your team. Don't forget that."

As Rouse talked, McNally's jaw muscles tightened, and his eyes narrowed, but without another word, he nodded and left Rouse's office.

CHAPTER 7

Kyle went to interview the woman who initially alerted the district about noises outside her kitchen window on the night of the third hooker murder. Petrocelli had interviewed Mrs. Ziomecki earlier, but Kyle found that witnesses often recalled something later, some detail that they hadn't thought of during the initial questioning. He'd had the obligatory kinesics training for interviews and interrogations. His best results came by allowing witnesses to take their time relating the setting, sights, and sounds while he constructed a framework of the scenes they described. He knew witnesses seldom remembered everything in an initial interview. Sometimes frightened, often nervous, they rushed through their recollection of the events and skipped minor important peripheral events. However, there was a downside; sometimes they began to conceive an alternate, reconstructed version, one that agreed with their personal beliefs and cultural upbringing.

Beat cops, and sometimes younger detectives, often became preoccupied with a hope for quick collars and gloss over more important methods of interviewing witnesses. Witnesses needed to be encouraged to take their time recalling details. It required patience and careful observation. Mrs. Ziomecki reported unusual sounds coming from an alley behind her apartment on the night before they found the vic in an alley near her home.

He knocked on her apartment door. The door opened a crack, and a frail-looking dark-haired woman with sorrowful eyes looked him up and down.

"Mrs. Ziomecki?"

"Yes. Who are you?"

"I'm Detective McNally from the Chicago Police Department. We spoke earlier about me coming by to discuss what you reported about Thursday night." He held his badge out to confirm his identity.

"Oh. Oh yes, that's right. Please come in, Detective."

She looked to be in her midforties. Her appearance, which once might have been attractive, now showed signs of long neglect. The shabby dress hung loosely and appeared washed more times than it wanted. Her hands might have once been slender and soft but were now chafed and red. When she noticed his look, she hid them from view. In contrast, her straight posture and carriage bore the markings of a once-proud woman. Her azure-blue eyes stared back at him but with no curiosity. McNally experienced a twinge of pity for this woman of faded beauty. Years of hard thankless work had marred her indelibly.

"I've already told the other officer what happened. I saw nothing more than I told him then."

McNally smiled. "Believe me, Mrs. Ziomecki, I understand. You've been very helpful. We appreciate the information you've already given, so my questions won't take much more of your time."

"That'd be okay, I guess. Please have a seat. What did you say your name was?"

"McNally, ma'am, Detective Kyle McNally."

"Don't mind me," she told him as he sat. "My knees sometimes give me trouble. I don't like to stand for long. Oh, I'm sorry, would you like a cup of coffee?"

"Why, yes, that would be nice. Thank you."

While she went to the kitchen, he looked around the small crowded room. Only a few pieces of furniture, a patched couch, and a worn green corduroy chair took up most of the space in the small room. A Formica-top table from the 1950s held the only lamp in the room. Dime store pictures covered the cracks in the plaster walls, and behind one of the closed doors, he listened to the voice of Bart Simpson on the television. The smell of fried fish lingered in the air, blending with a heavy pungent odor of a cheap cigar.

After she'd brought him his coffee and sat down again, he took out his notepad. "Can you recall for me the events of the other night, Mrs. Ziomecki, what you told the other detective? Tell me everything you remember, please. The smallest detail might be important." He waited as she gave the question some thought.

"Well, as I think I told the other policeman, when I first looked out the alley, I saw no one. Or at least I thought so, but then I swear I heard someone moaning or crying."

McNally's eyebrows rose at this. "Crying, ma'am?" He'd reviewed Petrocelli's report earlier, which said nothing about any sounds. "Sorry, I don't remember reading that from your earlier interview. You're saying you heard someone moaning. Anything else?"

"Well, I don't know about that, but something happened outside. It sounded like crying, and I remember thinking who would allow a child out so late on such a cold night?" She seemed to struggle for a moment, trying to recall more. "Well, I heard some banging around too, like somebody knocked over a garbage can or something like that. And after that, there were thudding noises. It sounded like someone dropped a bunch of heavy garbage bags if that makes any sense."

"And were you able to see the person making these sounds out of your window?"

"No. Not at first… I gotta say it scared me. Between the crying and thumping, it could wake up my old man. He don't like bein' bothered after he goes to bed. He gets mean when that happens." Her eyes were wide open now.

"Take your time, Mrs. Ziomecki. I need you to recall any details. So then there were crashing and thudding sounds?"

She repositioned herself on the chair and rested the interlaced fingers of her hands on her lap, shoulders relaxed. These were good signs. She'd already been more receptive to recalling events than in her first interview. Though the minutes ticked by, Kyle didn't push. He'd let her recall the events in her own good time.

"So anyway, when the noise stopped, I looked out the window again. That's when I saw old Benjamin weaving down the alley. It was the second time that night."

"Benjamin. Who's Benjamin?"

"The local neighborhood drunk. He's homeless, always carries his hooch under his rain slicker so no one steals it." Mrs. Ziomecki chuckled. "Not that anyone would. He smells like he hasn't bathed in months." She drew a deep breath. "I feel sorry for him. He's harmless. I sometimes leave a plate of leftovers for him on the back porch if I see him come around after dinnertime."

"So you saw him in the alley the night you telephoned the police? Two times?"

"Uh-huh, but the noises were during the second time he came around. I'm not sure why he came back. He always goes away for a few days after he's fed."

She began to laugh now, low and hoarse, deep in her chest. By the time it escaped her mouth, it sounded more like a whistle. "Old Benjamin is like a big old Tom cat. Gets his belly full and disappears—at least till he's hungry again."

"Describe Benjamin for me."

"He's a skosh shorter than you, I'd say." She smiled a thin tight smile and continued, "And skinnier. Around fifty, I'd guess. Gray hair, a bushy white beard—looks like a poor man's Santa. He always wears an old green rain slicker with a hood, even in the middle of August."

"Did he wear the slicker when you saw him that night?"

"He always wears the slicker," she said, now trying to hide her chapped red hands under her thighs. "Oh yes, he had it on." She nodded her head up and down several times as if to reassure herself about what she had seen. "At least the first time he did. I didn't see him the next time 'cause the streetlight was behind him. I only made out his shape that time. But I'm sure I saw the outline of his coat. He walked real different, sort of weaving back and forth down the alley. Must have hung one on." She paused and ran her fingers over the soft folds of material in her faded blue dress.

"Anyway, so it's late, and I'm busy cleaning up the kitchen from the dinner dishes by that time. I turned off the light and came in here. That's when I heard a crashing noise. Thought old Ben came back and was digging through the garbage again. Mory…" She nodded her head toward the closed door. "That's my old man. He was trying to sleep 'cause he gets up at three in the morning, and so I got mad. I opened the kitchen window to yell at him for making so much noise, and that's when I heard a brief crying or moaning. The thumping came after that. I thought he must be real mad, but it ended quick, though, when I yelled. The next thing I saw was Benjamin running like dogs were chasing him back down the alley. Never saw him run so fast."

"Anything else?"

"Funny, he never even turned around when I called to him."

McNally stroked his chin and raised an eyebrow. "So you saw Benjamin twice that night? Did he normally he act like that?"

She reached up and touched her lips as she thought about the question. "You know, at first I felt certain it must be Benjamin. Thinking about it now, I'm not so sure."

"So why do you now think it may not have been?"

"Well, in the years I've known Benjamin, I'd be surprised if he'd wake up in a burning house. Occasionally, I'd chat with him if I saw him coming for a plate. Said he got shot up in Vietnam and one leg ended up shorter than the other. I've seen him stagger when he's drunk, but he didn't stagger that night, more like deliberately weaving from one side of the alleyway to the other."

She leaned closer to McNally and pointed her finger at him. "Nope. Whoever I saw leaving the alley that night moved more regular than old Benjamin ever did."

"You said it was dark. Are you sure of what you saw?"

"I'm positive. Remember, I said the streetlight lined up behind him? It was in front of him leaving and the man's outline. This man wore a hat. Benjamin never wore one." She sat up straight in her chair and smiled, now believing in her heart that old Ben did nothing wrong.

"Where can we locate Benjamin to ask him a few questions?"

"I'm not sure. He lives all over the neighborhood and doesn't keep to a regular schedule if ya know what I mean. Maybe the mission a few blocks over has seen him. He sleeps and eats there every now and again if the weather's real bad."

"Is there anything else you can think of, Mrs. Ziomecki? Do you know his last name? Could you describe his hair and eye color? Was he bald? Would you say he was a white guy?"

"He had a dirty-blond head full of hair, and his eyes may have been green, but they mostly looked red by the time he came around for a meal. I never knew his last name. Ben's what everyone called him. When I called the police, all that racket outside upset me. There were only a few hours until Mory's alarm went off. They never came until the next morning. That morning, they didn't ask too many questions. They were too busy running all around here, outside in the alley, stringing up that yellow tape, and bumping into each other." She scowled. "I've still got mud stains dug into my rug where they'd tracked through."

McNally noted several large dark stains in the light-green rug. "I'm sorry. I'll have the City send someone over to clean that up for you, Mrs. Ziomecki."

"Oh, it's not that important. It's not like I live in a mansion full of nice stuff or anything. Until this minute, it didn't even occur to me it might not be Benjamin leaving. Nope, it wasn't. Like I told you, he always wore his slicker with the hood pulled over his head but never a hat. The person I saw the second time wore a high collar pulled up around his ears and a big coat all right, but he wore a hat—you know, one of those broad-brimmed ones like in the old detective movies."

McNally stood and held out his hand to the woman. "I appreciate your help, Mrs. Ziomecki. Your information has been most helpful." He handed her his card. "Please call me if you think of anything else or if Benjamin comes back."

She smiled and let go of his hand. For the first time, she took close notice of the detective. Her cheeks flashed pink as she realized how she must look to the detective. She ran her fingers through her shoulder-length hair, trying to preen herself at the last minute. He was a handsome man, and she was a woman, not so old she didn't notice. She opened the door for him. He thanked her again and left. She looked after him with a wistful smile. The handsome detective looked back at her, but only saw a bone-weary woman in a rag dress.

When she turned back into her home, she scowled at the closed bed-room door and cursed her life for the first time in a long time.

He felt that Mrs. Ziomecki had told him all she knew. It would be impossible for her to ID the second visitor, but maybe Benjamin saw something if he'd been in the alley Thursday night. Hopefully, he'd remember it.

He'd made some progress… but Kyle McNally was still a mile from comfortable about this case.

CHAPTER 8

Senator Wayne Reynolds hunched over his mid-nineteenth century inlaid leather-topped English library partner's desk. It was his proudest possession, and he'd paid dearly for it. It came with papers attesting that John Brown originally used it, the clandestine second husband of Queen Victoria.

The senator reviewed the speech he planned to give at Northwestern University. He committed himself to speaking for the Citizens Against Inhumane Treatment of Animals (CAITA) foundation at the university-sponsored fundraiser. One of his campaign promises had been to strengthen the growing national lobby that would aid them in banning animal experimentation. That and his promise to John Marshfield, the chairman of Tomorrow's Promise, the political action committee Marshfield sponsored, were the reasons he agreed to speak to them.

The senator was a rotund man, just this side of morbidly obese and shy of six feet tall. Though not totally bald, that, combined with puffed-out cheek pads and a jutting jowl, made him appear like a large hairless orangutan. But despite his appearance, like the orangutan, Reynolds possessed a keen intellect.

If there were causes to support and promote and if the campaign contributions kept rolling in, he knew how to feign interest better than most. From the outset of his political career, he'd schemed how to turn this into a lucrative venture for himself. And anyone who dared stand in his way would regret it.

I've kept my risks minimal. By God, my future is secure.

He chuckled to himself. He knew when and how to manipulate others. They voted for him the first time for his charm and charisma. For his second term, his support and ultimate reelection came from wealthy, politically connected backers and their PACs. He was now in his fourth term. He understood that his reelection had less to do with the issues he backed and more with the influence he'd gain on Capitol Hill. And armed with that rationale, he'd summarily vindicated himself for reallocating a few dollars from the campaign funds into private accounts.

The senator's future was bright, very bright. He'd have to remain vigilant, however. A single slip at this point could make it all disappear in a cloud of shredded paper.

Unannounced, his secretary came fluttering through the door in her usual disruptive manner. Betty Kuntz, at sixty, easily looked ten years older. Her wardrobe had name brands bought from discount outlets decades beyond fashionable, and her shape was classic pear. Her complexion held the gray pallor common to lifetime smokers and made more unattractive by the deep lines and creases of a hard life lived with an abusive, alcoholic husband, five years dead now. Bitterness shaped her worn, withered life and left her disenchanted with men and covetous of her quiet, cloistered private life.

She had worked in the senate offices for the past twenty-seven years, and for the past six, she'd been in a thinly masked passive-aggressive relationship with Reynolds. She possessed an overinflated opinion of her value at work but managed the senator's busy calendar for him with minimal problems. That was the main reason he kept her. Betty lived for her daily routine—not for the job, but for the perks she'd attained over the years through seniority and a knack for her savvy bullying of the younger staffers.

In self-defense, she'd developed the habit of cowering and mock shriveling before his vile-tempered attacks. Most days were easy as the senator spent little time in his office. When he'd begun campaigning for another term, she figured she'd only need to make it another three years with him until her retirement. Though her boss was a pompous liar, in a heartbeat, she'd happily document his many corrupt machinations and frequent peccadillos. But she needed this position, and if they impeached him, she'd likely find herself in a more detestable situation. She would manage this one and keep her complaints to herself.

No, she wouldn't let him force her out, and he wouldn't dare fire her. She'd found his little black book when it fell out of his pocket once, unnoticed. When she returned it to him, she'd made a copy of it and highlighted the list of his many female paramours. Imagining that most were either prostitutes or fetish-pleasers, she had him right where she wanted him.

Reynolds lifted his head to address her. "What is it? I told you not to disturb me this morning."

"Forgive me, Senator," she sniffled. "I've brought the cup of coffee you asked for." From learned habit, she began trembling at the rage she saw on his face. Her hand lurched, and the coffee cup flew off the saucer, spewing the contents over the senator's prized silk Tabriz carpet. In her initial attempt to catch the cup, she scalded her hand and shrieked from the pain. The cup ricocheted off her hand, shattering against the senator's mahogany desk. She dropped to her knees, attempting to retrieve the pieces of the shattered cup and with forced tears coursing down her cheeks.

She'd never seen him this angry. His lips and chin were trembling.

"LEAVE IT! JUST GET OUT OF HERE!"

"I'm so sorry, sir. If you'll allow me to—"

"My dear Mrs. *Klutz*, if you favor continued employment with me, you will remove yourself from my office *at once*! And do *not* disturb me again today. Do you understand? You can take care of this mess after I've gone."

Relieved by the offered chance to leave, she sighed. "Yes, sir." She picked herself up with most of the pieces of the broken cup and left his office. She closed his door behind her, threw the broken cup into the trash can, and swung on her heels to glare at his door.

"I hate you!" she spat. She'd make him sorry. He'd choke on his cruel words. He hadn't called her klutz in years. If it weren't for her coming retirement, she'd tell him.

Hey, fatso, why don't you stick my mouse up your fat ass, cable and all. I'm outta' here! With that, she began to giggle to herself. *Oh yeah, I'd give a year's worth of pension to see my Apple stuck between his cheeks!* She relished being able to laugh at him and smiled triumphantly. "Betty Kuntz, you are amazing."

Still chuckling to herself, she saw one of her call lines blinking.

"Senator Reynolds' office, how may I help you?"

Pause. "Senator Reynolds, please."

She would follow his orders to the letter. He would get no further phone calls this day. Her grin bordered on evil as she envisioned his face, red and puffy with rage. "I'm sorry, sir. The senator has a committee meeting this afternoon and left instructions he needed to prepare for it beforehand. If I may take your name and—"

"The senator *will* speak with me, I'm certain. Please tell him it's John Marshfield." The unearthly calm in his voice disarmed her.

"One moment, sir. Let me see if the senator has left for his meeting yet."

Betty Kuntz pressed the hold button and watched it flash for a few seconds. She knew the senator would not want to take this call. And no way in hell would she offer herself as his sacrificial lamb twice in the same day.

She pressed the line one button. "Hello. Mr. Marshfield, I'm sorry. The senator has already left for his meeting. So please, I have your number and will—"

Before finishing her preprogrammed announcement, she heard a soft click on the other end of the line. Marshfield had hung up.

She jotted a quick message and placed it on the senator's in-basket. Mr. Marshfield was peeved when told that the senator wasn't available. She also knew that Marshfield wasn't a man you said no to. And if he refused the call, she'd only followed his orders.

Good. Let him squirm.

"What goes around comes around," she mumbled, perusing his calendar of appointments. "What goes around comes around."

CHAPTER 9

The moon's soft reflection outlined the silhouette of a large man seated, staring pensively through the wide bay windows of his office. He was a lonely man who had gained so much during his life, though it all seemed so futile in retrospect. He took nothing from life he didn't earn or deserve. Now faced with what he knew he must do, John Marshfield sat alone with an overwhelming feeling of emptiness steeped in destiny. He laid his hands, palms down, on his shaking legs and lowered his head to his chest as he closed his eyes. Dark thoughts clouded his mind.

His philanthropic project, Citizens Against the Inhumane Treatment of Animals (CAITA), had been his vision and legacy for the future, his innermost reason for existing, the culmination of his life's philosophy and ethics. It seemed so simple to him then.

But now, all that had become irrelevant. Once again, he faced what he knew he must do to make things right. The serene view from the office bay windows stood in stark contrast to his current reality.

His world had unraveled...

I know indeed what evil I intend to do,
but stronger than all my afterthoughts is my fury,
fury that brings upon mortals the greatest evils.
                                        —Euripides

CHAPTER 10

Whoosh!

Thin slivers of light seeped through the slits of swollen eyes, a cruel reminder she was still alive. As the savagery of the attack rose, her perception seesawed between dim awareness and flickering flashes while still conscious of the excruciating pain at each pendulum swing between. Her lungs struggled for air beneath broken ribs.

Our Father in heaven…

Whoosh! The bat crashed down again. Her torso heaved in response from the blow to her stomach.

Deliver me from the evil one…

Whoosh! Instinctively, though too late, she tried to raise her arm to avert the blow. It wouldn't move. This time her whole body spasmed in protest. The weight on her chest grew heavier, and even in her semiconscious state, she felt mounting pressure in the arteries of her neck. She prayed they would explode. At least then death would come swiftly, mercifully. Blood gurgled in her throat as she struggled to swallow.

Amen…

Whoosh! Her nose and cheek shattered, causing blue and white lights to burst in her brain. Her reality unraveled. A detached observer now, she witnessed the death of her body. In its place, a new and compelling sense released her from the unspeakable pain.

And then she died.

CHAPTER 11

His fingers clawed at the clothes, tearing and ripping everything as he searched. His breathing was low and labored as his frustration mounted. He prowled from room to room, mauling everything in his path. Bloodshot eyes darted from side to side, searching every nook. As he moved through the apartment, the destruction increased. When he'd spilled out the last drawer, a low angry growl gurgled from deep within his throat.

Whores. Diseased witches. I am the ferryman who escorts you home.

Swollen, bloodshot eyes bulged, deformed by desperate anger. Spittle coursed down his chin from the corners of his maw. Visions of their pain both teased and tantalized him when their bodies writhed in delicious agony. That was the enthralling part of his quest; he dreamed of and daydreamed about those moments. They all begged for release. and he always dutifully obliged.

Goddamn it, where is it?

His eyes blazed with insatiable hunger—a deep, core-stirring ache recalled by images of their delicate soft skin torn from muscle beneath his mighty strokes. With deliberate strides, he returned to the bedroom. Though infuriated and unsatisfied, he bent to retrieve the consolation prize, a small golden ring.

Slut.

CHAPTER 12

An earlier driving rainstorm had slowed to a misting drizzle by the time Detectives Kyle McNally and Liz Dumont pulled up to the crime scene. From the first officer's report, the patrol car arrived to investigate a body found on Center Drive in the middle of the Graceland Cemetery by their security.

Upon his arrival at the scene, the patrolmen found a woman's brutally battered body leaned against a memorial. After a cursory check for vital signs at 6:22 a.m., Thursday, Officer Jorge Martinez radioed dispatch and requested the Mobile Crime Unit, the medical examiner on call, and detectives from the Homicide Unit. He cordoned off the area and secured the scene.

The victim was found propped and posed against the memorial monument of Allan Pinkerton in the Graceland Cemetery on Chicago's near north side. It was home to a variety of dead notables from various worlds, including Marshall Field, Jack Johnson, and Edith Rockefeller McCormick. Though it wasn't much of a leap to link this one to the three previous hooker murders, there were important differences. The signature Chicago White Sox card came from Dick Bertell's 1965 season, his first with the team, matched earlier victims marked with White Sox collector cards.

But with this one, the card had been left in her mouth, not her vagina, like the previous vics. Even though her panties were missing, there were no visible signs of vaginal mutilation. And finally, if this was the Slugger's work, why'd he bring her here, so far from the

Canarytown neighborhood? It's uncharacteristic for serial actors to change locales without provocation. With no identification found on the vic, she'd be tagged as another Jane Doe.

After the medical examiner completed the preliminary exam, Detective McNally questioned her for details. Dr. Hartley provided him with a quick summary including body temperature, estimated time of death, and the damage to the vic's torso, head, and extremities.

But she stopped short there with a shrug of her shoulders and a terse dismissal. "That's all I've got now. You'll know more when I do." Then she turned her back to him.

"Look, Doctor, some of that's obvious to me, but can you tell me if there's any evidence of sexual assault or telltale signs of the killer's size, weight, or handedness?"

Turning back to him with an icy stare, she said, "No, I can't. Not yet."

Beyond the earshot of the ME, Dumont said, "So this is the one they call Dragon Doc. What a bitch! But why here, Mac? How'd he get her here in the middle of the night? And if this is our guy's work, why here?"

A nearby security guard overheard her and said, "We've got 24-7 security in this place, Detective. We schedule our rounds every four hours but saw nothing unusual until spotting this body. We found her about an hour ago. I suppose it's possible we missed it on our 2:00 a.m. round. But we rarely get much action here after closing, except around Halloween. We checked the perimeter after we found her and found someone had cut a chain on the gate of the maintenance entrance on Clark."

Puzzled, Liz said, "I'm still missing the connection. This wouldn't be the Slugger's work, would it? A copycat job? Why here in a private, secure graveyard on the north side and in front of a tombstone of some old dead teabagger, Pinkertoes, or whatever?"

"It's a taunt," McNally replied. "Pinkerton was one of the first detectives in the country. His agency received credit for preventing an early assassination attempt of Abraham Lincoln. He also provided security for the railroads operating out of Chicago's national rail hub. His earliest company logo had an all-seeing eye. It's said that's the likely origin of the term *private eye*. I think the Slugger is taking a poke at us. Maybe he's changing his game."

"That's a stretch, Mac."

With furrowed eyebrows, McNally replied, "Maybe. Maybe not. He's been excellent at covering his tracks so far. This may be a signal he's getting bolder. He may try to bring us into his game. It's not a stretch to think he's making statements for our benefit—invitations, if you like. Or this one could have some special meaning for him. Bertell only played part of the season with the White Sox in '65. He injured himself, and they replaced him. I'm curious to find out if that 'interrupted season' might have a symbolic meaning."

"Yeah, like what? You think his girlfriend yapped too much and hated baseball and so he *interrupted* her life?"

McNally wasn't listening now. He stood in the rain, a dark scowl on his face. "We're done here. Let's get back to the car."

On their way out, McNally hailed Officer Martinez. "Good work here, Jorge. You handled the scene like a pro. Thanks."

"Man, I gotta say, this is the worst I've ever seen. I almost lost it. I wasn't even sure it was a woman at first. Her face looked like mashed potatoes and ketchup, like a coyote had chewed on it for a while."

"I hear that," Liz said.

"Do me a favor, Martinez. Keep this to yourself," McNally warned. "We don't want any murmurs about serials or copycats, right? And do me another favor, would you? Say hello to Commander Davidson for me. Tell him we miss his ugly mug around our headquarters since his promotion. He's a good cop. Tell him he still owes me a beer, okay?"

After the second murder, theories flew in as to what motivated this asshole. They bounced up like popcorn in a hot pot—from the Illinois Department of Law Enforcement (known ironically as IDLE), to the FBI. So far, the Fed's psychological profilers were describing a thousand alienated loonies the Chicago PD already had on file. They were in a hurry to find him and tag him for the psychopathy checklist, their profile instrument. And the division shrink held on to his pain and power theory. More bullshit. All that analytic garbage began two vics ago, and Mac was still short on leads.

CHAPTER 13

By midday Friday, the department had the missing person report on one Karen Clayton: Caucasian, twenty-four years, 5 feet and 3 inches, 110 pounds, blond hair, and brown eyes. Her mother, Marian Clayton, filed the missing person report. She'd become worried and contacted her daughter's friend Frank Butler after Karen had missed a luncheon date and hadn't called to cancel. Frank Butler tried to contact several of Karen's friends and coworkers. No one had seen her in two days.

On Friday afternoon, Butler went to her apartment and discovered she wasn't there. He began telephoning the hospitals. By Saturday morning, he started calling the area police stations. One of the districts in Area 3 informed him they had delivered a Jane Doe to the morgue Friday morning that matched the sex, height, and weight of Marian Clayton's daughter.

* * *

On Saturday morning, after an early call from the department and with only four hours of sleep, Detective McNally, unshaven and short-tempered, arrived at the County Medical Examiner's Office. Dr. Hartley was the ME on staff. An investigator directed him to examining room three. The victim had been so mangled that even her mother couldn't identify her. And her murder didn't exactly match the Slugger's profile. Serial actors are reluctant to change their methods. They reveled in consistency. To date, the first three victims had been prostitutes found on the streets in Canarytown, near the Back of the Yards neighborhood on the south side. This one, though uniquely crafted, had the same stink.

Before entering the examining room, McNally scanned the missing person's report and the information reported by her mother. Her daughter attended DePaul College, where they found her car in the parking lot.

A woman sat on a bench in the anteroom with head bowed, weeping. Kyle approached the woman and addressed her, "Pardon me, Mrs. Clayton?"

"Yes?"

"I'm sorry to have to trouble you. My name is Detective McNally. I'm the lead investigator on this case. I was wondering if you were able to identify the victim. Can you tell if it's your daughter?"

"I was cautioned by the medical examiner that it could be nearly impossible with the harm inflicted on her body."

Three walls lined; it had four rows of small steel refrigerator doors. One drawer sat open, and a shelf on rollers was pulled out from the wall. In front of the draped body stood a tall thin man, bent over and head bowed. The ME had pulled back the top of the plastic sheet and turned the body on its side, exposing her back. The man bowed his head and nodded to the ME.

Dr. Hartley stood next to him, her face dispassionate. She appeared to be asking him questions.

"Is that Karen's friend Frank Butler with the body now?"

"Yes, it is. He's a friend of Karen's. He volunteered to drive me over and help with the identification."

"Please excuse me, Mrs. Clayton. I'd like to arrange an interview with you later, but right now, I'm stepping into the exam room. Will you be all right here by yourself, or would you like me to get an assistant in here to keep you company?"

Through swollen, tearstained eyes, she whispered, "No. Thank you, though. I'm certain I'll never be fine again."

He moved into a near corner of the exam room, taking in the activity where the preliminary autopsy was conducted. Seeing the victim's uncovered head caused a familiar tightening in his stomach by what he saw under the bright lights. The disfigurement of the victim startled him more under the glare of the examination room's bright lighting. Hanging on by a few scraps of shredded skin, her face was an indistinguishable mass of jellylike flesh surrounded by wispy patches of hair.

The doctor whispered something, and the man fixed accusing, pain-filled eyes toward her. "No, I'm positive it's Karen." He hesitated, then whispered, "She once told me she had a pink four-leaf clover tattoo on her lower back."

The ME's tone held no hint of compassion; her manner was all business as she referred to Karen Clayton as *it* or *the victim*. McNally sympathized with the man.

"Yes, there's no doubt. She said she didn't even tell her mother. She thought it would upset her too much."

By the time the doctor noticed McNally in the room, Butler seemed to regain his composure. The detective took closer stock of Butler and thought he might be older than he first appeared. He looked to be six feet tall, with a slim, wiry build. He had a narrow forehead and small brown eyes that were closer together than you'd expect for a man his size. His course brown hair had fallen in disarray across his forehead, and he had a pair of wire-rimmed glasses held from limp fingers. Butler seemed to ignore anyone else in the room as he continued to stare at the corpse, tears running down his cheeks.

McNally needed to question Butler, but as he walked toward him, the man raised reddened eyes to Dr. Hartley and told her he'd like to be alone with the body.

She responded, "That's fine, Mr. Butler."

McNally caught her eye and motioned for her to accompany him out of the room. She re-covered the body and left the room. They walked past Mrs. Clayton and down the hall several doors. When she halted in front of a small windowless office, he stumbled into her. She turned, surprised, and he offered a lopsided grin in response.

"You may remember me from the Graceland Cemetery. I'm Detective Kyle McNally, in charge of this investigation." He held out his hand. She ignored it.

Ahh, I see now. Bitch!

"We've met," Hartley replied.

He smiled at her abruptness. "I glimpsed you, Doctor, when you examined the victim at the scene the other morning."

"I remember."

Bitch!

"Have you scheduled the autopsy yet?" he asked.

"No. We don't even have a verified ID, although Mr. Butler seems convinced it's her. I've requested fingerprints and dental records."

McNally found her cold indifference irritating. He remembered hearing some disparaging chatter about this one, but he hadn't made the connection before now. At the crime scene, she conducted herself professionally. He'd expected no less. Now she just appeared insensitive and cold.

Bitch!

She said, "How'd he identify her with her face beaten like that? And her body is so bruised and swollen that—"

The muscles in McNally's jaw tightened from the bite of her sarcasm, and he did his best to hide what he thought. "My concern, Doctor, is that after seeing the face so horribly beaten and swollen, the victim's friend still seems convinced that this is the body of Karen Clayton."

She did not hide her impatience and instead became defensive. "I doubt if he knew with certainty." Because the detective's expression remained unreadable, she added, "I'll have a positive ID when we get the fingerprints back."

"That's it? That's all you can tell me? The body's been cold for two days, Doctor, and what you've got for me is one vague possible ID and a—"

"All right, Detective. This is what I am sure of right now. From the postmortem lividity, her death occurred hours before being found at the cemetery. The small muscles in the face and neck are already showing signs of rigor. My guess is seven to ten hours. The perpetrator beat her with a solid round object, like a club. There are no initial signs of rape despite her missing underwear."

"Excuse me?"

"That's as close to laymen as I get, Detective. I can't give you any more until I have completed my examination."

McNally didn't want to let her off the hook so easily. "Then does this one appear like the other recent beating victims from the south side? Or could it even be a copycat?"

"Sorry, but I've got bodies lined up in the corridor." She waved her hand toward the six gurneys edged along each side of the hall. "It's been a busy week. You must be patient."

Her clipped reply only intensified his annoyance. His jaw tightened. "Doctor, I don't want to be here any more than you want me here. I'll get out of your way as soon as I have what I need."

He wanted to walk away. Tired, hungry, and needing a drink of something stronger than coffee, he began rubbing the back of his neck. "Okay, let me start over, Doctor. There are questions I need immediate answers to. I'm still about a mile away from comfortable on these recent murders, and if you can help me out, it would be a great favor. Frankly, Doctor, I need something."

McNally saw her hesitate to say something and then changed her mind, so he blurted, "During your initial examination, did you find anything unusual, anything that would separate this murder from the other similar beating vics your office received? You must have heard something about the previous three. They were autopsied here too." He leaned forward. "Lay terms are helpful, but if you'll answer the questions, I'll muddle through. I don't have the time to wait for you to type a formal report and hand it to the state's attorney. I apologize, but I need something more substantial to investigate." His words hung in the air between them. He left it at that.

"My best estimate would place the time of death between ten and twelve o'clock. Closer to eleven, I believe. I observed severe trauma to the head. The body cools between one and two degrees per hour. When I recorded the body temperature, it measured eighty-six degrees. Calculated with the external air temperature, I estimate the body died eight or nine hours before they discovered it."

She continued, "When death occurred, the body must have laid on its right side for a time, long enough to cause the whole lower half of her right side to collect the blood and turn deep purple in color. Although it's premature to speculate, Detective, I'd say the killer moved the body to the cemetery and left it in a sitting position, where cemetery security found her. The direction and pattern of the blows tell me your killer is right-handed."

McNally took a moment to consider her evaluation as Hartley flipped open her notebook and made notes. She paid no attention to him, ignoring his presence. She had been cooperative, even if only to get him out of her hair.

"Then I'll see you at the autopsy, Doctor. Please call me when it's scheduled."

She nodded and retreated through an open door.

He returned to the examination room, hoping to speak with Frank Butler, but by the time he got there, both Butler and Mrs. Clayton had left.

CHAPTER 14

Detective Jerome Peterson, the newest recruit to the area, hollered across the room, "Hey, McNally, pick up line two. Dragon Doc wants to talk to you." Spontaneous laughter broke out around the squad room.

McNally, just preparing to leave for the Clayton girl's apartment, revealed little more than controlled impatience as he answered the phone.

"McNally here." Silence. "Hello, may I help you? Doctor, are you there?" After several seconds and as he was about to hang up, he heard a whispered reply.

McNally cast a deep scowl at Peterson. "Was that supposed to be funny?" Peterson had allowed the doctor to hear his rude remark. McNally noticed the indignation in her voice and didn't blame her for being angry.

"Detective McNally, had I known I stood in such high regard down at your district, I would have suggested that you seek the expertise of one of the *male* medical examiners from our facility. I don't like being made a mockery of."

He tried attempting to make light of Peterson's remark. "Please, don't take it like that, Doctor. The guy's a dolt. It's my suspicion he was likely raised by wolves."

"Nonetheless, this may be a good time for me to take a step back as lead ME on this case. We have several qualified pathologists working here. I'd be more than happy to refer this autopsy to another."

McNally's initial embarrassment had ebbed when he replied, "Dr. Hartley, I assure you that although the man was out of line, he did not mean to compromise the professional relationship this department has always maintained with your office. One individual's careless remark shouldn't reflect on the department, but for that, I apologize."

"Well, I've scheduled the autopsy of the victim found at the cemetery for this afternoon. Do you still plan on attending?

"Yes, I do. This is a murder investigation, Doctor, and the faster this department gets your findings, the greater the likelihood we'll be apprehending this killer sooner rather than later. You and your office's cooperation are vital to our mission."

Dr. Hartley ignored his attempt to placate her. "Yet given what I overheard, I think I should postpone it until I can request a replacement."

He realized he was on thin ice. "Doctor, although it can't be unheard, I hope you will complete the autopsy yourself. I'm on my way out the door, but I'm asking you to perform the autopsy as scheduled since any time wasted would be a setback to my investigation. But no matter who does the autopsy, I must know the findings as soon as possible. Today would be best."

The seconds ticked away as he waited for her response. None came.

"Look," he said, "I'm not accustomed to humbling myself over the phone, but I'd like you to reconsider this. I can't afford the lost time." She sighed again. His voice lowered to a whisper, "Please, Doctor, let me at least buy you a cup of coffee to wash down my humble pie. I don't want to lose the expertise of a pathologist with your ability," he pleaded. Kyle would bend no more.

"All right, Detective. That's enough. Consider your apology accepted. And I'm prepared to meet you halfway, but by the end of this day, forget the coffee. I'll be wanting a glass of wine," she said, sounding soothed. "We can discuss that after. It's scheduled for three o'clock."

"That would be nice, Doctor, and I'll make it there on time."

"In that case, I'll see you later. If there's any reason you can't make it, I'll have the results delivered to your office after I've finished."

His tension eased as a lopsided grin replaced his scowl. "See you at three, Doctor."

"Oh, and Detective," she said.

"Yes."

"Somebody needs to put a muzzle on your Detective Peterson."

"I'll see to that myself. Trust me."

McNally hung up the phone and sauntered over to Peterson's desk. His anger didn't stem from his having to apologize for someone else's rudeness but that his carelessness might have delayed the autopsy and damaged the relationship between the department and the medical examiner's office. He'd grown tired of Peterson's constant smart-ass attitude from the day he came on their team. Peterson had the lightest caseload of anyone in the unit and somehow always appeared to accomplish nothing. He rarely lifted anything heavier than a Twinkie. Most suspected that Rouse placed him on the team to serve as his "inside" man. Because of that, the unit called him *shroom*. They all kept him in the dark and fed him bullshit to take back to Rouse.

Everyone expected the shit would hit Jerome square in the face. Usually, Weller kept them apart, but at this moment, nobody volunteered to save that doofus's ass. They all watched as McNally grabbed the edge of Peterson's desk with both hands and leaned over him, his jaw clenched tight. The only sound was the occasional ring of a phone and the soft whirring from the fans.

Detective Henderson finally broke the silence. He called from across the squad room, "Hey, McNally, I think you may need to bed the doctor to make up for Peterson's verbal diarrhea."

"It'll be a cold dark day in hell before she gives you the key to her chastity belt anyhow," a voice piped in from another corner of the room.

Henderson's comment diverted McNally, and he turned away from the frightened Peterson. "If I wanted to get laid, it wouldn't be anyone you assholes know."

When the jokes died down and the laughter ran its course, he warned Peterson, in a loud voice, that he'd be happy to reshape the idiot's nose for him if he ever repeated a stunt like that. Peterson covered his public shaming by lowering and shaking his head.

Kyle grabbed his keys and picked up his leather jacket and briefcase.

"Where you headed?" Liz asked.

"I want to run by the apartment of the girl ID'd Friday. And I'll need immediate follow-up by the Mobile Crime Unit since my only suspect hasn't turned up yet. Then I'm stopping to interview a woman who is a classmate at DePaul. If you need me, you can page me."

"Yeah, sure. With that and smoke signals, I might get lucky and reach you—"

Not skipping a beat Detective Petrocelli piped up, "Hey, McNally, so when are you gonna jump into the twentieth century and get yourself a cell phone?"

"How about when you start shaving, smart-ass?"

As laughter broke out, the tension in the room disappeared.

"Oh, and, Liz, if Sam should drag his limping, lazy ass in, tell him I'll catch up with him in the morning."

Though she cloaked her feelings, Liz's eyes were wet and dull. In the past, even with their heaviest caseloads, he always had time to share a beer and conversation with her. She blamed Rouse for the pressure he put on him. Kyle spent most days on the street. She saw him less these days—maybe five or six times since the killings started and never for an after-work brew.

Her lips tugged down at the corners. "No problem. Anything else?"

"That's it, Lizzie." He didn't fail to notice her black mood. He promised himself that when he caught up with some free time, he'd meet her for burgers and a few beers like old times.

After Kyle left, she walked to the women's john. Outside the washroom, nobody had a hint of the depth of Liz Dumont's misery. The silent sobbing never escaped the cinder block walls. Ten minutes later, she returned to her desk, her tears wiped dry and her face freshened.

CHAPTER 15

Late that afternoon, Detective Weller hobbled into the squad room. He'd been given clearance to return to full duty. Most of the first shift were out on assignments. Peterson, Ramirez, and Dumont were still at their desks. Ramirez was about ready to leave for a dinner break. Since the task force operated in shifts, a few detectives would go home to catch a few hours' rest then return to pick up where they left off. Nobody got much sleep these days. They teamed up in pairs, and each was given their own list of interviews, suspects, and victims to work with. Weller, McNally's usual partner, had been out-of-pocket in rehab for his ankle and was busy with a trial he had to testify at over in the Twenty-Sixth Street and California Avenue Municipal Courthouse. His testimony completed, he arrived at the deserted squad room and deposited his large bulk with much grunting and groaning into his chair. He hoped to catch Kyle for some beers and a dog after work.

"Hey there, Lizzie. McNally say where he was goin'?"

She looked at her watch. "He's heading over to the Clayton apartment, an interview, and then out to the county morgue."

Sam, his ankle still wrapped, recognized the edge in her voice and figured she and McNally had a row. "Did he want me to catch up with him?"

"Nope. He'll catch up with you first thing in the morning. If you need him, though, you can try his beeper."

Sam, pissed that Kyle still treated him like an invalid, got up and ambled over to the duty roster.

Kyle's phone rang, and Liz picked it up. She hoped it might be the ME calling to cancel her appointment with McNally.

"Hello. May I help you?" Her eyes widened, and she lowered her voice, saying, "EZ? This is Detective Dumont. I'll be talking to McNally, so tell me what you want, and I'll give him the message."

She looked around the room and cupped her hand over the mouthpiece. "No, I'm not alone. You're positive about this? Sure. Give me a number where I can find you. As soon as I'm at another phone, I'll call you back to arrange a meet. Wait for my call, EZ, okay? You wait for my call." And then she hung up.

She bolted from her seat, told Ramirez she'd be heading out, and asked him to tell Mac she needed to speak with him.

CHAPTER 16

McNally arrived at Karen Clayton's apartment building on Deming Place in the Elmwood Park area. It was a quiet, tree-lined neighborhood a few blocks from Lake Michigan. An elegant old Catholic Church stood on a corner down the street. It was a stone-and-brick four-story apartment building dwarfed between two taller apartment houses made of concrete and red brick. The architecture boasted early twentieth-century character, having high windows with leaded stained-glass uppers over each. Its ornately carved double doors, made of solid oak, contained a large etched-glass window. The wrought-iron gate appeared to be the work of an old-world artist with a flair for Victorian design. Round turrets on each corner of the building faced the street. The steps leading up to the building were cobblestone with iron banisters running up each side. The dense, well-manicured shrubbery reached around the sides of the building to the back. Thick green ivy clung to the brick, reaching its tentacles high above the second-story windows. McNally knew the neighborhood and that its residents were a mixture of middle to upper-middle class.

As he waited for the manager to answer the doorbell, he sorted through the questions he had concerning Karen Clayton's death. Did the killer know her, or did he choose her randomly? Did she know him? If so, maybe she knew something about him? If not, why'd he choose her? Is it possible she'd done something to him? And did he know where she lived, given he left her close by?

Okay, Mac, what's the link?

After entering through the security door, McNally waited for the landlord to speak with him. An elderly woman with blue hair and wide gray roots peeked from behind the chain securing the door.

He held up his badge and said, "Detective McNally, ma'am, Chicago Police Department. I would like to ask you a few questions regarding one of your tenants."

The woman's eyes began to blink. She stuttered, "I-I'm h-here alone. My husband will b-be back tonight. You come b-back then."

"I beg your pardon, ma'am, but I'm conducting a murder investigation, and it's important that I have a look at Ms. Clayton's apartment. I'm sure you understand."

"Sorry, Mr. Detective, but no one gets in no apartment without my husband's say-so. You come back later. Talk to my husband, like I said."

McNally saw from her averted eyes and pinched lips he'd get nowhere reasoning with her. He took a card from his pocket and tried to hand it to her. For a second, she drew back.

"I'm sorry to have bothered you, ma'am. Please have your husband call me at this number when he gets home."

She frowned, snatched the card from him, and closed the door.

As he left, he stopped to scan the names of other residents on mailboxes. He looked for a name on the second floor close to the Clayton apartment, 2B. He spotted a W. Schaefer in 2A. He pressed the button several times, and when nobody answered, he left.

Outside, McNally noticed a worn brick path leading around the side to the back of the building. He wanted to look at the back entries. Outside, a wooden staircase ran up from one floor to another with a broad landing on each porch floor. Dense thorny Russian olive trees and shrubbery surrounded the lower staircase, offering privacy to anyone who might enter or exit. He tried to gauge the distance from the back of the apartments to the next closest building, and though the yards were postage stamp size, the trees and bushes made it difficult to see from one building to the next.

McNally moved to the center of the small backyard and surveyed the tall buildings lining the street five hundred yards behind the apartment house. The neighboring buildings stood behind a row of trees and shrubbery. He made a mental note to assign someone to question the residents living in the front apartments on the adjacent street. McNally walked up the wooden steps to the first-floor level of the building. Stepping onto the landing, he heard a sharp tapping sound. He turned to look and saw the blue-haired woman scowling at him. She waved her arms and shouted through the closed window that her husband wasn't home and he must leave. Though both surprised and amused, he nodded in acknowledgment.

The landlord's wife scowled, not an unusual reaction for city dwellers. It was as natural as breathing air. He didn't blame her. He hadn't shaved in two days and looked more like a mugger than a detective with the police department. Badge or no badge, he understood her worry.

Seated back in his car, he closed his notepad and radioed dispatch.

Ramirez answered his call. "Go ahead, McNally."

"Detective Dumont still there?"

"Negative. She took a phone call and left."

"Is Weller there?"

"He came in, but cut out right after Dumont."

"Did he say where to?"

"No. I was on the phone when he came in and left before I talked with him."

"I'm on my way to interview Sally Kendwall, a classmate of Ms. Clayton. Contact me on my pager if you need me."

"Ten-four."

CHAPTER 17

Arriving early to meet Dr. Hartley, he spent the time reviewing the few notes he had on Karen Clayton. Little useful information came from Frank Butler during his repeated phone conversations with the desk sergeants while attempting to find her. His frustration mounted given the many conflicting facts of this case. He'd have to return to Clayton's apartment later. He hoped he'd find some answers there.

So why the differences? The differences baffled him, but the similarities maddened him. Same perp? His gut told him it had to be. So why a different signature and the staged site? Damn it. Think, Kyle! Clayton wasn't some transient or runaway turned hooker. She'd have a history that included people who knew and cared about her. He'd start by tracking back before her disappearance.

None of this made sense, not this far from his MO. McNally often picked up on a small bit of evidence, something mistagged or otherwise overlooked. From pictures, computer information, and personal notes, he got a better sense of the victims and their personal life, sometimes missed after a sweep of the property. He had a keen intuition for uncovering even the smallest pieces of useful information.

Butler claimed to be close to Karen Clayton and might know something about her routine. Early on, McNally tagged this as Slugger's work and thought it possible the woman might just have been in the wrong place at the wrong time. A deep scowl creased his face as he reached down and lifted the mic off its cradle to call into the station. He'd have Liz begin on a preliminary background check on Butler.

Out of the corner of his eye, he noticed some familiar objects on the floor. He reached down and grabbed several wide gold foil cigar rings and half a dozen discarded wrappers. If Sam Weller, his partner and best friend, was here, he'd bust his chops for leaving those goddamnit things everywhere.

CHAPTER 18

McNally hated autopsies—*really* hated them. The rooms were cold and dry, the air was thick with chemicals, and the ME's all thought "bad corpse" jokes were de rigueur. During the last one he attended, the jokes centered on a stiff-with-rigor-mortis penis.

Fifteen minutes after his arrival, Dr. Hartley found him waiting outside her office doorway. "Hello, Detective. I'm late. I've been behind all day."

"Hello, Doctor. We're good. I *just* got here myself."

She missed or ignored the thinly veiled distemper in his tone. This duty fell about a quarter of a mile from the top of his favorites list, and he'd prefer to skip it altogether. But he really wanted clarification about the circumstances of this murder, and it couldn't wait for the final report to determine how far the similarities went, even despite the fact it meant working with this walking stiff who'd held him up.

"Good, but it'll be another ten or fifteen minutes before I'm ready for Karen Clayton."

"Should I come back later?" he said, sounding a little too enthusiastic—even to himself. "It'd be okay. Don't worry. I have a baker's dozen things to do too…" He held his hands up in front of him, in mock defense.

"Now, now, Detective. Are you getting cold feet?"

He swore he glimpsed a devious smile flash across her lips. He smiled and nodded. "Oh no, these are like going to the movies for me."

Once inside the well-lit laboratory, the temperature must have dropped by twenty degrees.

He thought, *They should issue parkas and gloves instead of these cheesy lab coats.*

That sensation came just before he recalled why he hated this duty so much. Chalk it up to the detestable smell of rotting corpses mingled with formaldehyde. It always made him gag. A bad night with a stomach flu came close.

Long ago, he'd learned not to look at the bodies. This behavior was a safeguard learned during his training days when attending autopsies was standard procedure for his classes. He'd discovered that mental preparation held his discomfort to a minimum. He focused on the sights and sounds of the surrounding laboratory and avoided employing any intellectual curiosity. He scanned the room and listened to the sounds. The drone of the fans ran together with the muffled sounds of Dr. Hartley's voice speaking cryptic jargon into a microphone. He blocked out most of the indecipherable technical babble and focused instead on the checkerboard of black-and-white floor tiles.

To most people, the lab looked like an ordinary operating room. But this was no regular hospital operating room. Raucous sounds of Heart belting out "Heartless" seemed an ironic complement to the medical carnage underway on the table. And the patient lying in front of him was dead and cold. The doctor, with her attendant standing nearby, bent over the corpse on the table. There were surgical instruments spread out on a stainless rollaway table, and bright operating room lights hung from the ceiling a few feet above the operating table. He knew that before he'd come in, they had cleaned the body and then weighed and measured it. The autopsy table sloped slightly from the center to a surrounding lip and had several faucets and drains to wash away any blood and bits of organic waste. The contrasting sights and sounds unsettled and yet fascinated McNally. The doctor worked fast but with precision, slicing up pieces of flesh and organs with only occasional pauses when the assistant gathered samples as requested.

Fighting instinct, he watched while the doctor sliced the victim's head from ear to ear in a perfect arc along the top of the scalp. Next, she peeled the skin away and draped it over the face. Her hair, now underneath the folded scalp, covered both breasts. A high-pitched whirring sound interrupted the steady noise of other sounds as Dr. Hartley cut through the skull with an instrument that was like but smaller than a carpenter's circular saw. She bent to within inches of the hole in the skull to examine the tissue and brain. The procedures were stark, cold, and graphic.

She lifted the brain from the skull and weighed it before placing it in a large metal container next to the body. Her crisp blue surgical scrubs had splattered blood and shards of flesh and bone in blotchy stains from the waist up.

Despite her reputation as a royal pain in the ass to deal with, Dr. Hartley displayed formidable efficiency. Though relatively new to the Cook County morgue team, she'd proved to be as capable and thorough as their best. She had testified in court for her technical expertise by both defense lawyers and prosecutors with similar success. He suspected that her Dragon Doc nickname amounted to a parting shot by one or more department dicks who tried unsuccessfully to hit on her.

McNally heard the hum of the air-conditioning fan again as his eyes traveled from the toe tag up the length of the waxy yellow legs to the naked torso. She cut a Y-shaped incision from the abdomen to the chest and then removed and weighed the remaining organs while her tech recorded. She took tissue samples and had her tech return the organs to the gaping cavity. He had seen enough. He'd moved way past his threshold for discomfort while witnessing autopsies. With feelings alternating between nausea and disgust, he swung on his heels and headed out the door.

The doctor joined him in the waiting room twenty minutes later. She had disposed of the stained gown and replaced it with a white lab coat. "All done," she said. "Let's talk in my office."

"Lead the way."

She turned her back on him and walked away. During the time he arrived and now, her frosty mood had taken a dive. To keep up with her, he had to walk fast.

"I observed a good part of the autopsy but wasn't able to follow all the medical terminology," he said.

"Is that so? I'm surprised."

Her condescending attitude grated on his nerves. Snakes on her head would've completed his vision of her. He decided he'd try another tack with her.

"I found your examination…enlightening. So clinical. How do you do it, Doctor?"

She spun and stared into his eyes. "In my job, Detective, I find it more tolerable to remain precise and clinical. It's a dead body, Detective, nothing more. If I wanted to know the people coming in through my door, I can assure you I would have chosen a different medical specialization. It wouldn't help your investigation if your pathologist burst into tears every time she cuts into a corpse now, would it? Consider your hasty assessment of me noted. And since you believe you know me well enough to share your opinion of me, then let me try to be more specific. If my official reports reflected a narrative of my feelings, the state's attorney would ask for another ME, and I'd lose my credibility. I haven't got the time, the luxury, or the inclination to get personal with all the victims who roll into my autopsy lab. Now does that clear it up for you, Detective?"

More snakes. If he had tried to provoke a rise from her, he couldn't have done a better job. Still angry and frustrated, he plowed ahead. "You're right, Doctor. It wouldn't be appropriate for the pathologist to be weepy during her description of how a twenty-two-year-old woman has been bludgeoned to death or unceremoniously dumped beside a tombstone at the cemetery now, would it?" He hadn't meant to take her head off, but at this moment, he didn't give half a shit.

A curious smile appeared on her lips. "Well, bravo, Detective. Now you've got me wondering. Do I personally offend you, or is that your own frustration showing? Is it possible that the victim isn't another nocturnal creature and your killer is a murderer with changing tastes?"

"Look, Doctor, I didn't come here to upset you. Can you tell me what you think we're dealing with here? Is this one by the same guy that's been keeping both our offices busy?"

"Yes, I've read the previous reports, and the weapon used on this victim appears to be the same. But for your report, this one hadn't been raped with the weapon like the previous victims." Her shoulders dropped a little. She moved one foot forward a little, and a small smile broke on her lips. He took it as a modest yielding.

"Are we done here, Doctor, or should I come back later?" His own smile softened. "Perhaps if I leave and return, maybe we can start over. Maybe better?"

"No, that won't be necessary." She exhaled, her words sounding conciliatory. "The truth is, I'm not unaffected by the pain and suffering of others. I did have a hard time with this one, and I took it out on you. For that, I apologize." And not waiting for his response, she continued, "That said, I've completed my exam. It will take anywhere from a couple days to two weeks for the lab results to come back." She started to fidget, adjusting her name tag and lapels, but then she gave up and jammed her hands into the pockets of her lab coat.

"I'd like to say something before you wrap up your judgment of me. These last two hours I spent with the victim were difficult…as with *all* victims who die a violent, senseless death. And even though you might think otherwise, not all pathologists are cold, heartless cadaver-loving bastards." With her eyes fixed on his now, she smiled. "I'm aware that seems to be your department's opinion of many of us."

"Apology accepted. I got out of line too. These murders are way too personal for me, and you caught the heat. That's on me."

She nodded, her smile becoming less tenuous. She stepped to the side of McNally and summoned the technician who assisted her during the autopsy.

"Yeah, Doc, what'll it be, stitch her and pitch her?" he said.

Hartley scowled. "You can finish up with number six. My autopsy is complete."

"No problem-o, Doc. She'll be all closed up and ready for the black wagon to pick her up in an hour. That be okay?"

"That will be fine. Give the funeral director a call when you've finished." She turned back to McNally.

"Truce?" he offered with arched eyebrows.

Dr. Hartley's cheeks flushed. "Truce."

"Where do we go from here?" he asked.

"We can discuss the autopsy if you like." She smiled. "And I promise not to bury you with cryptic medical terminology."

"That'd be a huge favor. I planned on staying up late tonight studying a copy of *The Bantam Medical Dictionary* to catch up. Listen, if you're up for it, can we meet after you're done here for a cup of coffee or a glass wine and discuss it?" he said with a slight hesitation.

She laughed at that, surprising Kyle. "A glass of wine would be nice. Are you sure you you'll be free?"

McNally nodded, encouraged by her invitation and relieved that she pivoted away from that aloof mechanical android he'd been dealing with earlier.

"I'll make the time," he assured her.

"Good. I can be done here by six."

With the tension between them subsiding, McNally realized the doctor harbored a hidden compassion for the victims who spent some of their last hours aboveground with her. His respect for her was growing.

McNally smiled, imagining she thought he still felt contrite from their brief but rocky earlier confrontations. He thought how different the doctor now seemed from his first impression of her at the cemetery.

As if reading his thoughts, she continued, "And, Detective, you don't know me well enough to believe I haven't earned the label your detectives stamped on my forehead. It will take more than a brief apology and a glass of wine to buy you a pass into my good graces. You might still find I'm every bit the bitch your team seems to think I am."

"Oh, I doubt that," he murmured as she turned to walk to her office. He watched her as she strode down the corridor, pleased that he stayed long enough to uncover the flip side of this doctor's complicated personality. He called to her just as she was about to enter her office. "Oh, and, Doctor, since we're working together now, perhaps you'd consider calling me Kyle?"

She stopped, pretending to give his request a moment's thought. "Seems like a harmless enough request. In that case, you may call me Mykel."

"Mykel it is." He enjoyed how it sounded when he said it.

"I've got several things to finish up here before leaving today."

"Not a problem. I'll be here to pick you up at six sharp."

CHAPTER 19

Marian Clayton had given Kyle the name of Karen's teacher at Loyola, a Professor Consuelo. He remembered seeing Karen talking with one of her classmates after class. Sally Kendwall was one.

When Sally Kendwall opened her door, the first thing Kyle noticed was her height. He guessed her at six feet, two inches and skinny as a BallPark frank. She had long brown hair pulled away from her face and held with a clip. Her large thick-framed glasses magnified her bright jade-green eyes surrealistically, not unlike looking at them through a fish bowl. But she had a genuine, friendly smile. If he had to guess, her look and stature resembled his grade school librarian.

He introduced himself, showing her his badge.

"If this is about that parking ticket I got last month, I'm sorry. I'd planned to pay it."

"This is not about a parking ticket, Ms. Kendwall. It's about a classmate of yours, Karen Clayton."

Concern flooded her face. "Do you know where she's been? She left our class early last week and hasn't been back."

"I'm sorry to have to tell you, but we found Karen dead last Friday."

"Oh my god," she said, the blood draining from her face.

"It was a homicide, and I'd like to ask you a few questions if you don't mind."

"What! I can't believe it. This is impossible to believe. It can't be true. It couldn't have been Karen, could it? I just saw her Tuesday night at class."

"I understand you were taking a philosophy course together at DePaul University."

"Yes, Tuesday and Thursday nights." Tears welled in her eyes and spilled down her cheeks. "Karen? No, no! Are you sure you're talking about my friend Karen Clayton and not someone else?"

McNally read the shock in Kendwall's eyes. "Karen Clayton's mother and a friend of hers identified her."

She covered her face with her hands and sobbed. Picking up a box of tissues on the table beside him, he offered it to her and waited until she composed herself. He gave her another minute, knowing it would be counterproductive to press her too hard.

"It occurred that night, after your class."

"But why? Was it a robbery?"

"No, it doesn't appear so."

"Then for God's sake, why? Who would do something like that? Such a sweet girl." She dabbed her eyes with a tissue and inhaled.

"I'm hoping you can tell me anything that may help us with the investigation," he said.

Then with a small voice, she said, "I'm sorry, but I don't see how I can be much help. I last saw Karen in class Tuesday night. She came on time but then left halfway through it." She tried to keep a brave face, but her voice trembled. "No! God no. She was the kindest person on earth and always spoke positively about her studies, her job, and the people she worked with."

McNally asked Kendwall a litany of questions before ending the interview.

"Thank you again, Ms. Kendwall. I appreciate your cooperation. If you can think of anything else, please call me," he said, handing her his card.

"I wish I'd have been more help. We'd become good friends. I admired and respected her so much. This is an unreal shock. Please find whoever has done this, Detective. The world doesn't need people like that."

When he got back to his car, Kyle reviewed his notes. *Who called the vic? Order phone records.* He added two notes to interview Karen Clayton's coworkers Chi-Tech and Frank Butler.

CHAPTER 20

Detective Dumont tried multiple times to contact McNally on his pager.

Come on, Kyle, pick up!

No luck. She'd met with EZ and wanted to be certain no one had tracked or tailed her. After what he'd hinted to her, it was best not to trust anyone at the station yet. First, she had to call to the unit in the off chance he'd left a message for her. She glanced at her watch.

"Peterson," the person on the other end answered.

Liz froze. She thought about hanging up. "Peterson, this is Dumont. Has McNally been back yet?"

"Nope, haven't seen him since you left." He chewed his food while he talked. "But somebody mentioned he'd be at an autopsy. Di'ja try his beeper?"

"Peterson, this is important. I need you to do me a favor"—she might as well be throwing a Hail Mary pass to a blind man—"when he checks in again."

"Hey, it's been busy around here. Hold for a sec, will ya? I got another call coming in."

"Peterson, no, wait!"

Too late. He had put her on hold.

Damn it!

When he returned, he continued chewing his food in her ear, and she was one deep breath away from going Vesuvius on him.

"Look, if he checks in, tell him I'll meet him at the Clayton apartment later. Tell no one else. You got that? Only McNally. Tell him it's important."

Silence.

"Peterson, goddamnit! Are you listening?"

"Yeah, yeah, calm down, Dumont. Don't get your panties in a bunch. It's urgent. I got it. And you'll meet him at the apartment, right?"

"Okay. You page him and deliver that message as soon as he calls back. You do that, and I'll buy you lunch for a week. Okay? Anything you want."

"That'd be expensive."

"Peterson! Just tell McNally what I said."

He stuffed a cold french fry in his mouth. "Okay. Chillax, would ya? I got it."

Liz sighed after delivering the message. She didn't want to hang up. "Peterson?"

"What? Ya know, my dinner's getting cold while we're talking."

"Is Detective Weller still there?"

"Negative. He left. Don't think he's coming back."

"Oh."

Peterson whined, "Why? Now I gotta message him too?"

"No! But you'd better give McNally my message."

Before Peterson replied, Liz hung up. Peterson shrugged his shoulders and popped a pickle in his mouth.

CHAPTER 21

Liz pulled up in front of Karen Clayton's apartment, where she planned to meet with Kyle. Since her conversation with EZ, she focused on her upside-down emotions. What he'd told her was big. Unreal. But his information convinced her. That was why she had to tell Kyle. He'd know how to handle this. She'd tucked EZ in a motel and told him not to open the door for anybody except her or McNally.

Her palms were sweaty as she rubbed them on her jeans. Kyle would shit when he found out what EZ had told her. All these months, everybody but McNally thought he'd lied.

EZ, I can't believe you're not a dead man already.

She rang the bell to the manager's apartment, and after identifying herself, a loud buzz admitted her through the security door. The manager, Abe Goldstein, peered through the peephole. Liz held her badge up to show him.

He opened the door and stepped into the hallway. He was a short round man with wiry gray hair and thick black framed glasses.

"Yeah. So what do you want?"

"Sir, I'm the detective you spoke with earlier about needing the key to Ms. Clayton's apartment."

"My Greta says a man came by earlier and said he'd come back for the key."

"Yes, that's right. My partner, Detective McNally, is also on his way here. But since I'm here first, I would like to get in and look around."

The old man frowned and shook his head. "Such a nice girl. Why would anyone want to hurt her? Maybe you should wait for other detective, yes?"

Liz tried not to seem impatient but insisted, "Sir, when Detective McNally arrives, please ask him to join me in Ms. Clayton's apartment. Now if you'll give me the key, I won't bother you anymore." She held her hand out to the old man.

He grumbled his dissatisfaction as he handed her a key from the ring on his belt. "I'm not giving out second key, so your buddy don't expect one, right? And make no mess up there. Karen was a neat lady. I don't want her things disturbed."

"No, sir, I promise I am not here to mess the place up. Only to look around."

Somewhat appeased by her answer, the old man nodded, turned, and closed the door, eager to return to his dinner.

Liz climbed the stairway to the second floor. Even though the building was in a nice neighborhood and well maintained, the wall covering recalled a sixties gold and blue flocked paper. The carpeting leading down the hallway had faded; it had multicolor stripes, reminding Liz of her grandparent's apartment in Evanston. She visited them often as a child, and though she didn't remember the interior of their apartment, as with most older city buildings, she remembered the same striped carpet in their hallway.

As she moved down the hall, she counted five doors. The dim light made it hard to see to the end. Three small glass sconces hung on alternating sides of the hall, yet only two were lit. Those lights lit the hall a little better than candles.

The only sound in the hallway was the soft shuffling her own shoes made on the carpeting. She ran her fingers along the wall and felt the soft raised textures in the paper. She guessed none of the other residents were home as there were no lights coming from doorways and no sounds.

Just as she began to curse the poor lighting, the sole bulb on this end of the hall flickered and popped, leaving her in near-total blackness. She reached for her flashlight before realizing she'd left it down on the front seat.

Stupid. Very stupid, Elizabeth Jean Dumont. I should go back to the squad car for it.

She was at apartment 2-B. A few steps farther, and she would be at apartment 2-A. She squinted, freezing in midstride as she saw someone hunched down, close to the floor at the end of the hallway. She gasped while reaching for her gun and crouching in a defensive posture. In another heartbeat, she realized her mistake and sighed. She'd only seen a ceramic planter filled with artificial green foliage.

Who's spooked now, Lizzie? You might've killed a plant.

Now she was at apartment 2-A. She pictured how the other detectives would react if word got around that she ran up against a sinister and dangerous philodendron. She started to insert the brass key in the lock and stopped to read the small wooden plaque hanging from Karen Clayton's door.

Wilkomen. Liz recognized it as the German word for welcome. *Cute, this girl was cute.*

She slipped the key into the lock. It turned with only the slightest hesitation, and the door swung open into a coal-black room.

CHAPTER 22

"Any place you'd prefer to go?" Kyle asked once Mykel settled into her seat.

"Wherever you'd like." She grinned, adding, "Just so the women have all their clothes on and we don't need a roll of ones to get in."

"Nah, not my style. But I know a little place not too far away where I go when I want to be alone. No one I work with goes there. The drinks are decent, and the atmosphere is nice. So unless you have your own favorite…"

"No, sounds perfect."

"The Resurrection Pub. It's quiet and has a comfortable, private feel to it. It's been my getaway spot for some time."

"I'll bet there's a story behind the name."

"Yeah, actually there is. It burned to the ground in the midsixties. Originally, it was a family restaurant, and they didn't serve liquor. If the rumors are true, the mob noticed the success of the place and approached the owners about serving their liquor. The owners refused, and so they torched it. After some, *ahem,* non-insurance-related negotiations, the owners rebuilt, but with the mob's help and a full bar addition."

Mykel laughed. "Interesting story. True?"

"Not sure. It happened more than thirty years ago. But that history added some mystery to its character." Kyle became quiet, thoughtful for a moment or two—comfortable minutes for Kyle but not for Mykel.

She started fidgeting with a pen she pulled from her pocket. "So, Detective, if you're thinking this was a bad idea or poor timing, I'd understand."

He raised an eyebrow, eyes crinkled in amusement. "Where'd you get that idea?"

"You stopped talking." And looking at the pen in her lap, she said, "I'm feeling a little awkward."

"Sorry, Mykel. Most of the people who know me tell me my attention takes a U-turn with some regularity. So far, this Slugger case hasn't panned out any real leads for me. I get a little obsessive about it. My partner, Sam, accuses me of being ADD." He grinned and continued, "I can be tough to read sometimes. Trust me when I tell you, I'm glad we're heading to the Resurrection together. I'm intrigued by this new you without the white lab coat." There was no hint of mockery or sarcasm in the answer.

As they pulled into the gravel parking lot of the pub, Mykel noted its quaint appearance. It reminded her of an old stone church. Beautiful shaggy bark birch trees surrounded the property, and though it was March and the trees were not yet in bloom, she could picture their loveliness in bloom. Colored spotlights illuminated the base of the trees, casting sharp, twisting shadows against the rustic stone walls. Near the entrance, a small fountain trickled water from a cherub's mouth and sprayed the stream into a pool at the base. The pool held a variety of coins, tossed with wishes for dreamers of true love. Over the entrance, a large wooden sign declared, "Resurrection Restaurant & Pub, est. 1955."

Her first impressions of this cozy little place nestled among the trees pleased her. "My, my, you are full of surprises, Detective McNally. This is charming. I love it already. I'm surprised I haven't heard of it before. This is close to where I grew up."

"I stumbled on it when I served a search warrant nearby several years ago. They serve an excellent steak when I'm hungry and don't feel like food on the fly. I use it as a private place to escape to when I need quiet to think and relax." He smiled while placing his hand on her elbow and with a sweeping gesture with his free hand said, "Shall we go in?"

As he entered the dining room with Mykel at his side, it stirred some uncomfortable memories from his past. He hadn't spent much time with civilian females in a long time. He'd given up on complicated relationships—too much maintenance. But he'd try not to unfairly judge this woman or assume she came with a beehive full of neuroses. There'd been a few of those along the way. Over the past twelve years since his divorce, each new relationship began with exhilaration, fire, and fury while focused on grand possibilities. But they always devolved as quickly as they began, leaving him with the not-so-memorable image of train wrecks. A couple had ended badly, and one epic breakup concluded with an out-of-court property settlement that had spiced up his life for a few months.

A waitress speaking, with a friendly thick Irish brogue, greeted them, "Will it be dinner you and the miss will be havin' on this fine and glorious evenin', sir?"

"Just drinks tonight, thank you," McNally said.

She nodded and coyly smiled back at him, motioning for the couple to follow her to a small table in the back of the tavern. The thought popped into Mykel's head that this man must get lots of attention from pretty women. At six feet two, jet-black hair, clear emerald eyes, and a body that looked well tended, he was a handsome man. And she found his charm oddly unintentional and guileless.

Once they sat down at the booth, the hostess leaned into McNally, placing a hand on his shoulder while waiting for their order. Mykel imagined they knew each other.

McNally, still smiling from their previous exchange, said, "The lady would like..." And he looked over to her.

"Have you got a decent California Chardonnay?"

"Yes, we have, ma'am."

"Then I'll have a glass please."

"And I'll have Maker's Mark on the rocks."

The hostess bowed her head to him and left.

When the waitress had retreated, Kyle glanced at Mykel, amused by her expression.

"Someone you're *familiar* with?" Mykel said with eyebrows furrowed in mock curiosity.

"Not *that* well. But since you mention it, she reminds me of a lady I recall having a bad relationship with." The grin on his face mirrored her own.

"And have there been many of those?" she said, returning his volley.

"Aye, indeed. Sad to say there have, lassie," he replied, winking while ginning up his best bold Irish accent.

Mykel relaxed a little. He hadn't laughed at her inquiry as feared. And he seemed to be enjoying this comfortable moment together with her.

"You needn't explain. Sometimes I feel I'm too reserved for my own good."

The waitress returned and set their drinks before them.

Kyle raised his glass to her and recited an Irish toast, "May we live long yet never outlive our happiness."

Mykel nodded, loving his brogue and grinning her approval, using the interruption to change the subject. "So no suspects yet on this Slugger case?"

"No. Truthfully, I'm feeling more frustration than I have in a long time." He shook his head.

She twirled the wineglass in her fingers. "Police have a thing about nicknames, don't they?"

McNally laughed. "Believe me, it's nothing more than giving the offender a useful moniker until we discover his identity."

She rested an elbow on the table with her chin on her hand and said, "Tell me something."

"Shoot."

"What will happen if you don't catch him? Isn't that a possibility? There are more than a few cases of serial killers who never got caught."

"We'll catch him—believe me. He'll make a mistake. And our methods for tracking and capturing these slime balls have improved quite a bit in the past ten to fifteen years. For example, we've learned that right-handed criminals often turn left when bolting the scene but throw away evidence to the right. Also interesting is that most of these perps, when hiding in buildings, hide near the outside walls. Those tendencies play into our hands.

"Other new techniques include geographic profiling to aide us in honing in on the killer's home base. They like to stay in an area they are familiar with, known as their killing field. His own kills, until this latest one, tags him as a missionary murderer, someone trying to rid the world of immoral characters. Karen Clayton appears more like a stalker victim or someone spotted randomly by the Slugger and then targeted. That's why this is a real problem for me. This one veered from his normal pattern. That's unusual."

He broke off, feeling he'd said too much. His frustration with this investigation bore down hard on him. For an instant, his brows knotted, and his mouth turned down. Then his face cleared, and he smiled at Mykel.

"I'm sorry. Let's change the subject," Mykel said. "I shouldn't have asked. Sometimes my timing stinks."

"No, sometimes I get weary of watching this cold-blooded urban drama play itself out. And there doesn't seem to be a thing I, or anyone else, can do to prevent it from happening. And my gut tells me this one's coming much closer to all of us before it's over. But enough of that talk. I'm sounding like a crystal-ball-toting, five-dollar psychic."

"Okay then, putting aside your turban for now, inquiring minds do want to know more about you," she said with an impish smile. "Tell me, were you born in Chicago?"

"No, I was born on Staten Island in New York. My parents divorced before my first birthday, so I remember nothing about my biological father."

"So how does a boy from the forgotten borough end up as a cop in the Windy City?"

"I'll give you the condensed version so you don't mistake me for a tell-all kind of guy."

Never losing eye contact with him, Mykel settled back in her chair.

"The way my mother, Aileen, told the story, she met Patrick McNally as a twenty-two-year-old Irish cop on temporary assignment in Manhattan. She worked in Central Booking as a dispatcher. She was twenty-one and strapped with a nine-month-old baby. I'm told he was a bit of a brat." Kyle winked and continued, "Patrick came over to assist in a joint investigation between Belfast's inspectors and the New York Police Department. Airport security fell far below today's standards. The manufactured explosives were assembled in New York and then flown to Ireland by Sinn Fein terrorists posing as tourists. They would arrive in Belfast, plant them around the city, and then hop the next flight back to New York. When they figured out how the explosives were getting into the city, they had already murdered five high-ranking officials.

"Anyway, Patrick met my mother, and according to her, she instantly fell in love. After learning she had no husband, he asked a cop he worked with to introduce them. It seems they liked each other well enough because by the time he returned to Ireland a few months later, they were married, and my mother and I returned with him. Even his strict Irish Catholic upbringing didn't dissuade him from going home with a ready-made family. Patrick adopted me not long after they married. He's the only father I ever knew, and to this day, we're close. Patrick McNally played a big part in my decision to choose a career in law enforcement." He paused for a moment with his eyes downcast.

Mykel maintained a steady gaze and a small reassuring smile.

He lifted his head, drew a breath, and continued, "Sorry, it's been a while since I've thought about Ireland. I liked it there—at least until the last part."

"No need to apologize, Kyle. You could find some rough spots in my past too. How long did you live in Ireland?"

"Thirteen years. My father worked in Belfast, but we lived in Belleek, a small picturesque town about one hundred miles away from the city. It sits right on the River Shannon and is famous for the Belleek Pottery factory. Their china is world famous."

"You're kidding, right? That's where you grew up? I've got a couple of pieces of their china at home. I've heard it's picture-book beautiful there."

"It is."

"What brought you back to the States? Did your father change jobs?"

"Not exactly. My father decided to send me back to the States. The country had a lot of religious divisiveness and reactionary violence back then, about a mile and a half from what it is today. It affected almost everyone in Ireland during those days. We were no exception. At fourteen, I learned just how monstrously humans can treat one another. My mother died when three Sinn Fein terrorists triggered a package bomb blast. The shrapnel mortally wounded her."

Mykel reached her hand across the table and placed it on his arm. "I'm sorry Kyle. I...I don't know what to say."

"Thanks, but it was a long time ago now. It tore me up for a while, but as with many of the pains from our youth, it has faded to a small dot in my mind's eye. After the funeral, my father decided to send me back to the States. That complicated my grief recovery. He feared for my safety since I saw the attackers. Later, I came to believe that wasn't his sole motivation. I'd become a constant and painful reminder of my mother, who died at thirty-four years old."

Kyle raised his glass in the air. "So here's to my sweet mother, the fair Aileen McNally."

She touched her glass to his and added, "To your mother."

"Well, this is special, huh? Here we've just met, and I'm burdening you with the origins of the Kyle James McNally story. If you don't mind, I'll pretend you forced it out of me." But then, grinning again and with a slight tilt of his head, he said, "Good thing this isn't a date." It was followed by a wink. "It's been a long time since I thought about her death. I hope I haven't bored the hell out of you, Mykel."

"So your father sent you back to this country..."

"Yes, I went to live with my mother's relatives in New York. I finished high school and went to John Jay City College, where I completed my bachelor's degree in criminal justice. And there, Madam Doctor, you have it. The rest is dull, I promise you."

Mykel shook her head. "Somehow I doubt that. Are you still in touch with your father?" she asked.

"Oh, sure, he and I are friends these days. We try to get together once every year to tip a few lagers and amiably argue politics and current police techniques. He never seemed to get over my mother's death, and he used professional dedication as his facade. Funny, but I've always suspected her death put a kind of barrier between us. He's never remarried and never talks about my mother, so I don't bring her up.

"But now he's become one of the leading experts on explosives and detonating devices working for Interpol. He travels the world, teaching his methods to professionals in law enforcement. The Chicago Police Department even hired him to train our explosives team a few years back." And with a wink, he said, "It took me a week to shake off my hangover from that visit."

Mykel's own laughter was open and warm.

"So now are you going recount your wonder years? It seems only fair to me, don't you think?" He noticed her blushing.

"Wouldn't you rather discuss the autopsy?" she said. "I might surprise you how dull my life has been."

He looked at his watch. "There's enough time to talk about the autopsy."

"But you said you're having trouble with the technical language."

"You're stalling, Mykel. Spill the beans about, baby Hartley, or I'll tell the waitress to hold your next drink."

"Okay, okay. I give. My early years didn't involve world travel like yours, but we had some turmoil of our own. You're lucky you still have your stepfather to call on. My mother worked two jobs to keep my brother and me clothed. My alcoholic father couldn't hold a steady job. Though he tried to provide, he spent little time at home with us. We lived in a blue- and white-collar suburb west of here, LaGrange. My brother and I both went to a Catholic school. That cost my mother dearly. To this day, I don't know how she managed. After two years spent waffling about what I wanted to do when I finished school, I realized I always liked science and anatomy, so I pursued medicine. Much to my surprise and my mother's relief, I received a scholarship to Valparaiso University. At first, I tried majoring in psychology, but it didn't take long for me to realize I didn't enjoy fumbling around in other people's heads, so I turned to forensic medicine. At the time, it seemed like a nice, safe vocation. Turns out I'd made the perfect choice—not to mention the liability insurance is way more affordable. The patients don't complain, and not one has threatened to sue me...yet." Her growing level of comfort and natural humor were bubbling up.

"So tell me, why do I feel like I'm reading a book and you have torn out the middle pages?"

She snapped back in mock defensiveness, "Okay, you got me. I floated, not a single plan for my future until my best friend told me she planned to start med school."

"Hold on. Are you telling me you haven't always been the single-minded, driven woman I'm sitting with today?"

Smiling, she continued, "I guess I thought she would have fun without me or something like that." Here her brows drew down, and her manner stiffened. "The summer before I started at the university, I lost both my mother and father within two weeks of each other. I had to postpone my entrance to school for a semester while I worked through the trauma. Thank God we had a dear family friend who literally saved my life from the desperation and depression I'd sunk into. So now, it seems, Kyle McNally, both of us have family misfortunes in common."

"Sounds like a real bad patch. Here's hoping our futures bring many more comforting moments than some of those from our past," McNally said.

She said, "It was difficult losing my mother. She anchored the world I'd grown up in."

Kyle saw the pain wash over her features.

"Anyway, somewhere along the line, I lost touch with my brother. I think he is on the East Coast, working for a shipping company, but it's been several years since we've spoken. He is a few years older than me, but we were never close. He left right out of school, leaving just my mother and me."

He regretted that he had insisted on *quid pro quo*. But at least he had a little more insight into the origin of Mykel's cool and sometimes even callous emotional makeup. He knew she'd told him more than she wanted. That was small consolation now.

"I think I still have time enough for another drink. How about you?"

"Yes, I'd like that. I'd like that a lot!" He raised his empty glass to the waitress, signaling the need for refills. "I have to check in with the precinct. There is an important call I'm expecting. Please excuse me for a minute?"

"Sure, go right ahead."

He left to call the station. Shaughnessy answered.

"This is McNally, any messages for me? I'm hoping to hear from Detective Dumont."

"I just found a message from her. Seems she's gone to Karen Clayton's apartment and would meet you there."

"What? When did she leave?" The muscles in his stomach tightened.

"I'm not sure. I just got here myself. Peterson took the message."

"Let me speak to Peterson."

"Don't know where he is. Someone said he left half an hour ago. My guess is, he's stuffing his face at one of the local eateries. His shift is over. He might not be back."

"That fat fuck!" McNally screamed into the phone. "When did Detective Dumont leave for the Clayton apartment? Forget it. I'm on my way over there now. If you see Peterson… Never mind, I'll deal with him later."

Mad at himself and madder at Peterson, he walked to the head to splash cold water on his face. When he returned to the table, he still had a tight expression on his face.

Mykel frowned. "Everything all right?"

"Unfortunately, no. I got a message that one of my detectives went to the Clayton apartment and I'm supposed to meet her there."

"Is there a problem?"

"The problem is, she left the message hours ago, but the duty officer who took it neglected to notify me." Involuntarily, his fists balled, and his jaw clenched. He had warned Dumont not to involve herself in this investigation. "I'm sorry Mykel, this has nothing to do with you. I would have stopped Detective Dumont from going to the Clayton apartment if I'd known earlier. But we won't be able to have that drink I ordered."

"It's okay. Anything I can do to help?"

"Thanks, but no. Dumont knows better. She's someplace she shouldn't be. She's not assigned to this task force."

"Then why would she go there?"

"I told her to call me if anything came up." And with a distant voice, he added, "She must have thought it important enough to hand-deliver."

"Oh. I think I understand." She reached for her jacket. "I'm sorry. You need to get back to work. I'll call a cab."

McNally motioned for the waitress to bring the bill. "I'm sorry to cut this short, Mykel. But at least let me run you back to your car and head over to the apartment."

"Listen, that'll hold you up way too much. Since I'm the lead examiner on this case, I have a personal stake. If you wouldn't mind, let me tag along. You're in a hurry anyway." She saw doubt flicker in his eyes, and she cut him off with "I promise to stay out of your way." She hesitated, refolding her napkin as he considered. "You won't even know I'm there."

McNally considered her request as he checked his watch. "Okay, but if I get hung up, I'll send you home by cab."

"Fair enough."

Watch close while I work now, feel the electric shock of my touch, open your trembling flower, or your petals I'll crush.

—Israel Keyes

CHAPTER 23

Detective Dumont stepped into the Clayton apartment. She swept her hand over the wall, touched a light switch, and flicked it up.

Nothing.

Down.

Nothing.

Shit!

The room was pitch-black. She stood motionless, waiting for her eyes to adapt to the infuriating darkness. The first light she detected came in dim and yellowish from a streetlight peeking around the edges of the window shades.

She took a step forward and froze, seeing a person across the room. "McNally? Is that you?"

What the fuck?

In this light, she saw someone lying on the floor. Glassy life-less eyes stared back at her. She took a deep breath, stepping toward the object. It was dark and unmoving; she took several seconds to identify it. It was a large porcelain doll placed beside a tipped-over rocking chair. In the dim light, it appeared to have a cracked face.

Relax, Dumont, you're too jumpy. No ghosts here.

She regretted her decision to come up here before McNally arrived.

This day damn sure won't go down as a keeper... Where in hell is he? He should've been here by now. Could he still be at the ME's? How long did a friggin' autopsy take? It started off bad enough, crying like a goddamn baby in the can. Then that crazy conversation with EZ. Was his ID solid? At least I got him stashed for the night. Mac could deal with him later. And where the devil is a working lamp?

"Christ, why didn't I grab my flashlight in the car? Not one of your best moves, Dumont."

I thought he'd be here before me. It took too long to get EZ calmed down and into the motel. I'll castrate that idiot Peterson if he doesn't give Mac my message.

She stood ten feet inside the apartment now, listening to the sounds around her. Rain splashed off the sill against the shade covering an open window.

An open window? Damn, I should've tried beeping him again. Why hasn't he called back? This is important! No, I'm certain this is the best way. I need to tell him to his face…

Huh? An open window?

She straightened her back and rolled her head on her neck to ease the tension.

Dark, dark, and darker. Liz scanned left and right, to the limits of her vision, to where the edges of the gray shadows turned black, trying to determine the layout of the room. But the longer she squinted, the more things seemed to move around her. She slapped a fist on her hip and cursed.

Okay, kid, one step at a time. Nobody here but me and the doll. I've gotta find a lamp or at least raise the window shade to get more light in here.

With the next step, she tripped over the back of a wooden chair that was on its side.

Jeezus!

Instinct made her halt and listen. Did she hear something? She struggled with the creeping fear taking up residence in her head.

"Fear is the great mind killer," she remembered from a book she'd read. Besides, what did she have to be afraid of? A chair, a doll, rain on the windowsill, the boogeyman? She bent down and rubbed her leg and slid the chair from her path. She took another long, slow breath. Still, she sensed something wasn't right here.

A shiver ran down her spine. The blouse beneath her jacket clung to her cool, damp skin, and stringy, wet hair stuck to her face and neck. She blinked several times, hoping to clear her dark-impeded sight.

Focus, Dumont. Find a lamp!

She brushed a hand across her face while turning, hoping to locate a lamp anywhere in the room. The moving shadows grew and shrank in the room. A blinding white light filled the room, followed by a booming peal of thunder that shook the building.

Well shit, I wanted more light... Now I'm blind times two!

Heavy drops of rain were pounding against the window as she stopped to let her eyes readjust. Her shivering was out of control now as she shuffled toward the window.

Baby steps, Lizzie.

She half convinced herself that if she closed it, it would remove the chill and clear her head. A second lightning blast illuminated the room, blinding her momentarily, followed by the rumbling thunder.

A sudden, powerful gust of wind whipped the curtains away from the window. She took two steps back, stumbled, and caught herself in time to avoid falling. She knew the storm made her jumpy, but for the first time since childhood, she felt an alien emotion within her—fear.

During the last flash, Liz had seen a small lamp at the end of a sofa. Still shuffling, she changed direction and aimed herself toward the lamp.

Baby steps.

She cracked her shin again.

Shit!

This time, the culprit was a coffee table. She wasted too much time in this frustrating game of peek-a-boo, hide-and-seek.

A low scraping sound froze her in her tracks, a nearly imperceptible change from the previous silence. The air moved behind her, somewhere in the shadows. To avoid revealing her location, she held her breath and listened. A primordial sense originating from self-preservation made the tiny hairs on the back of her neck stand up, warning her someone else was in the room. She raised her right arm across her chest and unsnapped the safety strap holding her gun in its holster.

"Who's there? Chicago Police! Identify yourself." Her warning sounded weak and hollow in her ears. She stood still, straining to detect any movement as she slid the 9 mm from its holster. Positive someone stood behind her, she swung around, dropped to a crouching position, and pointed her weapon.

Again she raised her voice. "Who's there? Identify yourself!" Her heart pounded loud in her chest, and she swore it echoed off the walls. "McNally. Is that you?"

Silence.

She searched the shadows for any sign of movement. Her mouth was powder dry as her eyes darted around the room. All the shadows were in motion now. She prayed for lightning, but only the raindrops pounding on the windowpanes cut through the silence. No other sound. No other unnatural movement. Like an animal on alert, her muscles were taut, prepared for action. She sniffed the air, testing it for any change since she entered the room. Nothing. She pivoted on her heels to find the exit to leave.

Where's the door?

Too late, she realized it had been beyond reckless coming here alone. A smarter cop would have waited in the car for McNally.

From behind, something metal and heavy smashed down on her gun hand, causing her to immediately lose the gun. Leaving her no time to react, an arm locked around her neck, holding her with Herculean power. She struggled for breath, pulling and pounding on the arm of her attacker, twisting and kicking with her lower body. Instinctively she used every defensive maneuver she was trained for. Seconds passed, her arm fell to her side, her body held fast next to her attacker. She never felt herself drop to the floor like a rag doll. She never saw the brilliant flash of lightning nor heard the explosion of thunder from the raging storm.

Elizabeth Dumont was dead.

CHAPTER 24

The night air became chilly after the rain ended. Mykel shivered, sorry they had to leave the cozy warmth of the tavern.

"This is the place," Kyle said, pulling in front of the three-story brownstone. "Ready to go in?"

"Yes, and I hope we'll find your detective friend was here and had left already. I've been thinking about our conversation on the way here. I imagine you might think it's easy for people in my profession to forget that the bodies we examine were once people—people who had jobs, homes, parents, friends, and children. However, I honestly try hard to remind myself of their humanity."

Kyle caught himself wondering how he would handle that grim occupation.

She continued, "On the surface, I may seem single-minded or even cold, but that's my own built-in self-defense mechanism. I don't think I'd be able to face the work I do day in and day out if I got involved personally in every case, every family, or every history like you have to."

He considered her words for a moment before responding empathetically, "I can't imagine how difficult it would be for you every day. You're right. I'd always considered coroners and morticians to be devoid of the capacity for emotional attachment to the victims. And though some I've known had a better sense of humor than others, I suspected they went home at night to colorless and subdued lives."

When he tried to compare it to his own professional and personal detachment, which for him was natural, he naively assumed their lives were different.

As they entered the portico, he said, "I understand what you're saying. It seems both our professions come with a basket full of stereotypes, and that can be exasperating. Whether a cop or a medical examiner, we have more in common than I thought."

Crammed into the tiny entryway, they waited for Goldstein to buzz them through the door. At first, McNally tried staring up at the ceiling. And then with a roguish smile, he said, "Cozy, huh?"

The heat rose in her cheeks. Oddly, though Kyle made her a little nervous, she recognized it as a feeling closer to exhilaration than anxiety. Mykel dodged the awkward moment and turned her back to him, saying, "So where's that landlord?"

As if on cue, a crackling sound interrupted the silence. "Hello! Who's there?"

"Detective McNally, Chicago Police Department. I came for the key to Karen Clayton's apartment."

Silence.

"Hello, Mr. Goldstein. I told your wife earlier that I would return tonight."

"It's too late. Come back tomorrow," the man grumbled.

"Sir, I can't do that. It's important that I get into the apartment tonight. I'm meeting someone here," he said, hoping the old man was wearing his hearing aid.

"Left without returning key. You get my key back first."

McNally's apprehension mounted as his patience plummeted. "Mr. Goldstein, I'm sorry, but I must see the apartment tonight. You've got to give me another key!"

"I got none left. I call key maker, and he comes out—costs me money. Now go away. Go find that cop. Get her key, and I see you tomorrow."

"Listen, Mr. Goldstein, you either let me in now, or I'll be back with a warrant. You will not like that either." He hesitated, giving Goldstein a moment to think. "It'll be late by the time I get back here. Is that what you want?" He rolled his eyes at Mykel, hoping the threat of a warrant would fly.

Seconds later, the buzzer sounded. They stepped into the hallway, where a bald man with a weathered face peered out at them through a crack in the door. He threw a key at their feet, grunted, and slammed the door shut.

"You don't forget. Bring my key back. I got no more," he barked from behind the closed door.

McNally stooped and picked up the key. They stood in the empty hallway and looked at each other for a second. He rolled his eyes, grinning.

"Let's get up to the second floor before he changes his mind and sends his wife after me."

"I don't imagine this is the part of your job that's advertised in the recruiting pamphlets?" she said, flashing him a mischievous smile.

"It's never this easy. Unlike in your business, my customers often grouse when I do my job."

"Why did I think you needed a warrant?" she said.

"Since the occupant is deceased, I don't. Dead people don't argue about their legal rights. But I didn't think he'd give up the key after giving one to Liz. I'll bust her chops about it in the morning and let her face the old man's wrath when she returns them both."

By the time they reached the narrow second-floor hallway, Mykel experienced an odd exhilaration rising in her. The dim lighting and antique wall sconces were like a scene from a Sherlock Holmes mystery. She hesitated when she realized she couldn't see to the end of the hall.

She said, "This reminds me of some Hitchcock movie—I mean, the darkened halls, the eerie silence, and all."

He thought she might need some reassurance, but when he turned to look at her, she had a playful smile and winked at him.

"Don't you worry, little lady. I've got a big bad gun in my holster," he said, wincing from his terrible John Wayne imitation.

"Then lead on, cowboy."

The key slipped easily in the lock of apartment 2A. But instead of opening the door, the bolt popped forward and locked it. McNally tensed and moved Mykel behind him. He pulled the Glock 9 mm 45 from its holster and turned to Mykel, putting his fingers to his lips, warning her to remain quiet.

He motioned for Mykel to wait in the hall. Then he pushed the door wide open with his left hand and held his gun steady in front of him. Cautiously, he stepped into the room and searched the adjacent wall for a light switch. He became a wary predator. His muscles were taut as he crouched while scanning the room and listening for any unexpected sounds.

He found the switch after the second sweep of his arm and cursed when it didn't work. He heard a soft whistling from an open window across the room. He pulled the penlight from his pocket and went to find the breaker box.

In the bedroom, he saw clothes pulled from their drawers, shoe-boxes emptied, and all thrown in heaps on the bedroom floor. He pushed some of the clothes aside in the closet and saw many of the dresses shredded on their hangers. He reached in and opened the fuse box to reinsert the master fuse. It wasn't in its place, but he found it on the floor beneath the box. He reinserted it, and the lights came on. He was searching the bedroom when he heard a creaking sound behind him. In a single deft move, he spun around, pointing his gun at Mykel's shocked face.

"Damn it, Mykel! I told you to wait outside." he snapped, holstering his gun. "I might have shot you."

"I'm so sorry. I didn't hear you, so I came in… What on earth happened here?"

He walked into the bathroom. "Looks like somebody turned this place upside down." He frowned at the contents of the medicine cabinet scattered around the bathroom floor, noting that their caps were still on. "Mykel, this is now a crime scene, so please take a seat on the davenport in the living room until I can get this sorted out." He followed Mykel to the living room and found the phone under an overturned end table and called the station.

"Homicide. Ramirez."

"McNally here. Any word from Dumont yet?"

"No. Nothing yet. I came back to catch up on paperwork, but you should remind her that me and her are partners now and she's not the Lone Ranger."

"I'm at the Clayton apartment. We've got a problem over here. The place has been flipped upside down."

"What happened?"

"Don't know, but get the MCU over here right away. This mess is new since their initial walkthrough, and I need it swept for prints ASAP."

"I'll send the lab boys over, though they ain't gonna be smiling this time of night."

"That's too damn bad. Their tech three's getting lieutenant's pay. They can drink coffee until it bleeds from their ears for all I care. Just get 'em over here."

"Anything else?"

"Yeah. Do me a favor. Have dispatch keep trying to reach Dumont on her radio and her cell again. If she shows up, drag her along."

"Will do. Anything you care to tell me about?"

"I'm not sure. It's a hunch. Oh, and call Weller. I want him over here too."

"Will do. And I'll keep after dispatch till they contact Dumont."

"Do that. Every fifteen or so." McNally's jaw tightened. "Is that fat jerk Peterson still hanging around?"

"Nah, his shift's over. Shaughnessy's here though."

"Forget it. It'll keep."

He clutched the phone until his knuckles turned white. He was turning to go downstairs when Mykel cleared her throat, reminding him he wasn't alone.

"What's up?"

"Shit, I'm sorry, Mykel. I planned to tell Goldstein we're expecting company."

"Lucky you, huh? I'm feeling useless here. I'd like to help with something," Mykel said.

"How about if you go talk to the old man for me?"

She laughed. "Besides that."

"Well, for now, please relax. I'm relieved your services won't be needed."

She knew he was holding back and not telling her everything, and she knew Detective Dumont's absence created his urgency to summon the lab team. She caught herself pondering a relationship with him. Would it go beyond professional? Were they to be lovers? Good friends? Where on earth did that come from?

A few minutes later, McNally returned to the apartment. He stepped into the room and saw Mykel waiting on the couch, appearing bored and distracted.

"Are you concerned that something happened to Detective Dumont?"

"I'd rather not speculate too far beyond what's in front of me right now. It's too early for that."

Mykel wanted to offer some reassurance, but there were no words.

"Listen, Mykel, there's no reason for you to stay here. It looks like it will be a long night. I'll arrange for an officer to give you a lift home when the team arrives."

"Thanks, Kyle. How about a make-up date for our discussion of Clayton's autopsy?"

"Date? Is that what this was, a date?" He grinned, then added, "Though I do like your choice of words."

CHAPTER 25

McNally needed time to focus his thoughts. He stepped out onto the back porch. He again considered the contradictions in this case.

If Slugger murdered Clayton, why the changed MO? Why on earth would he take the chance of going to the vic's apartment with the police sniffing around? Could it be it as simple as a search for another trophy from her? Not likely; it was too dangerous. So what did he look for? This case was a mile from his usual MO. What the hell?

The minutes dragged as he waited for the crime techs. He rolled his head from side to side and clasped his fingers behind his neck to stretch. Angry at himself, he recognized he'd become distracted by so much irrelevant shit. He'd lost his focus on the larger questions.

How does Slugger choose his victims? Is it random? Does Clayton's murder signal a sudden change in his motivation or just a one-off? A simple trigger that clicked in his head? What would he do next? Concentrate!

He double-checked the bedroom and bathroom again, paying no attention to Mykel.

I think he must have known this girl. Otherwise, how did he know where she lived? Did she know him?

He pivoted back to the more immediate question of Liz's involvement.

What did Liz find that could be so urgent she had to meet me here? Why didn't she wait? Goddamn it, Dumont, where in the nine circles of Hades are you?

He hated unanswered questions. McNally had to be smarter; netting Slugger would only happen if he thought like him. He also recognized an unfamiliar sensation in himself—claustrophobia.

Christ! Think, McNally!

Mykel watched as Kyle paced the floor. He took a deep breath, wondering how the city's MCL unit could take so long. He glanced over at Mykel and scowled.

He said, "Don't like the waiting."

"Knock, knock," a voice boomed from behind them. "What in the name of a flaming bag of shit on the front porch have you got yourself into now, McNally?"

Kyle smiled as Sam Weller walked through the door, ankle wrapped, and wearing sneakers, looking way past his usual disheveled appearance. Four technicians followed him, each carrying large black cases.

"You're a sorry sight, Weller. I hoped you'd make it tonight. This one's taken a nasty turn."

"I dropped back by HQ for my messages. Ramirez tried to fill me in. What have you stepped into here?"

McNally made a waving motion with his arm. "Long story short, Liz knew I'd be coming here tonight, and the message I got said she planned to meet me. I never caught up with her and found the place like this."

"Looks like somebody got real angry here, buddy. I doubt Lizzie did this, so who did?"

"That's what I've been kicking around."

Sam stepped out of the way of the technicians, giving him a chance to admire the attractive woman sitting on the couch. "You gonna introduce us, Mac, or am I gonna have to play twenty questions?"

"Oh, sorry. Sam, Dr. Hartley, the ME assigned to the Clayton autopsy."

Weller beamed. "Ma'am, I'd heard there was a looker working in the dead zone. A pleasure to meet you," he said with a slight bow.

"Sam, behave," Kyle warned. "Mykel, meet Detective Orville Goff Weller, my partner and a man who's been around police stations since Democritus first identified the atom. That explains his ornery disposition."

Mykel laughed and offered her hand. "It's nice to meet you, Detective."

Weller took her hand and grinned. "What he meant is, I've only been around since they split the atom, ma'am. And you can imagine with that name why everyone calls me Sam. But please pardon this dumb look of confusion, but is there a body around here that I ain't seeing? I mean, are you here on business?"

"No, she came with me. We were discussing the Clayton girl's autopsy when I got the message that Liz would meet me here."

Mykel excused herself, stepping out to the hallway to clear the way for the techs, who were busily setting up their operation.

Weller turned to Kyle. "Hartley? As in the Dragon—oh, my bad."

"Put a cork in it, Weller."

"Sometimes words spill out without warning when my brain takes a holiday—automatic, like a gumball machine. But, Mac, that still doesn't clear up how in the devil's name you and her end up here together. Shock theater, fella... Shock theater."

"Forget it. Let's get to work. But first I've got to arrange for a ride for Dr. Hartley to get back to her car."

Weller ordered one of the three uniformed men to guard the door and another to cover the building's entry. A third one chauffeured the doctor back to her car. They would prevent any unauthorized personnel or nonresidents in or out of the building.

Kyle went out to the hall to say goodbye to Mykel, while Sam did a walkthrough of the apartment.

"Mykel, we've arranged for a ride back to your car for you. Sorry about the bumpy ride this turned out to be."

"Hey, don't give it a moment's thought. You've got plenty going on without that. I enjoyed the evening despite the problems you've run into here. I'll look forward to our next chance to get together."

"As will I."

He went back into the apartment and found Sam in the bedroom.

"Christ! What a mess." Weller turned and faced his friend. "So what am I looking at here?"

"Still working on that."

"Okay." Weller put his hand on his friend's shoulder. "Now you want to tell me again why she'd come here? She's not even working this case, right?"

From beneath a furrowed brow, he stared levelly at Weller. "Haven't got a clue, Sam. I left her instructions to contact me if she needed me. Don't know why she didn't."

"Did you you check your beeper lately?" Sam asked.

"I got distracted, waiting for word from my CI. He promised to get back with me about Henry Lucas's location. I told her she should contact me if he called into the station. She knew I planned to come here tonight to have a look at the place. Ramirez saw a scribbled message on Peterson's desk about Liz trying to reach me. Never did check the beeper."

Weller grunted. "Peterson? That useless sack of shit. Let's shoot him and put him out of our misery."

McNally's jaw clenched. "Trust me, I'll take it out on his ass next time I see him."

"I saw Liz running out when I came back to the squad room today." Weller waved his arm over the room. "You think she might've run into whoever did this?"

"Maybe. We don't know where she is yet. If she walked in on this, I'd like to think she'd call one of us. She wouldn't simply close the door and leave. Trouble is, the manager downstairs says she came, but he never saw her leave."

"Wouldn't be the first time that little renegade didn't follow orders."

"What the fuck is that supposed to mean?"

"Forget it. I remember the heat you took for that mess in Chinatown."

"Liz had nothing to do with it. That screw up was all on me."

"Somehow you always get stuck defending her, don't ya, Mac? Forget I said anything. When she got here, the place was probably still clean. At least that's how I see it. She tired of waiting and left.

She'll show up. Always does." Weller placed a reassuring hand on McNally's shoulder. "Listen, my friend, it's obvious how tight you two are. Hell, the three of us shared many a brewskie together, but I'm serious now when I tell you to relax, buddy… This case is eating your lunch."

"There's no blood," McNally said, shrugging.

"Well, I ain't gonna say anything you haven't already thought, and you won't like me saying this out loud, but we're dealing with Slugger here, not Jeffrey Dahmer. Slugger does his best work outdoors."

McNally lowered his head. "Okay, but if Slugger did this, we still don't have an answer why he staged Clayton at Graceland or why he came here and trashed her apartment. He had to be looking for something, right?"

"And…what else?"

"I'll try to fill some gaps since you've been in court and on restricted duty with your ankle."

"And whose gaps are you filling—"

"Christ, Sam! Get your whore dog mind under control for five minutes, would ya?"

"So sorry, buddy," he said, feigning hurt. "I missed the bulletin saying you'd lost your sense of humor last week."

"Yeah, yeah. At this point, I'm thinking he might have left something here he didn't want anyone to find. Or if she didn't know him, she may have had something he was after," Kyle said.

Sam responded, "But that still doesn't answer whether Liz ran into him here tonight. She still hasn't checked in at Area 1."

"He's a ruthless son of a bitch, but there's nothing that proves Liz came here before or after he made this mess."

Weller jumped in. "Yeah, it's more likely she changed her mind and left—and forgot to return the key. Like I say, 'Don't go scratching for trouble if there's no shit in the litter box.' We'll find out more when the lab boys inventory the evidence and deliver their report. If anything's here, they'll find it."

"He's gonna fuck up, Sam. You can bet your ass on that. And when he does, I will be there to escort him straight to hell."

"Okay," Weller continued, "so see if this fits with your idea about her murder. I'll assume the Clayton woman *was* just another random target. History says that's how he picks his vics, right? Then if I'm the Slugger, I pick her out on the street because of her looks, her clothes—oh, what the hell—because I like the way she swivels her hips. Anyway, I'm seeing something different about her, and it stirs my sick fantasy factory. And so I trail her, looking for my opportunity. I follow her from her work to her school and wait for an opening. It's possible, right?

"Now I see her and take my shot. Keep in mind, she's different; lived well, by the look of this place; a popular lady with friends and a few bucks in the bank. But our man's a smart and careful predator. Now if I were the Slugger, why in hell do I risk my tuchus and come here, even if I find an address on her driver's license. To get my rocks off messing up the place and get away with a couple pair of panties?

"So again, where's my motivation? Sounds a little thin, pal. Maybe some smoke, but no fire there, methinks. There's something going on here, but it doesn't look like a murder site. More like the wrath of a jilted boy *or* girlfriend," Sam said with a wink.

Kyle didn't believe that. What *would* bring him back here? Not for a pair of panties; he'd always taken them before leaving the women. Even if this was random, Slugger wasn't sloppy enough to leave anything he'd have to come here to find. And even if he grabbed her here, which Kyle doubted, he'd never been that careless before. This wasn't some mindless, reckless psycho, or there'd be a trail a mile wide by now. This killer was smart enough to slaughter his prey, avoid detection and capture, and move on to his next kill. He'd never moved his vics before, and he'd never left them on a stage like this one.

No, Slugger reveled in his handiwork and looked forward to the torment of each one of his models. Here was a living, breathing bogeyman. He'd grown exhausted from his effort to rent space in the Slugger's head. Like Sam said, it wore on him. With each new victim, his own anger grew. And the familiar sense of control he'd had in past cases seemed beyond his grasp in this one.

"The FBI has a handful of psych geeks in Quantico," Sam said. "Have they worked up a profile yet?"

"Yeah. They have our reports and the autopsy results from each vic. Those idiots won't find anything useful until after we've solved this one."

"Sam, do me a favor and put a team on the photos taken from the crowds around the cemetery. I want identities and interviews of any unknown gawkers from the crowd standing gathered at the scene. I suspect they're the usual TV news camera zombies, but we might see something. If this is the Slugger, the change in this MO started me thinking that he might hang around, watching us work the location where we found the body—and particularly since I think he tried to rub our noses in it by placing her in front of Pinkerton's monument."

"Will do, Mac."

Kyle continued, "So putting aside the mess we've got here for a moment, these are the facts and guesses I'm left trying to sort out, like where did he murder her? We find her viciously beaten and propped up against a gravestone in a staged pose. Her car's left in the campus lot, no signs of a struggle. She left class early. Why? Witnesses say she got a call, and it appeared to bother her, bother her enough to get up and leave class. We still haven't found her phone yet. Did he snatch her in the lot, or did she go freely? She wouldn't get into his car unless she either knew him or he mugged her, right? So then let's say she might have known her assailant. I'll bet it all started in the school parking lot. Even with no evidence to support it, it's my best guess she knew him and got in his car willingly."

Kyle started pacing around the room.

"If I look at it from that angle, then the killer had some other reason and didn't just beat her with a bat, sexually assault her, and leave her at the scene like the others. Imagine it was personal this time. He knew her and had some grudge against her. Or she had something he wanted, which is the more likely. He takes her to a place where he can take his time and tries to find out what she has and where she keeps it. He wants to look this one in the eyes as he questions her. But why leave her in the cemetery? To piss me off? Really? If he needed something she had and couldn't find it on her, he might come here to find it. Could it have been something she had that revealed his identity?"

Sam didn't interrupt McNally. He knew his friend well enough to realize he did this with every case that landed on his desk. He'd think it through from a dozen different angles before settling on one that fit the case to a tee.

Kyle stopped pacing and looked at Sam. "Sam, I'm convinced we won't find a connection to the other vics, and it's more likely he knew her. We've got to find her phone, Sam. I think that's how we connect the dots, buddy. That seems like the most likely explanation for the right angle turn in Slugger's MO. I'd bet the Sears Tower she knew him."

Weller followed McNally out of the room. "So you got it stuck in your gut that the Clayton girl knew Slugger. I guess I can run with that, but"—he flipped his hand toward the mess in the room—"that leaves us with bupkis, Mac."

"Not if my theory is correct and he knew her. He believed something was here he had to find to protect himself," he said with more conviction.

"Well, I'm no shrink, buddy. Can't say for sure what he's thinking," Weller said, shrugging with hands raised. "Maybe he's only a sadistic fuck all coked up with a joystick in his hand?"

"Come on, Weller. That'd be too easy."

An hour passed with no new discoveries. The techs finished sweeping everything from the fireplace to the broom closet. They were waiting for McNally to call off the search. They'd labeled every collected bag and box, and all would end up in the evidence locker for McNally to sift through later.

McNally left Weller standing in the kitchen, regurgitating ethnic jokes with a tech three. He passed them unnoticed and walked out on the back porch.

Outside, the air felt cool and humid. A thick, low-lying fog had partially obscured the ground below. He filled his lungs with the night air and listened to the sounds of the last of the rainwater echoing down the gutters of the building.

Then from down in the backyard, he heard "Sir, we've got something…"

CHAPTER 26

McNally leaned over the balcony and saw two of the techs dressed in black rain slickers, the word *police* in large yellow letters across their backs. They were squatting on the brick path, holding their flashlights over a patch of muddy ground.

"Tell me the son of a bitch dropped his wallet."

"Nope, but something as good. There's a near-perfect footprint in the mud here."

The tech cleared leaves and loose debris from the area surrounding the impression. McNally went down to join the two hunched figures. He listened as they discussed the shoe that made this imprint.

Corporal Joey Santini said, "This one's fresh. Rain didn't wash out the tread. Look here." Then he pointed with a twig, looking up at McNally. "No water in the grooves. That's a good thing. The old lady's given us a break here."

"Old lady?" McNally asked, imagining blue hair and recalling the window where he'd seen Mrs. Goldstein earlier.

"Yeah, Mother Nature," the tech replied.

"Do you recognize the brand of shoe?" McNally asked.

"Can't say I remember this one from memory, but it's a sneaker—that's for damn sure. Don't worry. We got a book back at the lab that has the design of almost every known sole made for man's comfort." He smiled at his partner. "This one'll be easy. Every groove and dent's intact."

"Okay, Jeremy, let's get a tent over it and make the cast. Get me my kit bag and water out of the truck."

"How long will this take?" McNally asked.

Santini raised his eyes to the sky. "In this weather? If the rain holds off, the quick-drying plaster we use shouldn't take over fifteen minutes before we can lift it."

Santini hollered at Jeremy's departing back to fetch his camera and tripod along with the other equipment. He responded by lifting his arm in acknowledgment before disappearing around the corner of the building.

Sam Weller joined the two lab techs gathered on the back porch, who were watching. "They find something?" he asked.

"A footprint, I think."

Weller chuckled. "Well, I gotta wonder... Maybe somebody walked their dog and left that print."

Santini frowned. "Nope. Not likely. Only one print here in the mud, and it's a deep one, like someone either heavy or carrying something. Maybe they got off balance and stepped off the path into the mud. Then they quickly stepped back on. You can see here how there's more mud along the path going out."

"Well, my man, we need a break right about now," Sam said.

The wind shifted, and a quick blast of cold air swept in from the north. Jeremy first placed a metal frame around the print and set up a tripod device centered over that. He attached a high-resolution camera to the tripod. He used them to take framed photos of the footprint from a top view.

After removing the equipment, Santini mixed the quick-set plaster. When ready, he poured it over the frame to cover the print.

Two hours later, the team finished up. McNally rubbed his eyes and ran his fingers through his hair. At just past one o'clock, he was dead on his feet. The lack of sleep over the last two days hit him like a brick to the head. He leaned against the living room wall, only half attending to the dwindling activity around him.

Sam looked over at him. "Mac, you know Dumont will turn up. Everyone, including the state boys, are turning over every leaf to find her. And think about it—how many times in the past have her man-related escapades caused her to be out of communication for hours or even a day at a time? Go home and get some shut-eye. I'll wrap up here. You look like warmed-over shit."

"Then I look better than I feel."

"A shave might help, but your eyes look like you're coming home from an end-of-the-world party, brother."

McNally frowned and ran his hand over his heavy day-old beard. "Okay, Sam, I'm leaving. Call me as soon as Dumont checks in."

"Will do."

CHAPTER 27

McNally headed home from the Clayton apartment at 2:00 a.m. and decided he needed a good jolt of Maker's Mark right about now. That and several hours of undisturbed rest sounded good. He'd given up hope of finding an open liquor store when he saw the flashing neon sign: "Lou's Liquors—Open."

Entering the small cluttered store, he recoiled from the pungent odor of stale cigar smoke, beer, and the oppressive aroma of an old air freshener. He nodded to the weary-looking cashier, who lifted droopy red eyes from the *Playboy* centerfold opened on the counter in front of him. McNally located the whiskey section in the back of the store. He grabbed a fifth of his bourbon and headed back down the aisle toward the cashier. Angry words made him pause midstride. He listened to the ensuing conversation between the cashier and someone who'd entered the store after him.

"C'mon, buddy, don't shoot me! I'll give you whatever you want. Please don't hurt me. Please!"

McNally groaned. "Shit."

A low menacing growl reverberated off the walls. "Fill the fuckin' bag, and shut your piehole before I blow your goddamn head off!"

Carefully placing his bottle on a shelf next to him, McNally crept toward the front of the store. He crept down the aisle toward the voices. He hoped the robber wouldn't spot him in the overhead security mirror behind the cashier before he reached him.

As he listened to the slurred, staccato words from the man with the gun, he moved closer. He slid the 45 out of his holster and moved into the aisle that gave him a full view of the gunman's back. At the counter, the man held a sawed-off shotgun, pointing it at the trembling cashier's face. McNally's distorted reflection in the mirror had so far gone unnoticed. Rather than risk lunging the ten feet that separated them, he inched his way closer, hugging the shelves. If he didn't move fast enough, the cashier might unwittingly tip off the gunman. Timing was critical.

As the clerk stuffed the contents of the cash drawer in a paper bag, the assailant yelled, "Hurry up, asshole! What the fuck are you doing? Forget the change! You got a safe? And don't you fuckin' lie, or I'll paint the wall with your brains!"

The cashier shook so much he dropped a handful of money on the floor, and it scattered in every direction. Before the quaking man stooped down to retrieve the scattered bills, the gunman reached over and dragged him by the collar across the counter.

With lightning speed, he jammed the shotgun into the cashier's mouth and spat, "You just ran outta luck, fucker."

McNally took advantage of the seconds given him by the cashier's clumsiness and covered the remaining distance between him and the gunman with two long strides. He pinned the barrel of his gun against the back of the gunman's neck.

"No, *you* just ran out of luck, asshole. Now hand over the shotgun," he ordered. "Nice and slow, fella, and you won't have anybody crying at your funeral tomorrow."

The gunman appeared to be a head taller than McNally and outweighed him by probably forty pounds. Black curly hair flared out from under a blue baseball cap that sat low on his head. He wore a long black coat over faded jeans.

"Don't shoot, man! I ain't gonna do nothin'. Christ's sake, don't shoot. Here, here, you can have the gun."

Just as Kyle reached for the outstretched weapon, the man spun to the side, smashing the barrel of the shotgun against his right shoulder hard, knocking McNally's gun hand away as he fought to maintain his balance. In defense, Kyle reached out with his left hand

and grabbed the assailant's shotgun barrel and attempted to yank it from his grasp. The man's finger caught on the trigger, and when Kyle jerked, a loud explosion filled the air. Glass and liquor from a display stand behind him spewed like a volcanic eruption. The shotgun flew from his grip while he fell back several steps. For a moment, the robber stood staring at him with a look of utter surprise painted on his face.

But his face transformed as his eyes widened and his nostrils flared. Kyle dropped to a crouching position and shouted, "Don't do it, man!" Even without being able to see his eyes through the dark glasses, instinct told him the man would dive for his weapon.

The man's lips twisted into a malevolent grin, exposing a wide gap between large yellow teeth. He met McNally's challenge like a bull staring down a red cape and dove for his weapon. McNally leaped to cut him off and succeeded by driving the man into the glass counter the clerk had hidden behind. The man's head crashed through the glass with a concussive boom. Broken glass from bottles and the display case flew in every direction. McNally's head bounced off the countertop, and he fell back on the floor, landing on top of the bloodied assailant.

With a loud groan and despite his wounds, the man pushed McNally off to the side and jumped to his feet. McNally rolled over and stood up a second too late to deflect the man's powerful kick to his rib cage. McNally winced in pain. Then he reacted and punched back, hitting the robber hard twice in rapid succession. The second one found its mark, and the man's crushed nose sprayed blood in all directions. Unconscious, he fell back on the floor.

Head spinning, McNally dropped to his knees and yelled to the cashier, "Call 911!" The cashier stood frozen with his mouth gaping open. McNally added, "While I'm still breathing!"

"Oh, oh, sure... S-s-sorry... You a cop or s-s-something?" the cashier stuttered, fumbling for the phone.

"Make the call. Tell them, 'Officer down.'"

His limbs were shaking as he tried to push himself off the floor and realized he had no strength in his right arm and his rib cage screamed for mercy. His arm gave beneath him when he noticed blood dripping from his jacket sleeve.

Terrific.

Sharp splinters of glass tore through his jeans. His arm hung at his side.

"Yeah, s-sure, mister. Were you hit? Is that your blood on your arm?"

McNally didn't answer as he fought to keep from passing out. Seconds passed, and he grew weaker until he had to rest his head against the shelf behind him. He focused his eyes on the blinking neon liquor sign at the front window, struggling to clear his head. He tried again to regain his feet, but he swooned and fell back.

The cashier raced around the counter in time to catch McNally before he hit the deck.

"Hang in there, Officer, okay? The cops are on the way."

McNally heard the sirens in the distance. The last thing he saw through blurred vision were two uniforms entering the store with their guns pointing at him.

"Great," he mumbled before losing consciousness.

The cashier screamed, "He's a cop, I think! Hurry, some guy shot him!"

CHAPTER 28

McNally's body twitched, and his eyes flew open. He could not remember where he was. He attempted to raise himself from his prone position but flinched from the pain in his right arm and ribs and then collapsed back against the pillows. Sam Weller sat in a chair beside his bed.

"Ow! What the...?" Kyle's eyes began to focus on his surroundings. Then he said, "Jesus, you're a splash of ice water to the face first thing in the morning."

His partner chuckled. "At least you got the time of day right. When I sent you home to get some shut-eye, my friend, I didn't mean for the rest of your life. What the hell were you doing in a liquor store at two in the morning?"

"I needed a drink. How long have I been down?" He tried once more to lift himself, this time rolling on his side. Rockets of pain shot down his arm. His wrapped shoulder had a mile of gauze around it and hung in a sling across his chest, and he had an IV drip plugged into his left wrist. He looked down at himself and frowned. "Tell me it's still May."

Weller looked at his wristwatch. "Yeah, but you've been out of pocket."

"Shit."

"Careful with that shoulder, Mac. They've got you bound up good, but you could still do some damage by moving around. I guess you tore a muscle or two. Do you remember anything that happened?"

"The wing's hurt, Sam, and my memory's a little fuzzy. It feels more like a screen door than a steel trap." He inspected the bandage on his shoulder and rubbed his forehead. "I'm a half mile from perfect, but I'll be okay."

"That so? You got a concussion from your fall. That's why you've been laid up here for a couple of days. The clerk reported you got that knock by bouncing your head off the store counter. A sore shoulder, two broken ribs, and a bad headache—it coulda' been a lot worse. The perp's shotgun blew away an entire display case."

Sam grimaced as Kyle tore at the tape holding the IV in place on his hand and removed the needle. He tried removing the sling from his arm. It was harder than he thought it would be, but he got it.

"To hell with all this, Sam. We need to get out of here. Go get my clothes, Sam. I need to get dressed so we can get out of here."

Sam'd seen the stubborn set of Kyle's jaw before and knew he'd be wasting breath arguing, but he tried anyway. "Don't be a jerk. The world's not gonna teeter off its axis with you off your feet for a day or two longer. Besides, the doc says he wants to run more tests on your melon before you're cleared to leave the hospital."

"Can't stay here, Sam. Too much to do. And I've already burned two days too long." His expression hardened. "Any word from Liz yet?"

"No, but every able body in the precinct is working it. We've cast a wide net to locate her. We'll find her," he said, trying to sound reassuring.

"Too much time's gone by."

Damn it, she'd have called by now.

"Nah. She'll turn up. She always does."

Kyle's jaw tightened. "Sure she will. Now we've gotta go."

Sam grabbed the pants from the closet and threw them to Kyle, chuckling. "News flash, Mac, nobody wants to see you in your Fruit of the Looms."

"What about my CI EZ? Any news?"

"Nothing yet. He's still blowin' in the wind."

"Sam, Liz is dead, and it's on me." This was as real and painful as his bandaged arm and ribs. He believed that, and the guilt suffocated him.

"Whoa, buddy, let's not start imagining the worst before we have something solid, okay?" Sam said.

"Yeah right. Now toss me my shirt, goddamnit, or I swear to the heavens, I'll take this bedpan and give *you* a concussion."

"Okay, I'll do it. But not on account of that lame-ass threat. I want it on record, I'm not agreeing with you. Anything happens, and it's hasta la fuckin' bye-bye to my ass, not yours."

"Quit your whining. Nothing will happen."

Reluctantly, Weller got him the rest of his clothes.

"Where's my gun?"

"The district commander has it."

"Then we'll have to stop by my place to get my other revolver."

Weller grumbled as he headed out of the room, "McNally, if it got around I was your own personal *do boy*, it'll ruin my bad reputation."

McNally still hadn't finished dressing when Sam popped his head back through the door.

"By the way, two uniforms from the shooting review team have been by here already. They need to interview you. What do you want to do? It won't be long before Internal Affairs will be sniffin' around to ask you some questions too."

"Fuck 'em, Sam… The district boys want me to dictate their paperwork for them. And IA can catch up with me when I'm back at headquarters." McNally grimaced from his pain. He'd already moved way past irritable. He held onto the chair for balance as he fought to remove the standard-issue hospital smock. McNally looked up at Weller, who was still standing in the doorway. "Come on, Weller, don't nag. Those boys will have to settle for the report from the store clerk until I've got time for them."

The pain in his arm was throbbing, and a couple of his ribs were fighting to see which one popped through his chest first. He cursed as his pants slipped from his fingers and fell to the floor. The room started to spin. He clutched the side of the bed.

Christ, not now.

In great pain, he slipped his body into a kneeling position and retrieved his pants.

By the time Weller got back, he found McNally dressed and standing next to the bed for support. He had a blanched face and features pinched with pain.

"McNally, you are one stubborn son of a bitch."

"And you worry too much. Did you get the gun?"

He took it out of his raincoat pocket and said, "Hope I don't regret this. But we better move quick 'cause I'm picturing Nurse Crotchety down the hall chasing after us any second. Where to first?"

McNally looked out the window. "It looks like nice weather for a funeral."

CHAPTER 29

In the squad car, with his head down and eyebrows crowding together, Kyle turned to Sam.

"I'm still stuck on whether Slugger changed his MO, or is it a one-off? It just doesn't fit, does it? I've been trying to make some sense of it. My gut tells me this isn't a copycat's work. The degree of brutality along with the baseball card rules out a copycat. The baseball card details still haven't made it to the press.

"Then staging the body like some sick cartoon caricature? When they stage them, it's for one of three reasons—he's deliberately trying to throw us off his scent or he's thumbing his nose at us or he's gratifying some fantasy of his. Take your pick. By placing the body in front of Pinkerton's grave, it makes me think he may be satisfying all three. And he knew her, Sam. I'm sure of it."

"Look, partner, how about we keep following the leads? Yeah, Slugger may have turned a corner here, but I'm not ready to take anything off the table yet. There's more we don't know than we know. Like why? Slugger didn't get his jollies from staging his victims before. We've learned he likes to display them like some kinda nutsy trophies, but he's never shown a taste for the P. T. Barnum shtick, has he? Yeah, he's got a style, like a dog marking a hydrant, and that's been his trademark. Serial killers don't change their methods or their geography, do they?"

By the time they arrived at the cemetery, the rain had become a steady downpour of sleet. They drove down a long driveway leading through the cemetery, searching for the burial site. Visibility was poor, and the wind turned umbrellas inside out. Sam chomped on his fresh cigar, but catching his partner's grim expression, he prudently decided not to light up.

"Good Christ, I'm sick of this never-ending rain!" McNally said between gritted teeth.

They found the gravesite, but after walking closer, they had difficulty making out the silhouetted figures huddled under umbrellas. The wind and rain beat against McNally's face, and he struggled to keep his coat closed over his sling. He grimaced, unable to stop shivering. Women were leaning against their men for support while the men stood with heads hung low. The priest spoke, and muffled sounds of sobbing rippled through the crowd. It reminded him of the call and response of a Gregorian chant.

Weller swore under his breath, "Damn, I'd like a cigar and a double shot of scotch right now."

"Roger that. This shouldn't take much longer. We got here late."

From the corner of his eye, Kyle noticed movement. A tall shadowy figure stood camouflaged beneath a stand of trees some fifty yards from the gathering. The wide umbrella and rain prevented him from seeing the man's face clearly, but it was obvious the stranger wanted to view the service from a distance. Kyle stepped away from Weller and walked a wide circle around the people toward the hilltop. As he passed the mourners, the group dispersed. He stopped long enough to scan the crowd of faces. By the time he turned his attention back, the solo observer had left.

Kyle was trying to pick out Karen's mother in the tight circle of people walking away when Frank Butler approached him, clutching the arm of a small delicately attractive woman.

"Detective!" Butler shouted, pulling the woman behind him. She clung to his arm, struggling to keep herself from falling. "I'm glad you're here. There's something about Karen's case I have been wanting to discuss with you."

McNally raised his hand in the air. "Mr. Butler, I've been meaning to speak with you too. But, I'm sure, given the solemnity of this occasion, whatever we need to discuss can wait." He turned to face the woman. "Mrs. Clayton, I'm not sure if you remember me from the morgue, but I'm Detective McNally, and this is my partner, Detective Weller. We're heading up the investigation into your daughter's homicide. We won't intrude on you here today."

"Thank you, Detective. That's kind of you. I believe we spoke briefly on the telephone the day I met with the detectives at the county examiner's office."

"Yes, ma'am. And I realize it's a difficult time for you, but I have a few follow-up questions I'd like to ask. I'd like to meet tomorrow if it's okay with you. I'll come by your home if that's convenient."

"That would be fine. But please tell me, have you learned anything more in the search for my daughter's killer?"

"Excuse me, Marian, but I have a few questions of my own for the detective," Butler interrupted.

McNally shot cold eyes at Butler. "I don't think—"

"Not now, Frank. I'm sure the detectives have a lot to do, and I'm cold and want to go home. People are waiting for me at the house," Marian said.

Intercepting the argument he saw Butler was itching to start, Kyle said, "We won't keep you, ma'am. We stopped to pay our respects. Mr. Butler, I'll reach out to you so we can discuss your questions at a more appropriate time."

"Thank you, Detective. Now let's go, Frank."

Weller had interviewed Butler while Kyle was in the hospital and reported him to be genuinely despondent over the loss of his friend. He wanted to help with the investigation. Sam left the interview convinced that Butler's sincerity in offering to help, overzealous as it seemed, was honest. But McNally had known people like him; they were almost never helpful and more often became troublesome.

"What a waste of time, huh? What say we go for a shot and a brew, my winged friend?" Sam said with a wink.

"I don't care. Just take us somewhere dry and warm." McNally dropped into the passenger side of the car. "I feel like dehydrated shit. It's possible you're right. This may not have been a good idea."

"So why'd we do this? We got enough dicks assigned to this case so we can afford to take a few hours off."

McNally rubbed his arm and growled, "Not now, Weller. Did you see that guy standing solo on the hill?"

"Yeah. Big son of a bitch. I'm six feet tall, but I got the feeling that if he stood right next to us, he'd still be a full head taller."

"That's the one. I started to walk over there when the service ended. I took my eyes off him for a second, but he'd left. You see where he went?"

Weller shrugged. "Nah, I had my eyes on the crowd. Probably someone on the outs with the family is all."

"Maybe."

CHAPTER 30

"Dispatch to McNally."

He picked up the mic. "Yeah. McNally here. Go ahead."

"What's your 20?"

"Cicero and Archer."

"Hold, please."

He clutched the mic tighter in his hand. "Maybe it's Liz."

A crackle came over the police radio. "McNally, come back." It was Ramirez.

"Yeah, Roy, what's up?"

"We've got Dumont's car. They found it at an abandoned warehouse parking lot behind West Parker Street, close to Clayton's apartment. Can you get to the precinct garage? The techs are waiting for you."

"Be there in thirty."

"Well, that don't sound good," Sam said.

McNally didn't respond, his face was turning to the color of chalk. Sam struggled with something to say, but the words wouldn't come. He decided to keep quiet and not make it worse.

Fifteen minutes later, Sam said, "Hey, Mac, you still got an open file on that snitch of yours they found belly up in the river a few months back?"

"Yeah, but it's an eater, gone nowhere. Trail's ice cold. Damn shame. Best snitch I ever had."

Weller concentrated on the road, chewing on the end of his still unlit cigar. "Problem, as I saw it, he forgot who he worked for. Got him killed. So you're still using that other guy, EZ what's-his-name?"

"Yeah. He's a useful idiot. Been keeping a low profile since someone offed his buddy, my former CI, Billy."

"Coincidence, that's all. Shit no one can prove."

"Seems like more than coincidence. Right after shouting about a leak in the department, he turns up in the river with a .22 in his head." McNally watched the buildings whiz by. "Liz believes him too."

"Yeah, but Dumont shows like a raw little rookie sometimes. She'd likely believe any harebrained story that took the heat off that broken bust. You guys got the worst end of that stick all right. And soon after, your new snitch starts whisperin' that it's our fault the deal there went bad. He would've said anything to point the finger in a different direction. I still don't get her stickin' with that broke-ass story."

"Knock it off! Why are you laying this crap on Dumont? Sam, people died."

"So? I say let 'em kill each other off. They're the bad guys anyway, right?"

Weller's cold indifference bothered McNally. "Well, it's a DEA problem now, not ours."

"And look how far they've gotten with it. Chinatown is the same stinking shithole it always was." Weller waved his hand in the air. "Ah hell, I don't give a good goddamn anyway. Just as well you're out of it now. Only good came of it is that you and me are partners again."

CHAPTER 31

Cold beads of sweat were showing on McNally's forehead by the time they pulled into the precinct garage. As they got out of their car, two men in greasy blue overalls eyed them with suspicion, their faces spotlighting their indifference.

The taller of the two wore glasses with thick black frames. They slipped down on his long narrow nose and hung precariously at the bulbous tip with a cleft in it that closely resembled an ass crack. His wan, pudgy face and large jowls spoke of a career spent with too much time in the lunchroom and too little time in the gym. He peered at the detectives over the top of the frames with pale watery blue eyes shrouded beneath deep hooded lids.

McNally stared into the unfinished face of a character from a comic strip.

Elmer Fudd is sweeping Liz's car?

He caught the flash of authority emanating from the man's cold stare, and he surmised this must be the man in charge.

The tall technician squared his shoulders and took a step forward, attempting to project confidence. He overlooked that his black police boot was about to come down on someone's dropped jelly roll beneath his foot. With the full weight of his body on it, a red blob shot out. His partner chuckled, then stumbled, almost falling himself as he tried to sidestep the spewing glob of jelly.

Meantime, Elmer attempted to break his fall by reaching for a nearby red rollaway tool cart. Unfortunately, the unlocked wheels offered no stationary support and began rolling across the garage floor as he tried in vain to hold on. In one last twisting, writhing effort the mechanic's knees buckled, and he fell, ass first, on top of the sticky mass.

Kyle and Sam eyed each other without saying a word, while the rest of the techs began derisively applauding and whistling, compounding Elmer's humiliation. Though a simple comedy of errors, the technician's glare showed that he'd be happy to blame the witnesses for his mishap.

He dragged himself up off the floor and began wiping his ass with a shop rag. Angry already at having to wait for the detectives, he now suffered the humiliation of looking like a fool in front of everyone in the garage. He hadn't met the two detectives before, but he despised them now, blaming them for being a party to his humiliation.

The set expression on the dark-haired man's face told the humiliated tech he was the one responsible for ruining his day.

"Nobody's touched that car yet, but we got a schedule to meet. Your late arrival has set us back at least an hour. So can we get on with it now, or are you gonna make me wait until you get a cup of coffee and have lunch?" His eyes squinted to slits as the tech kicked the jelly roll in their direction. Moments passed, and no one said a word.

McNally preferred to walk a wide circle around altercations with anyone on the same side of the law. But this was far from a normal day. And the tech chose the wrong time, the wrong place, and the wrong cop to think he had the upper hand. Kyle's patience evaporated with a new stab of pain in his ribs. There'd been too much wasted time on the bungling character smirking at him. His frustration over Liz's disappearance burned in his gut like hot coals. A tight, insincere smile stretched across his face.

McNally got right in the man's face, grabbed his shirt, and pushed him hard against the rollaway cart. "It doesn't look like you boys wasted *all* your time working this morning." The pinned technician saw the angry detective nod toward the counter covered with coffee cups, doughnuts, half-eaten sandwiches, and ashtrays filled with cigarette butts.

Glassy blue eyes no longer challenged McNally, but he had no inkling of the consequences. He attempted a moment of false bravado to save face. "Well, you can shove it, mister. We'd be finished by now if we didn't have to wait on your lazy asses before starting on this car." A wiser person would have read the warning signs from the shift in his opponent's stance or the narrowed pupils in his green eyes. Instead, the technician's confidence grew with the snickers starting to rise from the crowd. Boldly he pushed his chin into McNally's face. "Now we stay outta your way when you do your job. You dicks stay outta our way when—"

"What did you say?" McNally's sudden bark startled him so much the tech fell back against the car.

The slow realization of the seriousness of his mistake dawned on the tech too late. He tried to speak, but the words died in his throat as a mighty hand clamped around his larynx. He had grossly underestimated the cop standing in front of him. And now, feet swinging inches above the ground, he struggled for breath.

"Whoa, McNally! He ain't gonna be any good to us dead. We'll be buried in paperwork for a year if you kill him." Weller stifled a laugh and decided to let the scene play out a little longer. He stood watching the technician's face turn purple and thought any second his neck would crack under the pressure.

Kyle ignored the warning and held his grip on the squirming technician's neck, squeezing his powerful fingers into each pulse point beneath his jaw. Like a dam weakened by a tear in the wall, his pent-up rage blew. He felt Weller's hand tighten around his arm.

"Okay, Mac, playtime is over. You can let him go now."

Startled out of his blind fury, before he loosened his grip, he again slammed the frightened technician against the cart and then lowered the shaking limp body to the floor. Everyone watched as the technician clawed at his neck, gasping for air. His bulging eyes stared up at McNally. None of the onlooking techs blamed the angry detective. They'd been wanting to do that themselves for weeks.

"The vehicle you are about to examine belongs to a detective that has, for no known reason, disappeared. How you perform your assignment may determine whether we find the detective alive or dead. You may have noticed by now I'm in no mood for *any* shit from you or anyone else today. I've seen your department's performance in the past and never had cause to want to strangle the life out of someone until now. Do we understand each other?"

The terrified technician rubbed his neck and nodded. He thought the man must be half insane and ready to kill him. He nodded meekly and turned his back on McNally.

"Now if you're finished with your bullshit, let's move along so you can get back to your job."

He twitched, his voice hoarse and weak. "Nobody told me about any detective missing. We'll get it done." Then almost defiantly, he said, "And we'll get it done right."

"Good. We understand each other then."

Weller watched them work on Liz's car and realized he'd been holding his breath. For the first time since they'd started working together, he feared the strain was breaking his partner down. He hoped this incident wouldn't reach the commander's desk.

Two hours later, the sweep was completed. Every square inch of the car was searched, dusted fibers and hairs were collected, and all were sent over to the lab for evaluation. The techs were thorough with their inspection. No one mentioned the earlier incident.

This wasn't a routine auto theft; nothing was missing from the car. Her shotgun was in the trunk along with a spare revolver and bulletproof vest. A list of personal effects found in the glove box of the car included a box of tampons, a brush, hair clips, a Target charge card, and even an unmailed envelope addressed to the Publisher's Clearing House sweepstakes.

Weller continued to chuckle. "Short of going back and rearranging the dickwad's face for kicks, doesn't seem there's anything left to do here, Kyle. It's late. Why don't we head over to the bar across the street for a couple of brewskies? Might help to numb the pain in your wing."

He nodded to Weller and threw his jacket over his shoulder. "Yeah, let's go." And rubbing his chest, he said, "My ribs are killing me." McNally dated and initialed the log the curly-haired technician thrust at him. "I'll expect to see the results on my desk in the morning."

As they were pulling away from the garage, the curly-haired technician covered his mouth with his hand and coughed. "Asshole!" He grinned and felt better.

CHAPTER 32

They walked into ladies' night at the *Office*, a small smoke-filled bar in the Canarytown neighborhood on South Halsted. It was packed and loud by the time they got there. They picked their way through a throng of gyrating bodies on the dance floor and headed to a small open space at the far end of a long mahogany bar.

Weller didn't take his eyes off the scantily attired women. If they knew a couple of cops just came in, these young prey would scatter like startled deer hearing the crack of a gunshot, and the place would empty faster than the Ravinia Pavilion in a thunderstorm. But damn, there was no law against looking and drooling. He knew he wasn't a stunt double for any Hollywood leading man with his craggy profile, so he caught 'em with his easygoing, winning sense of humor.

The jukebox screamed, "Devil with the blue dress, blue dress *aawwnn!*"

Weller sat with a sly grin plastered on his face as he watched the dancers writhing and bumping hungrily against their partners. "Ain't it grand, Mac? All these pretty ladies just begging for a good porkin'. It's long been my theory that the drunker they get, the younger I look. Case you're wondering, that's how I corral all that puss 'n' boots I crave."

McNally shook his head and sighed. "Jailbait, Weller. Watch your step, or you'll have a count of statutory slapped on you by one of these little girls' pissed-off daddies."

"Hard time is my fantasy." He spread his arms toward a small gathering of young ladies sitting in stools around a high bar table on the edge of the dance floor. "Would you look at 'em, Mac? All dressed up and no one to blow. Damn shame," he said. "Damn shame."

"You old perv. You wouldn't know what to do with that young stuff. You'd be dead inside ten minutes. And then I'd be looking for a new partner."

Sam puffed out his chest and straightened his shoulders. Then glancing down at his prominent gut, for a nauseating split second, he realized that he had become little more than a sad, distorted reflection of his former self. He was just another middle-aged cop of Irish descent, skating by until retirement, trying to slide through his last couple years with the force. Transferring over to Property Crimes had crossed his mind. It would be easier, almost cushy. Trouble was, he hated those suits over there, and it would put him too close to Commander Kennesaw, an even bigger dick than Rouse. That idea got nixed quickly with him being a short-timer. He'd ride it out, God willing and if the creek didn't rise. And besides, a transfer request might trigger a review of his sketchy arrest history. He'd looked the other way and granted some ill-advised favors in the recent past that wouldn't stand up to a closer review. Mac had no reason to suspect him, but he didn't need that—not now, not ever.

"So you doubt my prowess with the ladies, my man? Then how 'bout a small wager?"

Kyle laughed. "I'll tell you what. When we finish here, I'll drive you by the Aragon Ballroom on Lawrence. You can bump rump all night and live the rest of your life loving the more *mature* ladies and avoid any worries about bending over for a bar of soap in the shower..."

"Hell, why don't you drop me at the geriatric ward at county since you think I'm so feeble? PS and oh, by the way, I ain't heard *you* braggin' much lately."

Kyle laughed out loud. He knew Weller and his theories about love all too well. There were two things he cared about in life—his cigars and his women. Their lifestyles were as different as their opposing politics. He liked it that way.

Sam ordered a shot of Jack for himself, Maker's Mark for Kyle, and beers. He was beginning to rehash the scene at the garage when a young woman with deep, sultry eyes leaned across McNally to reach for her cocktail, her breast brushing his arm.

"Hi, I'm Hallie. You new to the neighborhood? I know most everyone that comes here." She flashed them both a sensuous smile.

Weller took a moment to admire her body. She didn't blush. She appeared to be in her midtwenties, and her inviting smile suggested that she might be looking for something on casual street from him. The men standing at the bar were staring at her shapely full breasts, pencil-thin waist, and alluringly rounded hips. The snug-fitting sweater emphasized the curves of her body right down to the skintight designer jeans that clung to her ass and legs. They looked like they were spray painted on.

After a few moments of getting-to-know-you conversation, she asked if they would like some company. A familiar grin sneaked onto Weller's craggy face, and McNally, thinking that was his cue to cut out, signaled the bartender to bring a round of drinks. Sam invited the woman to join them. She liked the attention and smiled seductively, excusing herself long enough to retrieve her coat and purse. Weller's shit-eating grin and wide eyes gave him the look of a lion ready to pounce on a fallen gazelle.

McNally lifted his drink in toast. "I'm not sure how you fool them, Weller, but it looks like you've got another one on your hook. For reasons I've never been able to figure, she seems to have the hots for you."

Weller laughed and said, "It's easy, son. I count on your handsome mug to get their attention and then slide right in with my loveable nature and winning smile to convince 'em I'm the one they want to spend the night with."

"I'm feeling a little used here, buddy."

"Well, don't let it hurt your feelings none. You show any interest in these ladies, and I'd be the one backing off. But since you live like a celibate priest most days, I feel obliged to reel 'em in. I like to think it's my charitable nature."

"And I noticed you didn't put your tongue back in your mouth until she left."

Weller flashed a toothy smile. "The way I see your problem is, it's been way too long since you loosened your tie and drank from any feminine cups that runneth over. I've known you these past ten years since your divorce, and you've only stuck with two women for any time. Admittedly, that second one turned ugly sour. I've seen it again and again with you, Mac. You turn tail and run the moment you think a woman gets too close. You take life and love way too seriously. You're snake bit, I'd say. And I'm telling ya, it's not healthy. For some reason, the ladies seem to think you're a fairly good-lookin' guy, Mac. You ought to sit back, put your feet up, and enjoy the time the good Lord grants us. Soon enough, you'll have the doves flocking around you."

Kyle lifted his tumbler. "Well then, buddy, here's to you, a guiding light in the dark tunnel of my tragic love life."

Weller tipped the last drop of his shot and ordered another. "Well, Mac, it might've been you instead of me. She's a tempting piece of trim, and that's what you need about now." Weller lowered his voice. "Yeah, my friend, she'll make my little soldier stand at attention and ready to deliver a twenty-one-gun salute!" He grinned into his beer. "And yes, I'm in the mood to offer her a free mustache ride."

McNally laughed. "You old lecher. One day the ladies will realize the low regard you have for them, and you'll end up with nothing but your limp dick in your hand. Though you'd never admit it, sometimes I think you'd fuck a raccoon if you could get ahold of one."

Weller thought for a moment. "Well, not quite. I put my foot down to little boys and farm animals. Hey," he bellowed, "ain't no law against having a steady diet, as long as it's legal." He scanned the bar. "I'm the lucky pick of the night if she's looking for a grown man to pork her. Sorry, pal."

They had their backs to the crowd and didn't realize the woman had returned and overheard the last of Weller's commentary. Without warning, a loud screech filled the corners of the smoky room. McNally realized which ax was about to fall—and where. Weller proved slower recognizing his faux pas. He believed he had paid her a compliment.

"You pig!" she screamed over the din.

The room became silent as everyone turned their attention to the oncoming train wreck at the bar. Sam, taken by surprise, sat frozen, helpless to avert the coming explosion. It was too late to apologize; he'd done the damage.

McNally wished he could fast-forward to just past the coming tornado. He turned his back to Sam, downed the shot, grinned at the bartender, and whispered, "Don't worry. It's not the first time I've had to pull claws out of his back." The bartender snickered and returned to minding his own business. If there was no bloodshed, he'd enjoy the show.

The offended woman's eyes blazed with anger. If she had a knife, she'd have stuck it in Weller's unprotected backside. Before he realized it, she slapped him full and hard on the face, causing his half-empty beer to splash down the front of him.

"You're a grade A asshole," she said. Grabbing her purse, she pushed her barstool with such force it spun in a half circle and flew crashing to the floor. Without another word, she pivoted on her heels and pushed her way through the gawking, hushed crowd. The smell of her sweet, floral-scented cologne lingered in the air, a cold reminder of what he'd be doing without tonight.

The resulting silence in the room was deafening. A hundred eyes were watching the man dripping beer. Chuckles and whispers began drifting through the crowd.

McNally lifted his beer to Weller and announced in a voice loud enough for all to hear, "Here's to my friend, the only man in Chi-Town with a leather tongue."

A brief spurt of laughter and applause broke out from the other patrons before they returned to their previous diversions.

As Weller tamped himself dry with a bar towel, Kyle downed his shot glass. The bartender set up two more to replace them. Kyle winked at Sam and smiled, savoring the growing warmth in his belly. The pain in his arm and chest had settled down and felt more like a bad sunburn. The amber liquid no longer burned with the first swallow and traveled down his throat with a comforting smoothness. For the first time today, he found himself on the right side of normal. He downed his shot in a gulp and raised his glass to the bartender again.

CHAPTER 33

"Hey, Weller!" a voice shouted from across the room. "This is the last place we figured to find you two."

"Sheee-it," Kyle groaned. He recognized the voice and regretted not going home to get drunk. He always tried to avoid any places that were cop hangouts. And today, he needed to trade "How do ya do" with a couple of dicks from the precinct like he needed an enema delivered by an orangutan. This place was blocks away from the popular watering holes. But given the average age of the patrons, he and Sam were out of place; these two weren't.

"Christ, how'd the Hardy Boys find us?" Weller grumbled.

"Maybe they weren't looking. Let's leave," Kyle said.

Weller responded in a caustic tone, "Hey, we were here first. I'll bet if we ignore 'em, they'll leave."

Sean Cavanaugh and George Musselli were known as the Hardy Boys around the squad room because they were bright, young, aggressive, and inseparable. Cavanaugh's head glowed twenty yards away with his florescent red hair and red-brown freckles splattered over his round pink face. He was twenty-six years old and not a whisker to his name. In sharp contrast, Musselli, the bodybuilder, had spiked short black hair and a perpetual two-day-old whisker growth.

Kyle liked them both, but right now, he didn't want to deal with them. Feeling tired and grumpy, he'd just slid past the proper side of tipsy. The last thing he needed was two cocky boots trying to score points with the vets.

Sam had already found himself another horizontal mambo partner seated at the end of the bar. He'd met her minutes before on his way back from the head. She appeared to be a skosh more age-appropriate for him. Kyle caught the bleached blonde running her hand up and down Sam's leg, teasing his family jewels and blowing in his ear. The scene struck him as comical. It wasn't the first time Sam's appeal to women surprised him.

Musselli spoke first. "Detective McNally, congratulations on the liquor store incident. You won't have any trouble with a review, though your breakout from the hospital didn't make the commander as happy as a cup of coffee and a bag of doughnut holes would've. He kept screaming something about your balls and a vice before he slammed his door shut."

Anger flushed McNally's face. The set of his jaw and narrowed eyes should have warned the newcomer to walk away. His had been pissed-off meter pegged and now pointed directly at Musselli.

Cavanaugh felt the heat. Now stuttering nervously and close enough for McNally to smell the garlic on his breath, he said, "I did take a message for you. I left it on your desk."

The deflection came as a welcome distraction for Kyle, and he grinned, noticing Cavanaugh's own gaze landing on the roving woman's hand on Weller's leg.

"What's the message, son?"

"Oh, uh, sorry. Sergeant Sherman from property asked if anyone knew whether you went through the evidence collected from the Clayton apartment yet. If you didn't, he's planning to assign two men to it. Said you liked to go over it yourself. They identified the shoe print from the plaster cast."

"Is that it?"

Cavanaugh stumbled over his words. "Huh? Oh yeah, and call Dr. Hartley at her office. Figured it might be important."

"Consider your message delivered."

Weller didn't hear the conversation, but from Kyle's body language, he understood this wasn't a good day to poke the bear. He hoped the two youngsters would finish their beers and beat a hasty retreat. Since somebody had to make the first move, he jumped in.

He grinned and winked at his companion with her long, thick fingers wrapped around his leg.

He said, "Now, boys, as you can see, we've got more important things on our minds." He faked a yawn. "And I'm thinkin' it's long past time I beat feet outta here." Downing the shot of sour mash, he winked at the woman hanging on his arm. "Yep, think it's time this lucky dog said *au revoir* and headed out of here. I'll find my way home, Mac."

McNally nodded. "Yeah, in the morning, Sam."

The blonde lifted her heavy frame off the barstool and smiled seductively at the young detectives as she passed them.

Weller stepped gingerly around the two. "Gentlemen, we'll be leavin' now." Then he turned to say, "McNally, why don't you give the good doctor a call? I got a feeling she might have a cure for what ails you."

Sam and the woman with no name disappeared into the crowd.

McNally turned his back on Cavanaugh and Musselli. Without a word, they retreated into the crowd. Alone at the bar, he lifted his glass to the bartender, motioning for a refill. He rolled the amber liquid on his tongue and considered Weller's parting shot. He always accused Kyle of being the worst kind of loner, miserable and unable to commit to anyone, not even his wife when he had one. His marriage became a near-total disaster.

He'd made several major choices in his life, yet the only one that consistently fit him had been his job. He was a cop—his sole identity. It was who he was and what he did. He drank a little too much and worked too hard. But those were choices he made.

He believed in fate. Everything that happened required no human intervention or act of will. He'd grown tired of bedding the many nameless, faceless women he'd met since his divorce. They quenched his primitive sweat-it and forget-it needs but were devoid of any meaning for him. He surprised himself by admitting that, at his age, he needed more than a series of quick flings with women. If his yin could be called a satisfying career, he'd sacrificed his yang, that aspect of him that craved connection to a loving woman. Kyle had to agree with Sam. With almost four months of comp time in the bank, this was a serious rut. He'd never used the vacation comp time because he had no one he cared enough about to reflect joy back to him. So with his love life in the shitter and a case that kept on kicking his ass, the immediate future looked mighty dim.

Damn! Could it get any worse? How pathetic!

I don't feel guilty for anything. I feel sorry for people who feel guilt.

—Ted Bundy

CHAPTER 34

McNally jerked awake from the echoing ring of his phone. It hurt. He tried to lie still, hoping to ignore the intense pain in his head, arm, and chest. Every time his eyes moved beneath closed lids, hot pain stabbed his brain, a sharp reminder of how he'd abused his body the night before. He moaned, regretting too many shots and one too many hours in the smoke-filled bar. He tried rolling over on his back and nearly screamed from the sudden jolting pain.

Jeezus!

He gave up trying to reposition himself and covered his pounding head with a pillow. Two minutes later, it started again. With great effort, he reached across the bed and groped for the phone.

"What!" he growled louder than he meant to. Even moving his jaw hurt like hell.

"McNally?"

"And this must be Shaughnessy judging by the pleasure you're taking calling me this early."

"No pleasure, Detective. Weller told me to reach you and tell you to meet him down at the lake front behind the Adler Planetarium."

"Why?"

"They found Dumont. He needs you down there ASAP."

His stomach twisted. "Tell him I'm on my way."

He swung his legs over the side of the bed and grabbed the nightstand to steady himself. His hands shook as he ran them through his tangled hair and down over his eyes.

He only stopped long enough for a strong black coffee; he needed to choke down a few aspirins as he drove south on Lake Shore Drive. He tried not to think about anything but the waves crashing on the breakers of Lake Michigan. Even with his sunglasses, the flashing glare from the sun off the water blinded Kyle.

How did this happen? What got Liz so upset the last time I saw her? Why didn't she just tell me? What was so damn important that she had to track me down at Clayton's apartment?

When he first met her, she'd struck him as a woman in a perpetual overdrive state, a bona fide type A. When she told him she would be the first female super dick in Area 5, he laughed. Even when she got a meritorious promotion to detective, filling an equity slot, she proved to be a quick study of life on the streets. In her first six months, she'd collared rapists, gangbangers, and armed robbers. This was way beyond a job to her; it was her obsession.

By the end of her first year, she proved to be better than nine of ten detectives who'd been on the streets for a decade. McNally's forte was gathering and analyzing evidence and arriving at accurate deductions from ambiguous clues. Weller's gift was an uncanny knack for milking valuable information during interviews from both suspects and witnesses. Dumont didn't bother with either of those finesse-oriented aspects of the work. She worked best when chasing down offenders, slamming them against walls, and slapping cuffs on them street side. She scoffed at talking to them beyond quoting Miranda. The chase and arrest were her highs, her Nirvana. Dumont never showed fear, never hesitated entering a dark room, and never balked at turning a corner while chasing down an offender.

With dark thoughts and a head like a hammered anvil, he spotted the flashing beacons from the squads and turned east on Planetarium Drive. A crowd of uniforms gathered near the rocky waterfront. He spotted Weller standing next to the ME wagon with the examiner. Sam saw him coming, and with long deliberate strides, he met McNally fifteen yards from the activity.

"Two fishing boats out early this morning came across a fifty-five-gallon drum floating about a mile offshore. They pole-hooked it on deck and popped the lid…" Weller hesitated, searching for the right words.

McNally read Weller's expression. "Tell me it's a mistake, Sam. Tell me it's not her." A blast of cold air lifted the collar of his jacket and stabbed his face with icy fingers.

Weller shook his head. "Sorry, Kyle. She's over there."

Bile rose in McNally's throat. His jaw tightened, and his perspiring hands balled into fists as he struggled to keep from vomiting. The inevitable stared him in the face. He'd denied it before now. Anger and guilt shaded his pain-filled eyes as he stared at the empty drum.

"My god…" he said. "How?"

"She has deep bruising on her neck, and the ME says she took several cracks to the back of her head, blunt-force trauma."

"The sick fuck murdered her and stuffed her in a can…" McNally's eyes grew wide, and his nostrils flared as he watched the technicians working methodically, taking hair samples, looking for any evidence under her fingernails, searching for any forensic evidence before removing the body.

"Son of a bitch! Fucking son of a bitch! This is a goddamn waste of time. There won't be any prints. We both know that."

"I'm sure you're right. But they are going to be at it a long while, so let's let them do their job. You're hurting. This sucks for all of us. You two were real tight. Remember, you're not the only one hurting…"

"Spare me, Sam. Let's talk facts. The fact is, when she needed me, I wasn't there. I might have prevented this if I didn't let my focus slip. And"—he moved his face within inches of Weller—"when I find this cocksucker, I'll put the barrel of my 9 mm in his mouth and blow his brains out the backside of his head. I swear he'll never see the inside of a courtroom."

Weller began to speak, but McNally's hand flew up, warning Sam to cease and desist.

"Don't even say it." He turned and walked around the south end of the property. Once out of sight, he doubled over. His body shook so much he had to lean against the building to keep from buckling to his knees. He vomited repeatedly. Sweat poured from his face. After he expelled everything from his stomach, he continued to convulse. Every organ in his body hurt from retching, and his chest felt like he'd broken another couple of ribs. Ten minutes passed before he could stand erect. Still shivering, he wiped the sweat from his forehead and turned to face the wind. Though his head still hurt, the earlier disorientation had passed, leaving his mind clear.

She's dead.

Time might dull the pain, but the guilt he experienced hit him like a locomotive. He'd get the deranged bastard who'd done this.

He walked to the water's edge and kneeled to fill his cupped hands with icy lake water, splashing it on his face and neck. Most of the crafts on the lake were commercial and held the last of the morning fishermen. The sun danced off the surface of the water, and for the moment, its brilliance held McNally's attention. He followed the horizon, searching for some metaphysical answer to this chaos. Where did he go wrong?

McNally bent to retrieve a stone from the rocky beach and skimmed it across the surface of the water. A seagull, thinking the stone was a morsel to snatch, swooped down, stabbing at it until it disappeared beneath the surface. Dismayed, it laughed *cha-choy* as it returned to its perch on the bow of a lone sailboat anchored a hundred yards from shore.

In that moment, McNally saw his world spiraling out of control.

CHAPTER 35

"This could've been you." Weller's words sounded more forceful than he intended, but he wasn't one to soft-sell the truth. He believed Kyle acted soft.

"Christ, Sam! Listen to you. It wasn't me. Liz is dead." His eyes filled with tears. Then softening his tone, he continued, "Doesn't this bother you? One of our own, a friend?" He scowled and walked away. He wanted to get as far away from this place as possible.

Then attempting to back it down a notch, Kyle turned and said, "Hey, buddy, forget it. It's not your fault. This whole thing makes little sense. First, a good kid's murdered and left in a cemetery. Then we find a good cop in the lake. I don't see how or why Slugger would make such a radical turn with these two. Except for one footprint that may or may not been her killer's, we've got no trace evidence in Clayton's place. No witnesses. No motives. If the Slugger did this, had he followed her to the apartment, or was he waiting for her? And this may sound crazy, but hear me out. Is it possible this could be a deliberate hit? Maybe a promise being kept by the triads after the Chinatown mess?"

"C'mon, McNally. Are you trying to suggest that failed bust marked her somehow? I've got a big problem swallowing that notion. As for no one seeing him, I don't expect many people were out, walkin' their dog in a frog-strangling thunderstorm. The rain would give him perfect cover. But you're right. He still had to get back to his car, which had to be near where he left hers. And sorry, but we turned nothing up from our canvas of neighbors near Clayton's place either."

He continued that line of reasoning and said, "He wrapped her in something and carried her down the back stairs. Santini said the footprint could've been deep enough for someone carrying the extra weight of a body. We'll wait for word from the ME to find out if someone murdered her before or after being taken from the apartment."

Sam said, "Yeah. Well, right now it's all guesswork. Won't hold up in court unless we find the exact shoe to match. Even though there's ten thousand of those shoes in this city."

McNally's patience had begun to unravel. His partner's logic infuriated him. "I'm not saying that's how it happened, only sifting through some possibilities."

The wind whistled cold, changed direction, and swept from the west out over the lake. McNally noticed the smaller fishing boats had disappeared from the horizon.

"Stay with me for a minute. Say he gets Liz to her car and nobody saw them. And he drives the car far enough away, a few blocks, to a place where it's well hidden. He goes back, gets his car, and moves it. Now he waits until he can drive her to the lake with no one seeing him. It stormed for the better part of the night, so like you said, nobody would be out. Hell, Sam, if he'd lit a bonfire on the beach, no one would've seen it."

Weller knew McNally struggled to put all the pieces together in his head on this case. He was good—the best, in Sam's long experience. It always surprised him how Kyle developed scenarios and worked the facts, however disjointed they were. He always became obsessive about assembling clues into a big picture view. That obsession had Sam worried.

"This is a nasty, fucking business," Weller mumbled.

"What?"

"Forget it. Just thinkin' 'bout all the bullshit in this case."

"Don't go belly up on me, Sam. We've got too much to do. If we're gonna catch Liz's killer, I'll need your full attention and that famous cop's intuition of yours to find her killer."

"Gotcha. So where to now?"

McNally glanced at his wristwatch. "I'm disappearing for a few hours. I've got some thinking to do. Cover my ass with Rouse, okay?"

"Yeah. Don't worry about him, man. Where can I reach you if I need to?"

"Use my pager number, but only if you have to."

"Got it."

CHAPTER 36

Back at the precinct, Weller sat and stared vacantly at the piles of paper on his desk. He couldn't concentrate. The squad room had the feel of a morgue. Rouse wasn't in, and both the sergeant and lieutenant had the blinds in their offices closed.

His thoughts drifted back to the shit storm he stepped into when Liz and Kyle worked together for her training. Sam figured out early on that she wanted to get closer to Kyle. He winced, recalling the time he'd tried to enlighten his clueless divorced friend. It wasn't uncommon for their daily routine ending with him and Kyle stopping for beers at Clancy's Tavern off Diversey.

Sam thought his friend would take the advice differently than he did. That day, he wasn't feeling any pain after a few three-fingered booster shots of sour mash, so Sam figured it was the right time to bring his friend up to speed on the ways of the world. In his typical clumsy fashion, he shared his take on Dumont and pointed out her obvious infatuation with his longtime partner.

Weller groaned, unable to forget the anger that washed over McNally, the ominous threat that followed stung his ears. "Weller, when did you become one of those pussies in the unit who can only get a hard-on by sticking their noses where they don't belong? Do me a favor, and stick to your cigars, your bad jokes, and your own sleazy lifestyle. I don't want to lose a partner to the gossiping ganders."

He accused him of being like Peterson, of all people. Peterson couldn't find his own dick in the dark unless he tied a string to it.

Deeply offended, Weller vowed then that that was the last time he'd play love shrink for his friend. He'd kicked that hornet's nest for the last time. It wasn't worth it. His foolish interference put a strain on their friendship that didn't heal quickly.

He sat chomping wistfully on the end of his cigar. The sign on the wall beside his desk read, "Thank you for not smoking." He grunted and muttered, "Yeah, right."

He had an overwhelming urge to drink a six-pack of Old Style at Mach speed. He was clearing his desk when Roy Ramirez walked into the squad room.

"Damn shame about Dumont," Ramirez said.

"Yeah, she was a good cop."

With a sigh, Weller scowled, feeling old and dried up. *Jesus, Kyle couldn't be more wrong about me. No matter whose lovely fingers are working on me, I'm as limp as a wilted carrot stick. I doubt if I could get it up right now even with my hands cuffed behind me and Madonna having her long slender fingers wrapped around my joystick. Everything's gone to hell lately. Damn, I need to refill my Viagra script.*

CHAPTER 37

McNally stopped for a quick Rueben and a slaw from the Lucky Dill Deli on Dearborn. Feeling a serious need for diversion, he spent the next few hours searching for pain relief at a nearby tavern. He arrived home after nine. As hard as he'd tried to get drunk, he failed. He didn't feel much like sleeping either. He felt restless, and his shoulder ached again.

He ignored the flashing light on his answering machine and grabbed a tumbler of Maker's Mark before lighting a fire and putting on his favorite symphony, Beethoven's Sixth, *Pastoral.* The dampness soon disappeared as the fire, growing in intensity, crackled and popped. Even though the room warmed up, a lingering chill shook him. The flames danced in complement to the music, even with the comforting aid of the bourbon. Pouring himself a second bracer, he sank into the chair next to the fire and put the bottle on the table beside him. He didn't want to think anymore and needed rest. This had been a day from hell. Tomorrow would come soon enough.

He lowered himself to the floor, stretching his long legs in front of him and propping his back against the chair. He closed his eyes and concentrated on nothing but the soothing sounds of the music and the blue-orange flames dancing and sparking in the fireplace. The tension began to ebb from his tight, aching muscles as the stabbing pain in his chest subsided. He lifted his glass and swirled the golden-brown liquid. A couple more of these, and he wouldn't care if a tornado tore the roof off.

He'd finished his second glass when he heard a faint knocking sound. Kyle thought he'd imagined it until he heard a second one. Rising to his feet, he cursed Weller. He'd be the only one coming by this late at night—and likely drunk to the gills. Kyle intended to rake Sam over hot coals, but when he opened the door, a look of shocked surprise replaced his scowl. Large dark-blue eyes stared back at him. A slow smile spread across his face. Dr. Mykel Hartley blushed in response. She was beautiful, and the sudden, surprising shyness only magnified her sensuality and allure.

"Mykel, this is a most welcome surprise. Are we making a late-night house call?"

"I…I'm sorry, Kyle," she said. "Please tell me if I'm intruding. I'm sorry about Detective Dumont. You said you two were friends. Then when they told me about your, uh, accident… I just wanted to see if you were all right." Her breath caught in her throat when she saw his arm in the sling. Seeing him standing in his doorway reminded her that their growing friendship was tenuous, so all the reasons for her arriving at his doorstep now seemed premature. Without speaking, she raised her hand in apology and turned to leave.

"No, wait. Please, you're here now. I'm glad. Come in."

Eyes downcast, she fidgeted with the strap on her purse. Her sudden changed posture and contrary response puzzled Kyle.

"Okay, Mykel, but at least stay long enough to warm up a little. You're shivering. Here, give me your jacket and go sit by the fire. All I can offer you is a beer or Maker's Mark. Or I'll dig up some tea if you'd prefer that." His smile held an invitation.

"A little bit of Mark would be nice, thank you." She stood in front of the fire, rubbing her hands together, enjoying its warmth. He was fine, and now she felt like an intruder. She had been at the morgue when Liz Dumont's body arrived. When she called the station, they told her that McNally hadn't been back to headquarters. Sam Weller gave her McNally's home address and phone number and suggested it would be a good idea to check in on him.

She left two messages on his answering machine, and after working late at the office, she thought she'd see if Kyle needed anything. She convinced herself that the "house call" was necessary. But after searching the detective's green eyes, her good intentions seemed trivial. He didn't need company. She had no right to presume he did. The blood rushed to Mykel's face as she realized the reasons for her being there were selfish. She just wanted to see him again. She retrieved her coat from the chair where he left it.

"Leaving already, Doctor? Is your patient so easily cured?"

"I'm sorry, Kyle. I thought you might like some company, but I've only made myself feel awkward and stuck you with an unwanted guest." Mykel refused to meet his gaze. "I wasn't planning to barge in on you. I tried to call first, but when you didn't answer, I got concerned. I made a mistake."

He lifted the coat from her arm, replaced it with the drink, and escorted her to the large overstuffed brown sofa facing the fireplace. "Please don't be so hard on yourself. I'd love some company tonight. Drinking alone wasn't making me feel better. Trust me, I'm happy you're here."

She took a nervous gulp of the burning liquor and started to cough.

He laughed. "Maybe you should try sipping it until you get used to it."

"I think you're right," she said, smiling.

She looked small and vulnerable to McNally as her eyes darted around the room. When their eyes met again, she bravely smiled, forcing him to laugh.

"Relax, Mykel, your intuition hit the mark."

Without replying, she repositioned herself and settled deeper into the couch, where she almost disappeared as she sank into the cushions. She struggled to straighten herself. He grinned, watching her fight against both gravity and the unruly cushions. She dug herself in deeper and tucked her long legs beneath her slender form. More relaxed now, she began to survey her surroundings with an interested curiosity. She liked the look and feel of his apartment. It was masculine, but not over the top. The coordinated effect gave her the impression he'd carefully chosen every piece of furniture, each art piece, and the many personal knick-knacks around the room.

Kyle enjoyed the shared moment in the company of this lady sitting across from him. Beethoven's sweet second movement, *Scene by the Brook,* provided the perfect complement. With the eye of an artist, he studied every detail of her beauty and form in the flickering firelight. A soft open-collared white silk blouse clung to her full breasts and tapered down to her small waist. Her faded blue jeans conformed to her small rounded hips, stressing her femininity. Though hidden from view, the memory of those long slender legs intensified his appreciation of this statuesque lady.

God those legs…

He had to fight the temptation to reach out, unfold them, and run his hands down their length.

"If you'd enjoy talking, I…I'll…" She stumbled over her words. When he didn't respond, she blurted, "How bad are your injuries?"

"They're mending. Nothing to worry about."

"Detective Weller told me you suffered a serious concussion."

"Nah, I'm fine, though my cracked ribs tend to be a bother. Sam exaggerates too much. He thinks it's in his job description." He took another long, admiring look at her before saying, "Do you have any idea how attracted I am to you?"

Her heart raced, and her cheeks flushed. This man beside her expressed an attraction she also had for him. His easygoing personality attracted her despite her earlier misgivings. She admired his self-confidence and undeniable charm. He was one of the most attractive and head-to-toe sexy men she'd met in a long time. Feeling his eyes on her, she realized that his penetrating gaze didn't make her uncomfortable. Like the proverbial Cheshire cat, she smiled provocatively.

Feeling a hot rush from the liquor, she blurted, "It's been a long time since I wanted to hear those words from a man."

"And it's been a long time since I've said them to a woman."

The room's warmth and ambience had a calming effect on her. They both sat silently, relaxing and gazing into the fire. She closed her eyes to enjoy the music and listened to the crackling logs. They were having an enchanting effect on her. When she reopened her eyes, he'd turned off the table lamp, and the flames from the fireplace cast a golden glow throughout the room. Kyle appeared peaceful and deep in thought. She unselfconsciously surveyed his strong profile and muscled body. The fire illuminating his face hardened his features, making him appear like someone just this side of sinister, though his pensive countenance didn't make her feel in the least uncomfortable. With his long masculine frame relaxing in the chair, she sensed his ease. How long had it been since she desired a man like this?

Or have I ever?

She watched him swallow the last of his drink and lean his head back against the chair. Now she had no regret in coming here. Her senses reeled, lethargic from the mix of the music, the fire, and the liquor, though deliciously excited by the man in front of her. She felt safe here. To her surprise, she craved affection from this man. She'd considered the idea he was the needy one, but watching him now, she realized her own powerful wants. As she stretched like a cat aroused from slumber, she wondered if Kyle had the same compelling thoughts.

As if reading her mind, McNally raised himself from his chair and took her empty glass from her hand. He refilled her glass and returned it to her without saying a word. Though his manner seemed dark moments earlier, his reassuring smile now warmed her.

When she reached for the glass her fingers faintly brushed his; he felt his pulse quicken. "This could be dangerous for both of us Mykel," he whispered as he bent over and kissed her.

"You may be right, Kyle. Maybe it's best if I leave," Mykel responded, sounding apologetic.

"No, that's not what I meant at all." He smiled reassuringly. "It's been a very long time since I have entertained a lady in my apartment as lovely and sexy as you."

Mykel thought she saw a flicker of uncertainty in his eyes, but his body language was all too clear. She returned his smile with warm understanding in her eyes, and feeling emboldened from the effects of the alcohol, she responded impishly, "So, Detective McNally, are you saying that you lack self-control when it involves members of the fairer sex? Then should I hope to be arrested by you if I'm ever caught breaking the law?"

He grinned back at her, and without any words passing between them, she allowed his large hand to cup the side of her delicate face. His thumb traced her lips, and she felt a lump form in her throat. His fingers slowly reached behind her neck as he removed his other arm from the protective cloth sling and pulled her gently up until she was standing in front of him. As he caressed the back of her neck, his free hand began to slowly unbutton her blouse.

"No, Mykel. I have no difficulty with self-control when it's necessary..."

She felt his warm breath on her face and gasped when his cool fingers stroked the back of her neck. She stood motionless, eyes locked to his, hypnotized by their green brilliance. She was a lamb hypnotized by a cobra. With a mind of its own, her body began to respond to his touch. He lowered his head to gently kiss her temples, her eyes, her nose. His hands freed her hair from the clip she was wearing, and she could feel his fingers lose themselves in the soft curls. He gently yet firmly pulled her closer to him until their bodies were touching. His warm tongue seared a path down her neck. Fire coursed through her body as her arms unconsciously locked behind his neck. Completely helpless to control her body's urging to his touch, she felt pure ecstasy, mindless of everything but the fire forming in the pit of her stomach.

He lowered his head and covered her mouth with his lips. His tongue explored the softness of her lips and the straightness of her teeth, searching, seeking, and drowning in her sweetness. She responded by shyly pressing her small tongue against his, gently at first, then more boldly. Her exquisitely soft skin was warm beneath his enormous hand as it traveled the length of her back, savoring the slightness of her body. Her breathing became broken, husky, her body urging him on. He lifted her lace camisole and cupped her breast with his hand. His fingers teased her nipples playfully, tenderly at first, but then he lowered his head and covered her hard peaks with his lips, sucking and playing with them between his teeth. She moaned in pleasure.

In one fluid motion, he effortlessly lifted her in his arms and lowered her gently to the floor. The room was dark around them except for the dancing firelight. He slowly removed her clothing, his desire growing with every touch of her skin. Her touch felt fevered against his skin after she unbuttoned his shirt and slipped her hand around his waist and down his back. They lay naked upon the floor and visually explored each other's bodies with slow deliberation.

"Mmmmm. You are a beautiful woman, Mykel."

In response, she raised her arms and drew him into their circle. As she pulled him down beside her, he encircled her body protectively with his strong arms. Covering her with long lazy kisses, he felt the tension in her body and noted the flaming desire in her eyes. She moaned as he continued to tease her with his tongue. His mouth moved slowly down the length of her, kissing and sucking the tender skin below her navel while caressing the softness between her legs. She arched her back, greeting his attention, moving her hips to meet his every touch. Throaty murmurs of rapture rose from her when he kissed her ankles and trailed his tongue along her calves, behind her knees, and along the soft inner side of her thighs. She began to move feverishly beneath him, urging him to go further. Under his patient guidance, her long legs unfolded as exploring kisses drew slowly and softly closer to the core of her raging desire.

When he slipped his hands under her buttocks and lifted her to his mouth, her passion poured forth in a torrent of rippling waves. She felt certain she would go mad as his tongue danced in ever smaller circles around her clitoris. She lifted her hips higher, inviting his tongue to go still deeper within her. All her inhibitions were now stripped away and replaced by a long-unmet sexual hunger. She had never been touched like this before. Her hands grasped the back of his head as her awakening instincts overtook her.

He felt her tremble, her supple body glistening from perspiration in the flickering firelight. McNally was surprised and excited by the fierceness of her desires. He could wait no longer. He was consumed by the need to have all of her. She was taunting him, urging him on. Now totally driven by his own lust, he was determined to have this tempting creature beg him for more. Coherent thoughts fled as primordial instinct took over, orchestrating his every move upon her heaving body. The increasing crescendo from the pounding of his own heart became deafening. He shifted his weight and slowly rolled her over on her stomach. He lowered himself to cover her back and neck with kisses. He inhaled her sweet scent and buried his face in her hair.

"Jesus, Mykel, you're so sweet..."

He pulled away just long enough for her to lift herself to her knees, and then for only a moment, he hesitated before entering her to savor the final seconds before the inescapable zenith propelled them to climax. He drank in her pleas for release as a man trapped in the desert tastes his first drop of sweet cool water.

"Now..." she cried. "Now!"

He began his descent tenderly, soothing her frustrations by whispering her name, "Mykel, I'm waiting for you."

The intensity increased, and they moved in unison to the consummation of their desires. Higher and higher their ecstasy rose until a cry of release escaped her lips, and Kyle allowed his own pulsing pleasure to be released, delivering his hot fire with the excruciating thrill of conquest he hadn't known in years. Maybe never.

Kyle lay next to her, exhausted and trembling, her head resting on his broad chest. He caressed her back and listened as she purred softly beneath his touch. Gently brushing strands of her silky hair from her face, he felt the desire to protect her. Her impassioned love-making had taken him completely by surprise. It was in direct contrast to everything he had learned about her before. He found himself thinking more about Mykel Hartley the woman and less about Mykel Hartley the medical examiner.

With a million thoughts racing through his head, one thing he knew for certain was, he didn't want to let her go.

She excused herself and slipped away from him. He stared at the dying fire and felt completely relaxed for the first time in weeks. When Mykel returned, she knelt next to him, and he reached for her.

She whispered, "It's my turn, Detective. Just relax."

She rubbed a warm scented washcloth on his body, her every movement sensual and erotic. She traced the lines of his muscular arms, carefully avoiding his bandaged shoulder, and then across his broad chest, traveling slowly beyond his abdomen. She placed velvety kisses where the cloth had traveled. Her long warm fingers tenderly stroked his face, his jaw, his neck. Slowly and sensuously, she worked her featherlight touch around his penis and down his legs. Time stood still as she performed miracles to his lingering desires. He became oblivious to everything but her fingers and lips on his body. She slowly placed each of his fingers in her mouth, tasting the salt from his perspiration. His groin ached for her as her caresses became bolder and more demanding.

Paralyzed by her touch, he felt excitement churning through his belly. His erection boldly accepted her teasing tongue, and he reached his arm downward and molded his hand around her soft muscular buttocks. He marveled at the talent of the student turned teacher. A low groan escaped from deep within his throat as he yielded to her tender kisses.

* * *

The dim light of morning crept through the blinds when he woke. Kyle looked down at the sleeping woman cradled in his arms. His lips parted with a smile reflecting deep satisfaction. His eyes tracked the tender curve of her back down to where it joined the petite, shapely breadth of her hips. Her black hair spread in gentle folds across her shoulders. He marveled at this picture of innocence. She was a most unexpected and surprising arrival into the structured, castaway existence Kyle called a life. He greedily coveted these last few minutes of peace beside this amazing lady with her many charms.

Kyle would like nothing more than to spend all day long, continuing his discovery of the mysteries behind his attraction for her. Unhappily, he only had these few precious minutes. His fingers reached out and teased a lock of her luxurious hair; her lips parted in an unconscious reply. She stirred in his arms, and with regret, he slipped his arm out from under her and slid from the bed.

Pulling the covers up to her chin, Mykel's thick eyelashes fluttered open. She propped the pillow under her head, not yet ready to leave the warmth of his bed. She sensed rather than saw that he'd left. Serene and happy, she stared at the beauty of the "Visit Ireland" travel poster on the wall. How Mykel would love to be standing in front of the rustic castle pictured in the foreground or to be walking along sunlit paths that led to rolling green hills and lush forests.

Blinking for a moment and remembering where she was, Mykel repositioned her long legs from beneath her curled body. She stretched and leaned back against the pillows, touching the spot where Kyle's head had been. Her fingers brushed a small folded piece of paper. She opened the note and read Kyle's apology for having to leave without waking her. He told her to make herself at home. He'd call her later. He'd scribbled "K" at the bottom of the message. She loved the informality of it. With a smile on her face, she eased her legs over the side of the bed and felt a pleasing sensitivity in her body that was a sweet reminder of their evening together.

CHAPTER 38

On the way into the station, Kyle got a beep from EZ. He stopped at a bus station's pay phone to call him back.

First words out of his mouth were "Where *you* been, man? I been tryin' to reach you and your lame-ass partner for days! What the fuck happened? She said she was gonna meet me. What the shit is goin' on?" he barked through the receiver.

"Whoa. Hold on, EZ. I got no word of this until a few nights ago, and a lot's been going on since then," McNally said. He knew he'd better not tell EZ about Liz. It'd scare him off. "They said you had something important for me when you called the other day. What did you want?"

"Nuh-uh, man. I got nothin' to say over the phone. The phones are all bugged, an' I'd be capped before you got halfway here. If you wanna meet, I'll be in our usual spot right away. You gonna be there?"

Just one mistake now and EZ would bolt. He'd gotten scared, and he wasn't stupid. He wanted to be sure he was safe before giving up anything.

"I'll be there. Count on it. Ten minutes. And, EZ, if your tip is solid, there'll be a nice payday for you," McNally said and hung up.

* * *

After his meet with EZ, Mac felt deeply troubled. The information EZ gave him would rock his world and cause a gravitational shift throughout the department and division. But before he'd take EZ's word as gospel, he needed to check on the results of the shoe print report from Corporal Santini and stop by the evidence room to verify what he now feared could be true.

Even though the mobile lab combed through Clayton's apartment with their cameras and baggies, he hoped to find something they missed or misreported. Or not. Frustrated and angry, he couldn't shake the feeling he'd missed something from his investigation of Liz's murder, but he now knew where to go to find it.

He was heading down to the evidence locker when Tony Petrocelli walked through the door, grinning from ear to ear.

"McNally, I'm gonna make your day."

"Really? I need some good news right about now. What've you got?"

"After that tip we got from your CI, we found Henry, and you'll never guess what we found on him."

"A baseball bat and a White Sox collector's card in his pockets?"

"Might as well be. Your informant was right on the money. Henry's a guy that thinks giving his whores' occasional readjustment therapy keeps them in line. He's a big fella too. At least 6 foot, 4 and every bit of 290 pounds. We found a small leather club in his coat pocket. It's like one of those you can find at the triple-X shops."

"Where is he now?"

"In the interview room, he's cuffed to the table."

"Okay. I'll give him some time to think about why he's here. I need you to do something for me."

Petrocelli returned a half hour later and handed the sack to McNally with a puzzled look on his face. McNally then reached into his desk drawer and grabbed something that baffled Petrocelli even more as they headed into the interview room.

"Henry, my man," McNally said as he removed the cuffs and told him to sit at the table. He placed the brown paper sack in front of the angry-looking man. "Thought you might be hungry, so we brought you some ribs from Mississippi Rick's on Thirty-Fifth Street. Dig in. We can talk after."

"We got nothing to talk about, pig!" Henry's eyes grew wide when he sniffed the aroma of the spicy ribs filling the room. Because of his arrest, Henry missed lunch, and he reached into the bag to pull out a thick slab of the juicy pork. He ate them savagely, gnawing each bone clean. When finished, he smiled, revealing several gold-filled teeth that made him look like the poster child for a Maxwell Street jewelry vendor. He also sported a gold necklace with a chain that must have weighed half a pound and a glittery gold Rolex watch too. He leaned back in his chair, licking each one of his fingers with care. He then tilted his chair back against the wall and clamped his hands behind his head, scowling.

"So, *Detectives*, like I said, I got nothin' to say. So why you been chasin' me all over the hood? I ain't done one thing wrong."

Petrocelli cut in, "Heard you like to beat your trim, Henry." He'd gotten angry, half by Henry's attitude and half because he had to drive to Rick's to buy the mope's lunch.

With that, Henry's eyebrows knotted together over squinting bloodshot eyes as he sat bolt upright, scooting his chair back and leaning in. "That's crap, man. I see what you're doin, and it ain't gonna work. I got my rights, and I wanna make a phone call."

"Relax, Henry," McNally said. "We didn't bring you in here to charge you. We just have a few questions. I've got no beef with you. We'd like to cover all the bases." His expression was serious as he pushed a cup of hot coffee in front of Henry.

"I know what it's like, Henry. Been there myself. You tell someone who works for you to do their job, and they don't. Before you know it, everything goes wrong, and you're getting real pissed. Maybe make you pissed enough, so you want to hit them—a little reminder to show them who's boss. Hey, they're swearin' at you, so you swear at them. It's easy to lose it. We all do. You didn't mean to hit them that hard. Nobody knows that better than me. Isn't that right, Henry? That the way it happened?" McNally shoved his hands in his jacket pocket and shook his head back and forth. And after a pause, he continued, "Shit, we all get mad sometimes, Henry."

Henry eyed the detective with distrust. He remained sitting upright but rubbed the back of his neck. He shifted his weight in the chair, turning away. McNally feigned nonchalance as he pulled a baseball from his pocket and began tossing it in the air rhythmically. He slouched against the wall, pretending not to notice Henry's growing agitation.

Henry tilted back in his chair and started tugging on the collar of his shirt.

"I never killed nobody. Like you say, I hit 'em once in a while, but mostly to keep 'em in line. But I don't kill 'em. You can't make me cop to killing 'em." Then he leaned forward and placed his hands on his knees and began tapping his feet on the floor.

The interrogation continued another twenty minutes. It wasn't McNally's intention at the beginning to play "good cop, bad cop," but Petrocelli's questioning was persistent and fired off with antagonism. A knock on the door interrupted the interview. An officer handed McNally a slip of paper, and he excused himself. When he read the note, McNally motioned for Petrocelli to cease. It confirmed that they had the wrong man. The note corroborated Henry's alibis for two of the murders.

He turned to the silent man who was sitting motionless with his head bowed down. "You like baseball, Henry?"

Henry didn't look up. He just shook his head without answering. The detective pressed on, "I asked you a question. Do you like baseball?"

Henry's eyebrows rose. "What the fuck are you—"

"Heads up!"

As if shot from a cannon, the baseball spun in the air across the room. In one easy fluid motion, Henry lifted his arm and caught the ball in his large hand.

"What the fuck, man! You tryin' to kill me?" Henry screamed.

Mouth slack, confusion settled on Petrocelli's face. McNally smiled, walked over to him, and took the baseball from Henry's hand.

"We'll be right back, Henry. Don't go anywhere." Kyle nodded for Petrocelli to follow him.

They stood outside the door.

"You mind telling me what the hell you did in there?" Petrocelli asked.

"Cut Henry loose."

"Say what?"

"The ME said the killer is right-handed. Henry caught the ball with his right hand and signed his name left-handed. He's a south-paw. Cut him loose. We've got nothing to hold him with. And we're looking for a wood bat, not one like Henry's little leather blackjack. His alibis are sound. We're wasting time. Let him chill out for another hour, and let him go."

Petrocelli sighed. "Okay, I guess you know what you're doing." He left to arrange Henry's release.

McNally stood in the hallway. "So do I, Tony." Then, softly, he added, "So do I."

CHAPTER 39

McNally returned from the evidence locker, feeling sick to his stomach. He knew what he had to do now. He took a small plastic baggy from his shirt pocket and looked at it again. It didn't show up on the evidence report. He'd also picked up Santini's report. This would hurt bad, real bad.

Two hours later, after reviewing the reports, McNally rubbed his tired eyes and stacked the remaining papers into a brown accordion file marked "Clayton Case #CH850." He reread the examiner's preliminary report on Liz that they rushed to him. Neck bruises were visible on the epidermis down to the dermis, and there were signs of neck compression with the hyoid, thyroid, and cricoid cartilages crushed. The contusions on her head were delivered postmortem. The cause of death: strangulation.

A red file on the corner of his desk caught his eye. He picked it up and held it in his hands. Billie Fong, aka Kickboxer, had been the best informant McNally had working Chinatown. Dead. He took a .22 caliber to the back of his head and was found floating in the Chicago River.

Kyle rocked back in his chair, closed his eyes, and massaged his temples. He felt conflicted, frustrated, and upset. But there could no longer be any doubt.

He got up and, on his way out, stopped by Weller's desk.

"Where you headed?" Weller asked.

"Out. Got some things to take care of."

Weller watched the scowl on Kyle's face deepen. "Hey, buddy, what's up? You okay?"

"Yeah, sure, I'll be fine. Forget about it. I'll deal with Rouse if he fusses. What say we meet for some beers later?"

"You're on. Just say where and when? I'll be there."

"Give me a couple of hours. How does Brewster's sound? Six o'clock good?"

"I'll have a shot and a brew waiting for you," Weller said.

CHAPTER 40

Just before six o'clock that evening, two black Chevy Suburbans pulled into the parking lot of the all-night laundry next door to J. Brewster's Spirits, in the middle of a quiet tree-lined street on the edge of Canarytown. The wind howled and whipped the air mercilessly. It rained so hard it seemed like Noah's preparations might pay off again. Two spaces away, a man exited his car and walked bent over to the second vehicle. He held his trench coat tight around him with the collar up and his Chicago PD cap pulled down low. They exchanged a few words before the man walked to the bar next door.

The owner of Brewster's was a retired cop from Area 1. Mostly, local cops and firemen frequented the place. Only a few neighborhood regulars even knew of its existence. It was a small private bar, one where nobody ever asked too many questions. The owner, Paul Brewster, bought it a few years before and renamed it in memory of his brother John, a Chicago firefighter killed in a five-alarm blaze at a chemical plant in Argo. On weekdays, the tavern always had a quiet corner available for private conversation.

As Kyle entered, Sam hailed him, waving him over. "Glad you made it, buddy. Hope you don't mind, but I got here a while ago and put my old nose to the grindstone, so to speak." He lifted a full draft, then spoke with a mock-pirate voice. "Aye, matey, it's a darty job, but me throat got plenty parched."

Kyle shook the water from his coat, and he tossed it over an empty chair across from Sam. "No, I don't mind."

Sam smacked the table once and signaled for the waitress to bring a tall draft and a shot of Maker's Mark for his friend. The flame that burned in the small round candle in the center of the table provided just enough light to illuminate their faces. Weller seemed nervous. His usual congenial smile became tentative, and his eyes were bright and anxious in the flickering light.

"So what's eating you, Mac? You've been chewin' on your lower lip ever since I saw you this afternoon."

A flash of lightning broke in through the curtained windows, followed seconds later by the inevitable rumble of thunder.

"Sam, I talked to EZ earlier today." The muscles on Weller's face drew tight, and his eyes narrowed. Kyle waited for him to respond. The ensuing silence was palpable. His partner and best friend sat quiet and still, staring into his half-empty mug as bile began to rise in his throat.

Seconds passed before Sam swallowed hard and replied, "I'm glad you brought him up. How much do you trust this fella? I mean, I know you're sorry for him and all. So when he started sayin' he believes a cop did it, how can you be sure he wasn't working for someone else? He coulda done it himself, right?"

"Sam…"

"I never met him, but I tell you, I never trusted that scumbag. From what little you told me, I got the impression he's the kind who'd say anything to make a quick buck or to save his own skin."

"Shut up, Sam! I know."

Fear and doubt washed over Sam's face as he stared into McNally's eyes. "You know what?"

"What EZ told Liz. EZ witnessed Billie's murder, and he's willing to testify. I've got him in a safe house. He told me everything, Sam, said you were the one who pulled the trigger."

Weller slammed his fist on the table so hard the round candle bounced in the air and almost upended. The atmosphere in the bar became heavy as all other conversation came to an abrupt halt.

An off-duty cop from Vice grumbled, "If you two are gonna start swingin', take it outside."

"That's plain bullshit! I can't believe you're sayin' this."

McNally held out a picture. "Recognize this?" The picture had all the detectives in the unit gathered for the lieutenant's birthday cake.

"What's this got to do with anything?"

"EZ saw this and fingered you as the shooter."

"He's a fuckin' liar then. Why didn't he come forward until now?"

"He wasn't sure where the shooter worked or his name either until Liz showed him this picture. Before then, EZ thought Billie's killer worked for the feds. He described the guy to Liz the day he called her, and she knew who he was talking about, didn't she?"

Weller stared into his beer without speaking a word.

"I'm certain you were on the extension when EZ spoke to Liz. You knew she would contact me, so you went to Clayton's place ahead of her." Kyle didn't wait for a reply. "You went up the fire escape and got into the apartment, figuring you'd take care of EZ later. You waited for her, Weller, and when she came in, you murdered her, drove her car to where you parked your car, and took her to Adler Planetarium. That's where you beat her and dumped her. I can't believe how bad you beat her, Weller. You were trying to make it look like Slugger's work, but you left out his key signature—the card. Your first mistake. That and the fact the autopsy reported a crushed hyoid bone. She died of strangulation, premortem."

McNally's hands were shaking so much his beer splashed out.

"You had time to stash her and then meet me back at the apartment. What were you going to do with EZ? He was a loose connection. Were you planning to go back and take care of him where Liz had left him? Did you believe he'd still be there?"

"Oh, c'mon, Kyle, that's bullshit! Who ya gonna believe? I've had a clean record for twenty-plus years. It's my word against a worthless piece of shit snitch! You know me."

Kyle produced the small baggy from his pocket. He slid it across the table. Weller stared at the contents and shook his head. He lowered his head, hiding his eyes as he pushed it back across the table.

"I spent the afternoon in the evidence room after we found Liz's body. I went through everything the techs collected and bagged from the Clayton apartment the night we were there. I found this with the evidence. They overlooked it in inventory when they brought it back here."

"It could've fallen out of *your* pocket, couldn't it? Besides, if they didn't place it into their report, it'll be inadmissible in court. You know that, Kyle. A good attorney will blow that story to hell and back. So you found a cigar ring. Big fucking deal. You can't prove it's mine."

Kyle stared at Sam incredulously. He wanted to punch his face in. "That's not all, Weller. I got the forensic report back on the sneaker print those boys took that night. It had a small notch missing from the heel. I remembered seeing the bottoms of your shoe when you wore your boot. That same notch was missing from your heel, Sam. There's a team from Internal Affairs on their way over to your place right now, searching your place. They'll pick up your shoes while they're there."

With that, he reached in his pocket and held out a crumpled piece of paper.

"And this is what it was all about." He waved the paper in the air. "Something of yours, isn't it? Says you owe someone a lot of money." His lips curled in disgust. "A fucking IOU! She died to save your ass from the mob."

"What the... How... Where'd you get that?" he stuttered.

"The techs at the precinct garage called me back with their report the day after we were there. They told me they found it under the trunk liner after we left." McNally leaned against the back of his chair, still holding the folded paper in his hand.

Weller reached for the paper.

"Sorry, not this time," McNally said, stuffing it back in his pocket. "You should have checked the trunk a little more carefully after dumping her in the lake. You're gonna need a good lawyer. Even old F. Lee Bailey himself couldn't get you out of this one."

Weller's eyes watered, and his face sagged. He hung his head as hot tears dropped on his folded hands.

"Why? Tell me why!" Kyle said, pounding the table with his fist, his teeth clenched and his jaw muscles knotted and bulging. All heads turned to look at the two men. "You son of a bitch, I demand an answer!"

Sam's voice lowered to a whisper. "It doesn't matter. You've no idea what it's like. Those guys owned me."

"Tell me. Tell me what turned a good cop into the killer I'm sitting across from!"

"Two years ago, I started living pretty wild. When the old lady left me, I went a little crazy. I spent all my money on women and booze. Remember, you had to save my butt with the commander more than a few times. Anyway, I got myself into bad trouble. A couple of loans from the mob. I used the money betting the ponies, football, basketball, whatever. Over time, it all piled into one huge shit basket of markers I couldn't pay back. Before I knew it, they came to collect. So this guy approaches me and says he'd like to help me out of my mess. All I had to do was a favor for his boss sometime, and I'd be off the hook. Start fresh. Free, he says."

"So Billie Fong turned out to be the payback?"

"I never thought they'd ask me to kill anyone. Honest to God, I didn't. I asked the guy that first day what he wanted, but he said he'd tell me when the time came. I thought it would be maybe turning my head a couple of times or letting someone get away with a heist. When they told me, I tried to tell Fong to beat feet outta town, but he started screaming about how he'd take me down. He wouldn't shut up. I had to shoot him." He wiped his face with his now-shaking hands.

"Sam, why didn't you come to me or the Organized Crime Unit?"

"You and Liz were partnered then. No way could I come to you then. I wanted to, Kyle—believe me—but I owed too much and didn't have the guts."

McNally's face muscles knotted and his eyebrows drew in.

"I figured once I completed the contract, I'd walk away—free and clear."

"You never walk away, Weller. Never."

"I didn't start out wanting to hurt Lizzie. It tears at my gut thinking about it. At first, I thought I might shake her up, scare her a little. But after hearing what she said to EZ, I knew there was no other way. She'd have spilled everything to you. I ran outta choices." He opened his hands out and held them palms up. "Mac, you got to believe me, I didn't wanna do it!"

McNally fought to contain his rage. He didn't trust himself to speak. Sam pleaded with him and tried to grab his arm. He jerked it away and shook his head. It was over. He wore a wire, so he had Weller's confession and now just wanted to get away from him. The rain outside had ended.

"You will come with me. You will turn yourself in. I won't cuff you, Sam. Not here."

Weller begged him. "Please, Mac. Stop a moment and think about our history. Please, turn your back and give me some time to get away. For old time's sake. C'mon, buddy. You owe me that, right?"

"I owe you shit!" he spat. "Get up and walk out the door with me, or I swear I'll beat you to death right here, right now."

Weller rose from his chair. All eyes were on him now as he turned toward the door with McNally following close behind. Outside, four men with FBI caps and jackets walked toward them.

"What's this?" Weller said, turning to McNally, "C'mon, Kyle. Throw me a rope won'tcha? Not like this."

Kyle stepped away from the group and watched as one man took Weller's gun and badge, then slapped the cuffs on his outstretched wrists.

"We're from the Federal Bureau of Investigation. Orville Samuel Weller, you're under arrest. I'll read you Miranda if you like."

"Weller, my advice is you cooperate. I swear you're gonna pay big-time for what you did to Liz. And you will answer for Billie Fong's murder. Give up names, Sam. It'll go easier for you. Don't go down without naming the slime you worked for." McNally then turned and walked to his car.

"Kyle, please," Weller pleaded, "we were friends."

In a whisper, McNally's said, "That ended the moment you took Liz Dumont's life."

Back in his car, Kyle rubbed his hands over his face, catching his tired reflection in the rearview mirror and not much liking the face staring back at him. The two people closest to him were gone. He reached into his pocket and retrieved the blank scrap of paper he'd shown Weller. The bluff worked.

As EZ told it, Billie knew the mob held a marker for forty thousand on a dirty cop. He wasn't sure who it was. Weller knew the hammer was about to fall. Turned out he was right. Now Kyle only hoped Weller would cooperate with the US Attorney as a small measure of atonement.

Kyle knew EZ wouldn't agree to pick a cop out of a line-up, out of fear. EZ said he'd told Detective Dumont out of desperation when he thought the murderer was closing in. That was when she'd grabbed the photo of the precinct party and took it to show EZ. He identified Sam upon seeing him in the photo and promised to tell what he knew about Fong's killer for a thousand dollars of "get him out of the state" money. Liz told him she couldn't okay any amount until she cleared it with McNally, so she dropped him in a safe spot. When she left him, she went to Clayton's apartment to meet Kyle.

A faint yellow and gold glow from the setting March sun broke through the clouds. It lingered on the horizon as he drove west. Kyle got no gratification from busting Weller, just a sense of calm from finding and nailing Liz's murderer. He felt like he'd been gut-punched as he crumpled the paper in his fist and stuffed it in the ashtray next to a gold cigar ring.

CHAPTER 41

"Wayne dear, I held dinner. I hope you're hungry."

Evelyn Reynolds eyed her rain-soaked husband stomping through the front door. He gripped a twisted umbrella in one hand and a dripping briefcase in the other. Given his state of dishevelment, she regretted greeting him at the door and took three steps back.

He stopped, glared, and ignored her. She didn't deserve a response.

Oblivious to the consequences, she looked down at the puddle of muddy water collecting around his feet. She cried, "Oh, Wayne, the floor!"

At this, his scowl turned venomous, further incensed by the dull, wounded look on his wife's face. His lips parted into a snarl, eyebrows drew down, and nostrils flared. "Why, you bitch! Take a look at me. All you can say is look at your floor?"

He took a step toward the hall table to set down his briefcase. With that step, his right foot slipped on the puddle in front of him. To correct the sudden shift of his weight, his left leg buckled behind him. He panicked and tried to regain balance by flapping his arms in outstretched circles. As a result, his umbrella flew from his hand, sailing through the air and crashing into the library door. His briefcase went whirling like a saucer across the polished floor and smashed against one of the carved Victorian table legs. The leg buckled and broke, causing both the table and the marble statue resting on it to crash to the floor. The statue shattered like a clay pigeon blown apart at a skeet shoot, the sound echoing through the house.

Evelyn gasped and threw her hands to her mouth. Watching her husband trying to catch his fall, she fought the impulse to squeal in amusement at his floundering and flopping around on the floor like a three-hundred-pound tuna flopping on a dock. She took a step toward her husband to help him up.

He glared at her and said, "You, get the fuck out of my sight!"

Reynolds was grunting and panting from his attempt to recover. He rolled over and rose to his hands and knees. At that point, he stopped, glowering at his wife, who could barely contain her mirth.

He said, "Did common sense abandon you when you had the floors waxed today? In case you didn't notice, we're in the middle of a fucking typhoon! You are and will always be dumber than a box of rocks!"

At this attack, tears of anger and shame began spilling down her cheeks. "How can you talk like that? I'm the mother of your children, by God, not one of those three-hundred-dollar hookers you run around with in Washington. I've devoted my whole life to making a comfortable home for you. And this is my reward? I never, ever deserved a monster like you!"

Any other time, she would have been afraid of the murderous look he shot at her, but her anger and frustration spurred her on. "If I hadn't been so protective of your children and the scandal a divorce would cause, I'd have left you years ago. I despise you!"

He heaved himself off the floor with surprising speed and began lumbering toward her. Now truly terrified by the rage in his eyes, Evelyn pivoted on her heels and ran through the dining room to the kitchen. She'd escape up the back staircase to her bedroom. She made it to the stairs but halted when she heard the crash of shattering glass. Without looking back, she knew her husband gave up the chase but would still punish her with another selfish act of domestic violence. Once again, fresh tears streamed down her face, but they never washed away the shame or pain of all those wasted years.

Reynolds headed into his study and strode to the bar to fix his usual bracer of Johnnie Walker Blue. After splashing the dark-amber elixir into his glass, he noticed an empty ice bucket. He flung it across the room and swore at his wife for not having it filled. "Fuck the ice," he said, raising the glass to his lips. "And fuck her too. Fuck 'em all."

Still dripping and chilled after his harrowing hallway Hail Mary, he needed this drink. The numbing sensation sliced through his tension. As he poured a second healthier shot, he pondered what a useless, burdensome bitch his wife was for all these years with her whining and cowering. By God, he'd set Evelyn up. He'd given her respectability, a mansion to live in, and enough money to indulge in the lifestyle of her choice.

All women possessed a fatal flaw, the thorn in the rose—poisoned self-interest. They were passionate and playful in the beginning, but they always regressed, sinking into a morass of self-indulgence and depression. Whores, all. Men were so much more predictable.

I should never have married! Is this my just dessert? Karma come calling? But she would be sorry. Yes, she would.

"Yeah, fuck her!" he shouted, looking up to the ceiling.

Long ago, they moved into separate bedrooms, not because he tired of the occasional underwhelming sex with her, but more because of her childish modesty and sensual timidity, which he found revolting in a woman.

"Cunt, she'd bite it off if I ever got her to go down on me."

He took a large swallow of his drink. If I hadn't needed her old man's support and money in the beginning, she'd have been long gone by now. He reached for the bottle of scotch.

After his second glassful, the warm, numbing effects of the liquor brightened his mood as he plopped into the chair behind his massive desk. He hugged his drink with both hands, and in this semi-euphoric state, his anger dissipated. He considered the near-completion of his master plan—a plan that would see his ten-year goal of generating enough income to free him from this life he despised and all these needy people that made him want to puke. He'd been living a lie long enough, and his plans were close to fruition. A couple more details to wrap up, and he'd leave!

Pleased with himself for his clever maze of deceptions, he heaved himself out of his chair to pour another drink. On the way back to his desk, the phone rang. He sat before answering.

"Hello. Wayne Reynolds speaking."

"Wayne, this is John Marshfield."

Reynolds reacted immediately. His eyebrows knotted, and his mouth turned down. He shook it off and grinned. "Why, yes. Hello, John. How can I help you?"

"I understand you are planning a fishing trip the weekend before your scheduled speech for us at Northwestern."

His stomach climbed into his throat. The only two people that knew of his plans were his secretary and his wife. *What the…?*

"Pardon me, John, but I assure you, there is no reason for concern. At present, those plans are only tentative. Though I've always found that time in the woods spent angling helps clear my head before important speeches like this one…"

"No, excuse me, Senator, but I don't care how you spend *your* leisure time. I do, however, care a great deal if it threatens success of my decades-long project and the future growth of Citizens Against the Inhumane Treatment of Animals, CAITA. I chose you for your reputation and influence in Washington. We've been working closely on this—some might say a little too closely—yet my sources tell me our lobby is losing ground on Capitol Hill. *Your* Capitol Hill. Wayne, I've had to ask myself if there isn't some other agenda in play that's caused you to become negligent. And that's not a question I enjoy entertaining."

"Look, John, this trip will give me a chance to close the loop on several of our key initiatives, the ones you and I discussed earlier—how I'll negotiate for senate approval and get you the subsidies for the newest CAITA startups in New York and Pittsburg. I've got solid support in the committee and plan to use this speech as a dress rehearsal for my presentation to the full chamber. I'll only be away two or three days, though nothing is final yet."

Reynolds pulled a handkerchief from his pocket to wipe his face, catching a stream of perspiration that started on his forehead.

"Trust me, John, I'll look into your concerns. Let me speak with my aides in DC and see if there's any aspect of this we may have overlooked, though I'm certain someone must have misrepresented the information you've received. The last time I spoke with my allies on the hill, our interests were front and center on every major committee and subcommittee, including appropriations, budget, and finance. And let me add, the senators are all pleased with the support your PAC is providing them. Why, I even have the ear of the vice president. This takes time, John, but we haven't lost our momentum." He licked his dry lips. "Believe me, you can rely on my leadership here. Everything is as it should be."

Before Reynolds spoke another word, he heard a soft click and the dial tone buzzing in his ear. He stared into the receiver as Marshfield's words sank in.

"You son of a bitch!" he said and then yelled, "Who do you think you are?"

He hoisted his corpulent body to its feet, steadied himself for a moment, and then staggered over to the portrait of his father-in-law. He lifted his glass high in the air and, with a grand sweep of his arm, bowed to the face in the picture. His body wobbled as he raised bloodshot eyes. "To you, your vacuous daughter, and all those sluts I say, here comes the fate you deserve."

His booming laughter echoed through the house.

From her room, Evelyn heard the laughter and knew he'd gotten drunk again. She closed her eyes and inhaled. He would pass out soon, oblivious to everything, drooling over her precious Chippendale leather-top desk. During the middle of the night, he would stumble up the stairs, crash through the door to the bedroom next to hers, flop in his bed with clothes on, and sleep until midmorning. She exhaled with a sigh, reached over, and turned out her light.

CHAPTER 42

"Please come in," Marian Clayton beckoned.

McNally shook the rain off his jacket before stepping into her living room. Her face didn't conceal the weight of her recent personal loss. She offered him refreshments as he pulled a notepad out of his pocket.

"No, thank you, Mrs. Clayton. I apologize for this intrusion during your time of mourning, so I'll keep this as brief as possible." McNally hated this part of his job. "Please tell me a little more about Karen and her work with the CAITA organization."

"It's all right. I'll be fine. If there's anything I can tell you that might shed light on why Karen was..." She lifted her eyes to the ceiling and sighed, hoping to stop the tears that threatened to spill down her cheeks. "I mean, if I can help you catch her killer, it might be easier to let go."

He asked her several routine questions and jotted her answers in his notebook. Who were Karen's known associates? Local hangouts? Personal habits? Any enemies? With the last of the background questions answered, he relaxed in the chair and asked Marian Clayton to tell him about her daughter, even if it seemed unimportant to her. He knew this part of the interview would be painful to her and did his best to reassure her it was necessary. He had to learn as much as possible about her.

"I loved my daughter deeply. We were close and shared everything with each other."

She stared at her hands folded on her lap. When she lifted her head, McNally saw the quiver in her chin and the tears that misted her gentle gray-brown eyes.

She stared at a spot on the wall over McNally's right shoulder. "I thought I'd be able to do this. Now I'm not so sure."

"That's all right. Please take your time," McNally said, his face softening, reflecting his empathy.

"I'll be fine. I need to talk about her right now. It makes my loss seem a little less real."

He continued, "One thing we learned is that your daughter took classes at DePaul in Lincoln Park. She left class at seven thirty on Wednesday, May 23. Did you speak with her that day?"

"Yes. Karen called me early that morning to ask if I'd like to have lunch with her the next day. She volunteered her free time, working with her animal rights group. We planned to drop off some information she'd collected and then spend the afternoon together. She was excited about news she'd received and wanted to tell me about it. I'd heard about a Monet exhibit at the Art Institute, and we planned to have lunch there while enjoying the exhibits."

"Any idea what that news concerned?" McNally asked.

"No. She gave herself completely to her work. Ever since she was a child, she wanted to protect the helpless creatures of the world." Marian Clayton paused and smiled. "She was such a gentle child. She'd bring home birds with broken wings, injured rabbits, even once a squirrel with a severed leg. He became a personal pet of hers. Every spring would bring another parade of injured or abandoned animals. Karen would always be there, ready and willing to take them in with loving care. Her undergraduate studies in veterinary medicine at UIC in Champaign reflected both her character and her passion.

"She picked up a few courses at DePaul, where she met a group of young people like herself, ones dedicated to conserving and protecting animals. She worked for a nonprofit organization called CAITA. Karen was excited about her work for them. I'm only certain of what she told me, but I think part of their mission involved organizing protests against companies using animals in product testing.

Karen once told me CAITA's influence reached as far as Washington. Whistleblowers contacted CAITA if their company used laboratory animals for product testing. They would then investigate those allegations."

"Were those demonstrations peaceful?"

"Always. They were never confrontational. From what she told me, most of their cases settled as the companies wanted to avoid adverse publicity. CAITA's influence was broad and persuasive. Karen received a lot of recognition for her work with them. It even earned her extra credit toward her studies at DePaul. But to answer your question, she would never agree to violence as an answer to their mission. The CAITA people are humanitarians, not terrorists," she added confidently.

"Is CAITA an acronym for something?"

She nodded. "Citizens Against the Inhumane Treatment of Animals. Though they're a small group compared to the larger national nonprofits, they've developed affiliations with similar groups nationwide. CAITA may be small by most standards, but their success has grown here in the Midwest. They target the cosmetic and household product industries. As a result, many have agreed to discontinue their animal testing programs."

"So its headquarters are here in Chicago then?"

"Yes. But she told me their vision is to influence laws nationwide. She always complimented the leadership and volunteers she worked with. They were certain that a bill would pass in Washington, prohibiting the use of all animals for research." Marian stared at a picture of Karen sitting on the end table. "She would have been a gifted veterinarian."

"Other than the protests you spoke of, what other responsibilities did she have there?"

"She'd take jobs with the companies that CAITA believed were engaged in animal testing and then stay long enough to investigate the rumors. They knew the libel laws and were careful not to falsely accuse a company of animal abuse before they investigated."

Panic flooded her soft features. "I would never have supported Karen if I thought it would be dangerous. Is there a chance her death had something to do with her work with CAITA?"

"We're not sure, Mrs. Clayton," McNally said. "I saw that her most recent job involved working for a company called Chi-Tech? Did she investigate them?"

"Yes, she was. Karen would stay long enough with companies to confirm or refute the complaints. She did the fieldwork, and the organization followed up." Marian smiled. "She thought of herself as an investigative reporter, a kind of Barbara Walters for the animal kingdom. She told me she kept a diary of her work. You'd learn more from that than what I've told you."

"Did anyone else know about this diary?"

"I'm not sure, but it's possible. She took it everywhere with her. Chi-Tech was her latest case. She stayed longer than usual there. That's where she met Frank Butler. He and Karen became friends, and she told him about her interest in working in their laboratories. She needed a special security clearance to work in their labs, and he helped her get it. I believe his aunt owns Chi-Tech, and he works part-time for her. I think he had a crush on her right off. Karen thought of it more like puppy love and never gave him much attention."

"I see." McNally found it difficult to gin up any sympathy for the bereaved man bent over Karen's body at the morgue, considering their recent confrontation at the cemetery.

"She told me she discovered no evidence of animal cruelty. I believe that's when she gave her notice and quit."

"Did she ever speak of any problems or issues during her time at Chi-Tech?"

Marian Clayton thought a moment before answering. "Well, yes, Karen mentioned one thing she found odd."

"What's that?"

"We were talking over dinner one night, and she mentioned that even though she hadn't found evidence of any animals, one lab she visited had an unusual smell...different."

"Different how?"

"She did not understand what it was. Not the usual laboratory smells, she said, like animals may have been there before, but it still had another lingering smell. She had a nose for it because of her lab work at the university. She checked and double-checked the labs and decided it was more likely used earlier for keeping animals."

"So she checked all the labs?"

"That's right. At least all those she had access to. The one lab she didn't check was private, and her pass didn't work. One of the lab assistants told Karen they converted it into private offices for Mrs. Butler, and she held the only entry key."

"Then Butler and your daughter became friends at Chi-Tech? Our information is that he's a lawyer at Butler, Jamison, and Newman in the Loop."

"That's right. He's only at Chi-Tech two or three days a month. A board of directors runs the company. Frank does some of their legal work."

"And the aunt?"

"Frank doesn't talk much about her. Karen said she is semiretired and lives in a condominium on the Gold Coast. Frank told me once she was an entrepreneur from her assorted-business ventures throughout the years. I believe Karen only met her once." She glanced at the anniversary clock on the mantel. "I'm sorry, but I don't know that much about his family."

"That's all right. Anything at all is helpful." He saw both pain and confusion flash across her face. "The more I can learn about Karen, the easier it will be to discover who might want to hurt her. Though if you would like, we can finish this later."

"No, thank you. Give me a moment. I'm trying to remember as much as I can."

When she spoke again, her voice became soft, and McNally wondered if she was speaking to him. She lifted her bowed head and wiped a tear from her cheek.

"It's so hard to imagine anyone who knew Karen would want to hurt her. It breaks my heart." She inhaled, struggling to speak.

"We're doing everything in our power to find the perpetrator, I assure you," McNally said, but his words rang hollow even to his own ears.

"Karen's friends may help you more."

"We have people assigned to interview Karen's other friends. Does Karen have any brothers or sisters?"

"No, she and I were the only ones left of our family. Karen's father died of a heart attack years ago, and there wasn't any family on his side. My mother died when I was eight years old, and my father raised me, though we are long since estranged."

"You mentioned a diary Karen kept?" McNally said.

She nodded.

"Any idea where she kept it? Or what she wrote in it?"

"Everything. Karen always kept her diary with her. She wrote in it every day. Her interest in it became a habit in her high school years. I gave her the first one for Christmas when she was fourteen, and she replaced it every year. I've kept her old diaries if you'd like to see them."

"Yes, I'd like to take them with me. I'm primarily interested in this year's diary," McNally said.

"Of course." Her lips curved upward, and her eyes softened. "She filled them with wonderful things. I believe it gave her a sense of having a family, I think. She always wrote her thoughts." Marian's eyes widened. "And may have even written in it on the day she..."

"It might be helpful. We didn't find a diary during our search of her vehicle or apartment, but you may come across it," McNally said.

"I'll call you if I find it."

He knew she wanted to keep talking about her life, but following a short pause, he rose from his chair. Her eyes followed his movement, and without warning, she straightened her shoulders as if to rise and then folded in half like a rag doll. She buried her face in her hands and wept.

McNally rested his hand on her shoulder. "I can show myself out." He left a card on the table beside her. "Please call me if you can think of anything else at anytime—day or night. My pager number is on the back."

By the time he left Marian Clayton's apartment, he felt disappointed, and his shoulder ached. He felt certain now that something in Karen's apartment had drawn out the killer on the night Liz disappeared. His trail of clues now pointed to her diary.

CHAPTER 43

There was a black Mercedes parked in the tow-away zone that fronted the police station. McNally didn't pay attention to the driver, only the license plate with the expired tag. He pulled in the reserved parking spot behind the Mercedes. Butler emerged from the car, red-faced and disheveled. His eyes were open wide with nostrils flaring. McNally's knuckles turned white as he gripped the steering wheel. He wasn't in the mood for any shit accusations from this one. He opened the car door, almost knocking Butler back into the street. Butler, unmoved by the near miss, puffed up his chest and lunged back, positioning himself within inches of the detective's face.

Tiny hairs stood up on the back of McNally's neck. Butler had just jumped to the top of his "Assholes I Don't Like" list. The jerk-off should have taken the hint by now. His repeated calls to the department and unreasonable demands for information on the case had pissed everyone off. This lawyer with a measure of public influence had become a flamethrower of ill will, and McNally was about ready to break out the extinguisher.

He stood his ground and waited for Butler to make one wrong move. That Butler met with Commander Rouse rankled him like a two-day-old hangnail. It shouldn't have come as a surprise. Rouse wanted his name in the spotlight as the man solely responsible for stopping the Slugger. It was laughable. If Rouse thought Butler could be of any help to him, he would chance fucking up the investigation. McNally needed to stop him before this gained any more traction.

Butler had become the irritating mosquito buzzing around his ear in the dark. McNally waved him out of his way.

"Detective, I thought I clarified that Marian Clayton needed to have counsel when you questioned her. You have overstepped your bounds, and I intend to tell your commanding officer about this."

"Mr. Butler, your concern for Mrs. Clayton's welfare is commendable but misplaced. I interviewed her concerning a crime. I didn't charge her with the crime. There was no need for an attorney to be present, and I've got a good sense that if she needed you there, she would have invited you. Now if you'll please step aside, I'm running an investigation."

Butler's eyes darted back and forth like a man struggling with what to do next. McNally noticed a nervous tick that caused Butler's jaw muscles to pulse. He presented his own closing argument, giving Butler no time to regroup.

"Let me caution you, Mr. Butler. Do not insert yourself any further. You wouldn't want to become a hindrance to this investigation, now would you?" He lowered his voice, narrowed his eyes, and smiled, giving him the look of a lion staring at dinner. "If you continue to pressure this department, we might construe your interest in this case rising above the level of personal interest. My commander is funny about civilians interfering in official police business. I want to believe you're only concerned with finding out who killed Karen Clayton. But others took it as a gross overreaction on your part. I'm sure that's not what you intend, is it?"

"But, Detective, you don't seem to understand. I'm only attempting to look out for the interests of a dear friend, a friend who lost her daughter in a brutal, senseless murder on our streets only a few days ago. I have a familial right to hear about your progress in this case. Regardless of my intent, by God I will find out if you and your department are mismanaging this matter."

For a split second, Butler appeared almost ready to launch at him. Before permitting him to make a serious mistake, he raised a palm to Butler. "Mr. Butler, be careful what you say and do now. You need to step back and trust our department to do their job. It may be difficult to understand, but as a lawyer of no small repute, you understand there are explicit rules that prevent us from sharing the details of an active investigation. Do I make myself clear?"

McNally had run out of patience with this arrogant dick, his temper teetering on the brink. He would do anything to avoid an altercation with this man in front of the station. Half the free world would love reading about police brutality on the front page of the *Sun Times*. It would be "Hasta la bye-bye" to his career if his face ended up on the evening trash shows, but Butler pushed all the wrong buttons. The only thing keeping his fist from Butler's face was the thought of his ass nailed to Rouse's wall.

He lowered his voice. "Come on, Butler. We're both after the same thing. To solve a crime like this one takes time. Now why don't you take a step back, and let us do our job?"

Butler's face paled, and he hung his head. He'd been rebuked and shamed. The rage from a moment ago had vanished. McNally worried that he might collapse in a crumpled heap to the ground. Instead, he started to speak, changed his mind, and walked back to his car.

McNally stayed a few minutes after the Mercedes had pulled around the corner and out of sight. Whether or not McNally liked him wasn't relevant. In his line of work, he'd come across more than a few pushy pigheaded civvies. Compound that with the fact he was a lawyer. Lawyers always felt they deserved a bigger slice of the pie than the rest of us mortals. And though Butler might be as annoying as a mother-in-law's surprise visit, underneath he's a wimp with an inflated sense of himself. He doubted if he'd be hearing much from Frank Butler for a while.

CHAPTER 44

Butler slammed the telephone down and began pacing back and forth in his spacious corner office, angry that his confrontation with Detective McNally got him nowhere. They weren't giving him any information about Karen's murder case, and when he tried, he got the same cock-and-bull story. Not only did they refuse to tell him anything relevant; they continued to refer him to McNally. He hadn't answered a single message.

Idiots! They're just wasting time.

Frustrated and angry, he picked up the closest object he found, a copy of *Sullivan's Law Directory*, and threw the thick book, which crashed against his office door. The projectile bounced off the door and hit the floor with a booming thud.

"Goddamn it!" he screamed.

His attractive young secretary, Ms. Swanson, who had large jade-green eyes and thick black hair, opened the door of his office. "Mr. Butler, is everything okay?"

He'd considered taking her for a romp once or twice, and it took a major effort on his part to quell that urge. The adage "You don't eat where you shit" had influenced his decision.

He stood up behind his desk and absently fussed with his tie. "Yes, yes, thank you. I tripped over a book I left lying on the floor," he said, rounding his desk to retrieve it. "Lost my balance, but I'm fine, Ms. Swanson. Thank you for asking."

She glanced at the *Sullivan's* by the door. "That's a relief. If you need anything, sir, I'll be at my desk."

He felt foolish. He almost never lost his composure, not in front of his subordinates. Surrounded by spies, he had never doubted that he was being watched. His partners were all jealous of his position and how he'd gained it.

Frank returned to his office after an extended lunch recess, where he'd caught up with McNally. Now, however, the smile on his face grew as he thumbed through the thick accordion file on his desk. This client would make him famous.

His father, Francis Butler Sr., would've been proud of him. He was the youngest lawyer to ever become a partner at the firm. But Frank knew that with his limited jury trial experience, the senior partners doubted his ability as a winning courtroom attorney. From the first, he'd expected their resistance, so he planned for the time he would need ammunition to deal with them. He dug covertly, and with the help of a scruple-challenged private dick, he discovered there wasn't one without juicy skeletons rattling around in their closet.

Old man Jamison had an appetite for hookers. He was the easiest one to turn. Frank's detective produced damaging snaps of Jamison. They showed his fat milk-white body standing over a bleached blonde with ruby lips sucking on his cock while he wielded a leather whip over her head. Best five hundred bucks he'd ever spent. It took less than five minutes to convince him. He agreed that Frank would be the right attorney for the Palumbo case.

Philip Newman was not so easy. A good Catholic boy with a gaggle of kids and a socially active, perfect little wife made him less accessible. No matter how deep Frank's detective dug, he'd found nothing. Newman didn't cheat on his taxes, went to church every Sunday with his family, and was a teetotaler. He was over six feet tall and athletic, in his midfifties, and was graying at the temples; he looked very distinguished and proper. But Frank could be patient. He was sure Newman had a fatal flaw, and he needed him to assure the vote from partnership would go his way.

And his prediction came true. In late November last year, Frank got a call from his detective. He wouldn't tell him over the phone, so Frank told him they could meet somewhere away from his office. Two hours later, he sat in a dark tavern, drinking club soda with lime and waiting for his sleaze ball detective, Ralph "Lucky" Stryker.

Stryker lumbered into the bar fifteen minutes late. Frank was furious.

"This better be worth it," Frank said. The darkened bar smelled of urine and vomit. Struggling against his initial gag response, he wanted to cover his nose with a handkerchief.

Ralph stared through beady eyes and smiled, showing broken yellow-stained teeth behind a mangy-looking three-day stubble. "Yeah, listen, what I got is worth more than the five hundred. I'd say at least a thousand?"

"Let me see what you've got, and I'll tell you what it's worth."

The detective's sly smile never faltered as he squeezed his three-hundred-pound frame in the chair across from Frank.

"The guy is good, squeaky clean, but I'm better." He ordered a beer and swallowed it in two quick gulps and signaled for another.

"I haven't got all day, Stryker. Tell me what you've got. And lose the grin."

Thinking he held the winning hand, Ralph's mouth fell open. He pulled an envelope from the breast pocket of his mustard-yellow ketchup-stained jacket.

"Right out of law school, your boy joined a firm south of here in Springfield, some thirty years ago. Landed a case where he had to defend a good old Redneck accused of pistol whipping an airman out of the Chanute Air Force Base. Left the poor slob brain dead. Made all the papers, big trial. No witnesses, so prosecution was real scared. Newman must have known this early on because the trial turned ugly. Mudslinging on both sides." Ralph gulped down his second draft and wiped the suds on his upper lip with his sleeve.

"Get to the point."

"Bottom line here is, out of the blue, the prosecutor hears from an old classmate of your lily-white, big-time Harvard graduate and sold a tale."

"What tale?"

"Seems Mr. Newman didn't have what it takes to pass the bar exam on his first try, so he had his friend take the second one for him." Then grinning, he said, "Aced it, I'm told."

"Christ."

"Hey, missy, bring me another brew!" he hollered to the waitress.

"Go on."

"Not much more to say. The case ended in a mistrial. Your pal Newman went behind closed doors with the judge. I'm thinkin' Newman must have had some powerful connections at Harvard on account of the judge kicking the snitch out of Dodge instead of him, so to speak. I tracked him down, chasing ambulances in Hannibal, Missouri. Ha! What d'ya think about that? The one that aced the exam for the other ends up an idiot ambulance chaser." Ralph took another gulp of his beer and let out a loud belch that turned a few heads at nearby tables.

"Okay, so give me his name and address."

"I got better than that." He produced a piece of paper from his pocket and waved it in Butler's face. "I talked to him, and he said for the right price, he'll testify what he knows to the Disciplinary Commission."

"I'll take that," Frank said, grabbing for the piece of paper.

"Whoa now, bucko! Now's when you and me discuss my fee." He smiled wickedly. "Two thousand."

"You said one thousand!"

"That was before I knew how bad you wanted this." He waved the paper in the air again. "For two thousand, you get the name of Newman's pal that took the test."

"Take a personal check?"

"Not on your life, shylock."

CHAPTER 45

Frank reached for the telephone and dialed Wayne Reynolds's office.

"Senator Reynolds's office."

"This is Frank Butler. Connect me with the senator."

"I'm sorry, Mr. Butler. The senator has left for an appointment. May I ask him to return your call?"

"No. I'll be in court this afternoon. I'll try again later."

"All right. Thank you, Mr. Butler. I will give your message to the senator."

Frank picked up the folder with his closing notes, placed it in his briefcase, and slammed the lid down. He planned to go over them before returning to court, but now, between Reynolds and McNally, both his time and patience had run out. The senator had become difficult to reach. He'd have to play hardball soon, and he was still angry that Marian had consented to a police interview without him. He didn't expect any help from the police, and after his talk with McNally, he felt they were no further along in their investigation than the last time he talked with them.

Idiots! He had more of a right than anyone to know of their progress on the case. *Keystone Cops tripping over each other.*

On his way to the elevator, he heard his name called.

"Frank, have you got a moment?"

He sighed, and his eyes shot to the ceiling. It was Burt Warner, a man who should have done the firm a favor and retired years ago. Since he wasn't one of the founding partners, he posed no immediate threat—just a pain in his ass. A confirmed bachelor and workaholic, Warner spent more time sleeping on the leather couch in his office than his apartment in Dearborn Park. Frank suspected he might be gay. Warner usually kept to himself, a token elder in the firm kept with the notion he lent it an air of respectability.

He occupied one of the most elegant corner offices on the floor, the prototypical example of someone who'd worked well past their productive years. Frank promised himself early on that he would get Warner's office. He'd been the only one of the six senior partners on the board that didn't vote in Frank's favor for the partnership slot. He felt the boy had to develop his knowledge through work and experience before he earned a partnership at Butler, Jamison, and Newman. Truth was, they didn't like each other.

"Oh, hello, Burt. I'm on my way to court, so I've only got a minute."

"That's all right, son."

You're not my father!

"I wanted to tell you I'm invited to your aunt's house for a cocktail reception Saturday night and wondered if you would be there."

Frank eyed him with disdain.

"If so, that might give us a chance to discuss your closing strategy on the Nesson-Palumbo trial. I am the first attorney at this firm to represent that family, and they are personal friends of mine. I believe I can offer you some timely advice."

Frank fumed. "That's kind of you, Burt, but I have everything wrapped up and am ready to present my closing arguments on Monday. The only help I'll need is finishing up the documentation, and I'm getting all the help I need from my associate. But I look forward to seeing you at my aunt's home."

"I understand, my boy. If I didn't think you could handle this case, I would never have recommended you to the young woman's father, Everett Nesson."

Whom does he think he's kidding? His was the one vote against my taking the case!

"Again, thank you, but that won't be necessary. Now if you'll excuse, I'm late for court."

"Arrogant, ungrateful smart-ass," Burt Warner mumbled after turning away.

* * *

By five-thirty, with face flushed, Butler wore a nervous smile. He'd expected the judge to declare a recess before five o'clock. He thought the prosecutor would wrap up his case today. His opponent's cross-examinations were worrying him. The jury had listened sympathetically to the arguments of the assistant district attorney, and that worried him. He'd have to work hard to woo them back. In the past hour, his objections were all overruled. This wasn't how he'd imagined it would go. His face had lost its color, and he'd become visibly nervous. Sweat soaked his collar. His client noticed and, at one point, asked if he felt all right. He reassured her and attempted to regain his focus. But it was impossible. He needed to put an end to this.

"Your Honor, may counsel approach the bench?"

The courtroom grew silent. The judge frowned over his wire-rimmed glasses, and the prosecuting attorney spun on his heels and glared at Butler.

"Your Honor? Please," the prosecution objected, "I'm in the middle of my cross-examination of this witness."

Judge Redmond motioned for counsels to approach the bench and covered the microphone with his hand. He said, "This better be good, Mr. Butler."

Butler paled. "Your Honor, I would like to request a recess. I am not at all well and am finding it difficult to concentrate on these proceedings."

"Does opposing counsel have any objections?" the judged asked.

"Yes, I do, Your Honor. I'm not finished questioning this witness. This interruption is unexpected and may damage the credence of my efforts thus far with the jury," Assistant District Attorney Harper replied.

"Mr. Butler, although it is against my better judgment to delay these proceedings, I have noticed your unusual behavior in the last hour and am forced to concede it might damage your client's defense to proceed. I trust you will resume these proceedings by nine o'clock tomorrow?"

"Yes, Your Honor." He bowed his head. "Thank you, Your Honor."

"Very well. I'll schedule your closing arguments for next Tuesday, the 12th. Court is adjourned until tomorrow morning at nine o'clock," he announced to the courtroom, "and allow me to remind the jury they are not to discuss this trial with anyone."

As the spectators began filing out of the courtroom, Frank Butler overheard a voice in the crowd say, "What the hell happened? It was just getting interesting."

"Nice dodge, Butler. But your delay won't keep your client out of prison," the disgruntled ADA said, pushing his way through the crowd toward the exit.

Frank telephoned his secretary for messages before he left the courthouse.

His secretary said, "You had two phone calls. Your aunt called and said you need to contact her immediately. And Senator Reynolds returned your call."

He didn't need to talk with his aunt now. He had some business to attend to back at his Chi-Tech offices. "Call my aunt. Tell her I'm in court and will try to reach her later. I'll try reaching the senator from my end."

"Anything else?"

"No. I won't be back to the office before you leave. Leave any messages on your desk. I'll get them later."

"Yes, sir. Will do, sir."

CHAPTER 46

It was one of those early summer days you'd dream about in January—blue skies, warm (not hot), and the aroma of lilacs in the air. Tony Petrocelli heard McNally's car horn from the street. They were heading for an appointment at the CAITA headquarters on South Ashland.

Five minutes later and while sitting in the car, McNally handed him a cup of black coffee.

"Thanks, Mac. It's been a while since I had a Saturday off," Petrocelli said, shielding his eyes from the glaring sun. "Seems unnatural. It doesn't feel right. Would you believe it? I left a perfectly good omelet for the cat." Tasting his coffee, he scowled. "Ugh, this is close to mud. What, you dig it up in your backyard?" He liked his with caramel macchiato flavoring. "And why did I think everybody but cops and waitresses were off on Saturdays?"

"These CAITA people would go eight days if they'd let them." McNally cast a world-weary glance at the young detective. "And tell me, when was the last time you had a Saturday off anyhow?"

"You mean since getting assigned to work this case with you, or in general?"

"In general," McNally answered.

"I was still at the academy."

"So listen, Tony, there's something you need to realize about Detective Weller..."

"It's okay. I've heard enough officially and unofficially about what happened to understand you had no choice. I guess what stuck in my gut is how he... I mean, she's one of us for God's sake."

At that moment, he didn't see a young inexperienced detective in Petrocelli's eyes. This reminded Kyle of himself as a young rookie. He'd been a lot less jaded then and still searching for answers to questions he wouldn't comprehend for another decade. People like cops in the detective bureau had way too many variables to deal with between the perps, the vics, and the snitches. Then there were the bad ones with badges.

"I can't say why he took that wrong turn. He took his eye off the ball. Things got out of control. You sometimes see it, even with the best ones. Some say corruption is one of Lucifer's virtue tests. In his *Inferno*, Dante associated it with greed and assigned it to the fourth circle of hell. If you're Christian, it's called avarice, the third deadly sin. Though I'm not given to spend too much time contemplating the religious angle, I believe that you don't have to be looking too hard to find it around you, Tony. And it's pass or fail. In my book, if you fail, you own it."

"But Weller—we all respected him. You know what I mean. You and him, I mean... Partners... Well..." Petrocelli struggled for words. "Ahhh, forget it. It all seems impossible somehow. This is me being naive, I guess."

With a half smile, McNally said, "I've always been able to keep my head screwed on straight with two premises: one, that people are three quarters of the way to crazy, and two, that I'm the best judge of who is and who's not. Anyone believing that mankind's destiny is the pursuit of virtue is taking a stroll down the garden path in their heads. Some people are good, incorruptible; some are not. And temptation is a powerful bait for those who tilt the wrong way."

Kyle knew that Tony was angry and disheartened by what Weller did. Somewhere along the line, he'd begun imagining Weller as a kind of folksy hero, someone who couldn't fuck up on a bad day with a gun to his head. Well, he did, and it was done. There was no undoing or changing it. McNally's anger and contempt went deeper, not only because of the people's lives he'd ended, but also because of the stink of personal bitterness he left in his wake.

"Well, let not your heart be troubled, Detective. This shouldn't take long. Then I'll drop you at your place, and you can get on with your life."

"To be honest, I didn't have much planned today. I hope I don't sound like a whiney complainer." He paused. "And I've got to admit I'm surprised to be working with you, Mac, even if it's only temporary. Everyone knows—uhh, knew—that you and Weller were the best team in the area together. Every rook out of the academy hopes to work and learn from the best." His cheeks flushed when he realized he sounded like a creepy ass-kisser.

Petrocelli's admission surprised him. He'd lost two partners to bad endings and couldn't help viewing this with a jaundiced eye, even if only for the short haul. But now, hearing something that smacked a little too much of blind admiration suddenly angered him.

"Whoa, whoa, there, Detective. Don't start sucking my dick just yet. Blow the commander if you want to rise in this unit. As far as I'm concerned, you're here to watch my six and help me get the job done. Besides, I'd never fuck a greasy Wop—asses are too hairy."

Petrocelli, realizing this was in jest, responded, "Fuck you then, you Mic Protestant!"

McNally blew out one of his rare hearty laughs, suddenly realizing he was taking his anger from the recent events out on the young detective. His rage, born from his best friend's deceit, was his to bear alone. What Sam did was incomprehensible and unforgiveable. It took all his strength to keep from punching a hole through something, but it was not Petrocelli's fault. For now, it was time to focus on finding a killer.

"Great. We're going to get along just fine, Nancy boy. One other thing you need to learn, Petrocelli. Be careful whom you spend your trust money on. It's valuable currency. If you're not careful, people will chew you up and leave you for roadkill. If you're looking for someone to teach you the ropes, I'll bust your balls, but you'll learn. The only heroes I've ever known sit in parks, chiseled from stone, or seen for eight bucks in the movie theaters. I'm flesh and blood and consider myself every bit as susceptible as the next man. Consider Weller's fall as your first real objective lesson in human frailty.

"What separates me from Weller is my genetic predisposition for guilt and shame. I have them. Now I know he didn't, at least not in the end. Don't look for any black and white handles—it'll disappoint you. There's a world of gray out there, and even I missed his tells. If you're looking for advice, Detective—and I'm not sure you should—focus on digging into people's backstories. Don't ignore your intuition. There're only one or two experiences that separate a good cop from a bad one. The good ones aren't always good. And like I found out, the bad ones can fool you. I think I sensed it with Sam, but I ignored my best instincts.

"And if we're speaking plainly, you need to know that I wasn't looking for a new partner, much less a wide-eyed young Turk like you. Don't fool yourself into reading it otherwise. You're here today because Commander Rouse assigned you. Truth is, I'd rather work alone right now. Anyway, we worked together with Henry, and it went okay. That's all. Understood?"

"Are you accusing me of wanting to suck Rouse's cock? 'Cuz that's not what's going on here."

"Good, now we're on the same page."

CHAPTER 47

When they entered CAITA headquarters, a restored warehouse on Ashland, a coffee-skinned black man with a wide toothy smile greeted them. "How may I assist you, gentlemen, on this beautiful sunny morning?"

McNally read Petrocelli's thoughts and shot him a warning look, which told him not to so much as snicker at the flamboyant receptionist. Both detectives presented their badges.

"I'm Detective McNally. This is Detective Petrocelli. Chicago Homicide. We'd like to speak to the manager on duty."

The receptionist put his hand to his mouth and, in a whisper, said, "Oh my, homicide. Is this about"—he leaned his narrow body over the desk—"Karen?"

"We're in a hurry. The manager, please."

"Oh, listen to me! I'm babbling on and keeping you men from doing your job. Let me run and fetch Thomas for you. He'll be able to help you both." He beamed and winked at Petrocelli. "Back in a tick."

"I think he likes you," McNally said dryly after the receptionist had left the room.

"Are you pulling my leg? He'd better not be hitting on me! More your type, McNally, a waxed-ass guy!"

"Relax, kid." Kyle grinned, unable to pass up the moment. "It must be the Dockers and your chest hairs peeking out from under your V-neck sweater."

"Shit," Petrocelli said, zipping his jacket to his neck. "I hate this."

McNally's laughter bounced off the walls. This kid was so naive, something he hadn't noticed before. He made a mental snapshot of the moment.

While they waited, McNally shuffled through the inbox on the reception desk in front of him. "Look at this. All these letters are from people pledging money. One hundred, one hundred seventy-five, seventy, five hundred dollars. This is quite a chunk of change sitting here. Most of these have personal checks attached to them. Jesus, a thousand bucks from an alderman."

The receptionist returned. Clearing his throat, he said, "Puleez, gentlemen, those documents are none of your business. What would our donors think if they discovered that the Chicago Police were scrutinizing the size of their donations?" He made a clucking sound and stepped between the detectives and his desk. With hands on hips and eyes narrowed to slits, he puckered his mouth, daring them to say anything.

Petrocelli leaned back in his chair like someone sidestepping a rattlesnake. McNally got caught with his hand in the cookie jar; otherwise, the entire scene would have been hilarious.

"Besides, don't you need a warrant or something to do that?"

McNally stared coolly into his nervous eyes. "Relax, no harm done, and I assure you, we're not interested in your donors or their wallets." He grinned. "I was just wondering whom to make my donation check out to."

They waited almost five minutes, and Kyle was about to question the delay when a tidily dressed man entered the room.

"Gentlemen, how can I help you?" His large mouth stretched into a lopsided grin. He had clear, translucent blue eyes and curly blond hair cut close to the scalp. His wide forehead gave him a scholarly appearance. Broad shoulders and an erect posture suggested that he might have a military background. He stood eye level to McNally and confidently shook his hand.

"I'm Tom Conway, manager of operations. Jimmy tells me you're here to inquire about Karen Clayton?"

"Is there someplace we can talk?" McNally asked.

"Yes. Follow me, and we can speak in my office. Jimmy, hold my calls please."

Conway's office was small and cluttered, making the large metal desk appear out of place. The two directors' chairs held stacks of papers, leaving the detectives with standing room only. The top of his desk had fliers and advertisements and several eight-by-ten glossy photos of disfigured animals and posters in varying dimensions bearing CAITA's logo across the bottom border. Conway moved the stacks of papers to one of the few remaining empty spots on the floor and motioned for them to sit.

"You've come to discuss Karen Clayton. Terrible, terrible loss for all of us here at CAITA. Please give me a minute to pull her file. It may be helpful as it contains a list of the companies she investigated for us."

"And I hope you won't mind if I take notes while we talk?" McNally said.

"No, of course not."

After retrieving the files, Conway returned and began thumbing through a manila folder labeled "Clayton, Karen." He said, "It's a damn shame about Karen. I've only been at this office for a couple months, but everyone who knew her said she possessed amazing ambition and perseverance. Yes, here we are." Conway handed the open folder to McNally. "That's a list of the companies in the Metro area that Karen researched. She would take work with them and investigate to determine if they performed any animal testing for their product development, and if so, we would step in to request that the company explore alternative product development options. Although we're not always successful, Karen had quite a surprising record of successes to her credit. Since she began working with us here, three of the largest manufacturing companies in the area agreed to suspend their animal testing after her reporting."

McNally scanned the lists of companies as Petrocelli reviewed the photographs. Tony blanched at the vivid snaps of the forlorn-appearing animals with legs missing, open sores on their bodies, and burned-out eyes. "Christ," he said, pointing to a picture of a white rabbit. "It looks like its fur has been burned away. And what on earth happened to its eyes?" He handed the picture to Conway, disarmed by the brutality.

Conway took the picture and smiled grimly. "Karen published several articles for our in-house publications on the cruelty and injustices inflicted upon the animals in these laboratories. We all admired her work."

"Please make a copy of this photo for me." McNally pulled the photograph from the folder and asked if Conway would also provide him with a list of the people in the picture.

"Yes, of course. And I'll make sure you get a complete copy of her file before you leave. This picture is from a fundraiser at the Hyatt two months back. Let's see. There's Karen. She's standing next to John Marshfield, the chairman of the board for CAITA, and on her left is Senator Reynolds, our main sponsor in the Senate. The people in the background are guests. I'm not sure I can identify everybody without examining the guest list."

"I appreciate that."

McNally examined the photo of Karen Clayton. His stomach knotted as he compared this picture to the mangled and bloodied woman he'd seen at the autopsy.

"Her mother mentioned a journal Karen kept, said she carried it with her everywhere. Did you ever discuss it with her?"

"No. I wasn't aware of any journal."

"Thank you, Mr. Conway. I'll make sure her belongings are delivered to Mrs. Clayton after we've cataloged them."

"That'll be fine."

"No. Jimmy admired her. That's all."

"Well then." McNally signaled to Petrocelli as he got up to leave. "Thank you for your time, Mr. Conway." He handed him his card. "Call me at the station if you think of anything else. My pager number is on the back of the card."

Conway looked at the card and slipped it in his pocket. "I'll call. Sorry, I wish I could have been more helpful."

As they were leaving the manager's office, McNally turned and asked, "One more thing, Mr. Conway. Did Karen ever mention a boyfriend to you?"

"No. No, I don't think she ever did. I had the distinct impression from her long hours here, and given her intense dedication to her work and school, she wouldn't have the time for a relationship."

As they left, Petrocelli grinned and said, "Wow. That was a trip through the twilight zone, huh? Strange people. And why that question about a boyfriend?"

"Something I recalled from an interview with one of Karen's friends. Do me a favor and read through those files. Tell me if you see anything that might need a follow-up, okay?" McNally said.

"Will do. Can we stop and grab some breakfast? Remember? The cat got my omelet. Or don't you eat either?"

In a funny way, Tony Petrocelli reminded him of a younger Sam. He nodded. "I eat."

As they pulled out of the parking lot, it started to rain.

CHAPTER 48

Senator Reynolds's blood pressure rose as he entered the garishly decorated foyer of Helen Butler's home. He took comfort from the notion that these fundraisers and the predictable litter of unfulfilled promises would fade from memory as he'd sit on the veranda of his future beachfront villa.

Sheer will guided him into a hallway where he'd suffer through dozens of sweaty handshakes and innumerable smudges of blush and greasy lipstick smears left by wrinkled hags whose beauty had faded sometime near midcentury. And despite his covert plans, this was an election year, and his constituents had expectations he couldn't overlook without raising suspicions. So as unwelcome as this was, he would show no less than his usual spirited panache.

Once the last guest arrived, Reynolds made a beeline for the bar. He needed a drink to make it through dinner since he had to cajole these frivolous aristocratic wannabe wives and their dull, monied husbands.

* * *

You certainly impressed your audience, Senator. And you've only just arrived. Your charisma with our cultural elite is enviable."

Reynolds's face flushed as he turned toward the voice. "Well, Frank Butler, I would have thought this kind of soiree would not be exciting enough for a man of your, shall we say, exotic tastes."

"Quite the contrary, Senator. I am a huge fan of yours, and as my aunt is sponsoring this gala affair, I looked forward to seeing you."

"And how is it possible I never knew that Helen was your aunt? I always think of you as being someone more likely to have been raised by wolves."

Butler ignored the insult. "I'm certain you'll benefit from that little flag waving speech. Aren't we extraordinarily patriotic this evening?" Then with an exaggerated sigh, he continued, "Insincerity suits you well."

Reynolds clutched his glass so hard his fingertips turned white. He'd maintain his distance for now. There was too much at stake for him. He'd learned passive avoidance behaviors long ago and had a lot of practice.

One of the partners from his law firm tapped Butler on the shoulder, drawing his attention. Reynolds used the opportunity to move to the other end of the bar and ordered a third double scotch.

The day Frank Butler Sr. dropped dead on a street corner in the Loop was the day Reynolds's private hell began. Butler Senior had been his personal attorney and longtime friend. The son was no reflection of the father. Within days of the old man's death, Butler Junior called for a meeting. The topic he said was of grave importance to the senator. And his secretary, in her typical passive-aggressive fashion, allowed Butler to barge in on Reynolds without so much as a heads-up.

He came in with a sardonic grin pasted on his face and wasted no time in getting to the point. He began by summarizing several irrefutable facts he'd discovered that concerned the shifting of certain campaign contributions into overseas accounts. He proceeded to bring his point home.

Butler had all the evidence he needed to prove that Reynolds and his father were engaged in serious money laundering. He could prove Reynolds had committed a federal crime by skimming from campaign contributions and that Frank Senior had helped to cover it up.

"I'm certain you had something on my father that would trap him in your scheme. But make no mistake, I am not the same weak, pathetic ally as my father. As we go forward, the rules of the game will change. Since you're in no position to retain another attorney who'll support this nefarious scheme of yours and since I have assumed full management of my father's practice, this is the perfect time to implement a fee for my, uh… Shall I call them maintenance and protection services?"

Those subsequent demands echoed in Reynolds's head. Butler found the complete financial dossier the day his father died. He would maintain the illicit arrangement Reynolds and Butler Senior had, but he demanded a monthly retainer for protecting the senator's secrets. Ten thousand dollars a month would keep him from trotting over to the FBI. It was then that the senator made his devil's bargain with Butler.

In retrospect, Reynolds damned his own stupidity. He knew old man Butler had a weak ticker. He regretted the way he allowed Butler to intimidate and manipulate him. But he was a hundred times wiser now. He had ammunition of his own to defend against Butler's threats. They were both hanging on to a life raft that only held one. Butler was a dead man.

The senator set his empty glass down. As he turned to leave, he caught John Marshfield standing just beyond the bar, looking straight at him. Had he heard his exchange with Butler? He hoped not. Either way, and in no mood to talk with him tonight, Reynolds only smiled and made a beeline through the crowded room, heading for the front door.

* * *

"Frank. Frank! Come with me."

He followed Helen Butler into the library.

"How dare you keep avoiding me! I needed your help desperately, and I am far too busy to wonder about your whereabouts. I asked you here tonight to assist me and not stand around, hobnobbing with my guests and drinking all my liquor!" Helen scolded.

"So sorry, Auntie. Was there anything *important* you needed from me? When we spoke earlier, I thought we'd covered your expectations."

"Frank, are you listening?" she said in a whisper as she pinched his arm.

"What is it, Auntie? Did somebody complain about your liver pâté? Or perhaps the champagne isn't dry enough?" His lips curled into a sneer as he continued, "Forgive me, but you didn't expect me to show any genuine interest in these pathetic little crusades of yours, did you? I'm at a loss for any rational reason you would invite me here. Besides, I have important affairs to attend to that have nothing to do with stroking these people's egos."

Butler turned and promptly walked away from his aunt in mid-sentence. He jammed his fists in his pockets and went to find Jeffries. He didn't notice the tall figure standing in the shadows, studying him with keen interest.

CHAPTER 49

The cloaked figure slipped through the double doors at the county morgue and snaked along the wall toward a light at the end of the corridor, almost invisible in the shadows. His squinting eyes peered through a small window in the door, watching the raven-haired woman seated behind the desk. He smiled, knowing she hadn't heard him. He wanted it that way for now—to watch her, to relish this moment before her deliverance. She had tricked him once before and escaped his grasp. This time, he would be more careful, much more careful.

Like a jackal stalking an impala, he waited patiently. He trembled with excitement from her closeness.

Whore! They didn't deserve to be pretty. They should be ugly, misshapen, like their souls. That's the way they fooled the others—all of them that is, except me.

His hands opened and closed into tight balls. It was her turn. His breathing grew so raspy he forced himself to control it. He mustn't frighten the doe. He had a plan. It had taken years to complete his mission. He'd already ferried two others of her confederacy to hell.

No one else saw the obscure blackened mark of the devil stuck to her like a stinking, rotting second skin. He alone saw so deep within her, knew who and what she really was. He stared at her hair in disbelief. It glowed like a dark halo above her. It cascaded temptingly around her face, and he recognized it as one more proof of the fiend that took possession of her years ago. This would be his bequest

213

to the world. She and her familiars would all burn for their sins. He alone had the power to destroy their evil and send them back to the fiery pits they came from.

Electrified excitement vibrated throughout his body, emanating from his groin. Yes, it was her turn. This would be the dance promised him so long ago. Only seconds separated them. He could take her any time, but he wanted to bask a moment in this thrilling closeness to his quarry. He inhaled through distended nostrils, longing to drink deeply from the bouquet of her fear.

I am calling for you now, Faith Hartman. You are beautiful, but it's cheap beauty, like a carnival Kewpie doll, and hides a hideous truth. You are pouting now, pretending to be reading, but you can feel me close by. You're teasing me because I'm watching, trying to tempt me like the others, but I will not weaken! I am the wall that will not crack, your deliverance, and I will not falter.

His excited body was drenched with perspiration though his lips and mouth were parched from harsh breathing. He stepped up to the door and placed his hand on the knob...

CHAPTER 50

Mykel lifted her eyes. "Is somebody out there?"

She listened for a moment before returning to her work. Though not hearing from Kyle disappointed her, it gave her a chance to catch up on a backlog of reports. She heard a shuffling sound in the corridor. Her eyes fixed on the empty window in the office door.

"Is anyone there?" she said this time.

Her heart began pounding as she grabbed the tortoise handle letter opener. With eyes fixed and focused, she eased herself from behind the desk and began tiptoeing to the door. As her fingers touched the knob, it rotated in her hand. She jumped back and gave a faint squeal with a quick exhale as she raised the letter opener in front of her, holding it with both hands. The door flew open, causing her to stumble backward. Regaining her balance, she backed herself up against the corner of her desk, clutching the letter opener to her chest and holding her breath.

McNally leaped in time to grab hold of Mykel's arm holding the letter opener. "Whoa. Hang on, killer."

She fell forward into his arms, shaking beneath his grasp. Her face was paper white, and her pupils were dilated and dark with fright.

He held her trembling body and whispered, "My god, Mykel, what is it?"

"I'm all right. I…I thought I heard something. I felt someone watching me." She clung to him fiercely.

"I'm certain you're alone here. I didn't see anybody when I came in."

Mykel's cheeks flushed as she released her hold on him and backed away. "I'm all right, Kyle. I thought I'd heard footsteps in the hallway, but I'm not sure. I may have imagined it."

He stepped back and took a quick look down the corridor. To reassure her, he said, "Give me a moment. I'll check again."

"No, please don't!" Fear cracked her voice. "It won't be necessary. It's nothing, I'm sure. Why are you here?"

"Would you prefer that I wasn't?" he said as a teasing challenge.

"No! I mean, well, that's not what I meant. I'm glad you're here. I only asked because you didn't call."

"I've been tied up with the Slugger case, but I'm free now. How's a cup of java sound to you?"

"Absolutely. Give me a moment to clear my desk, and we're out of here."

"Great."

While she cleared her desk, he went back to the hall and noticed an open door to the office across from hers. The door was closed when he came in. He entered and flicked on the lights. The room appeared undisturbed, though he noticed a faint musky smell in the air. Someone had been here. He searched the room, confirming it was empty. He decided not to alarm Mykel by mentioning it.

Back in her office, he said, "Now I get the expression 'quiet as a morgue.' This place turns into some kind of Sandals Resort at night, but for dead people. No children and plenty of privacy, right? Any other live ones hanging around here with you?" he said with a lopsided grin.

Her laughter floated like a feather in a breeze. "No, sorry, I'm the only undead one here. And I'm quite impressed, Detective." She paused. "I knew hidden somewhere in the recesses of your psyche, you possessed a sense of humor—desert dry but a nice change from your serious side. You are not the first in a long line of self-proclaimed comedians that poke fun at my profession. So do you want to go for that cup of coffee, or did you plan to hang around here all night, wisecracking—just you, me, and your riotous humor?"

The fine lines around his eyes softened. "No, that wasn't my intention. Were you working alone tonight? You were spooked when I came in."

"The janitor may still be here, but he must be on another floor by now."

As he opened the door for her, he said, "But, Mykel, do me one favor, please."

"What's that?"

"In the future, when you're alone in your office after hours, keep your office door closed and locked."

"Oh, why?"

"I'm a cop. There's a lot of crazies out there, and it'd make me feel better."

"Will do, Officer McGruff," she said with a smile and a nod.

"Good. See? You're already listening."

As hard as he'd tried to lighten the mood, sitting in the car with the engine running, he sensed a slight nervous edge in Mykel. He caught her profile and noticed her fidgeting with a pen, clicking it absently. Should he tell her he enjoyed her company and that feeling hadn't happened in him for a long time? Was it too soon to tell her that during the short time they had known each other, he had grown comfortable being around her? He hesitated now because for years, he'd worn a mask of indifference with women. Still, he liked the amorous sensations she stirred in him. Even before his brief marriage ended in disaster, he had dug an imaginary hole and buried himself in his work. He'd been suffocating emotionally by the choices he'd made.

The next words were difficult for him. "Mykel, there're some things you should know about me right up front. I haven't had a meaningful relationship with a woman for a long time. I must appear awkward to you, but honestly, you're someone I enjoy being with. If you feel like we're moving too fast, let's both agree right now not to play the games two people often trip over in new relationships, things like 'I think she meant this' or 'Did he mean that?' Let's not fall into that trap. I've never been any good at predicting the future.

"All I've known for the past ten years is my work. Those who've been around me awhile would accuse me of being a loner whose lifestyle is incompatible with any kind of serious relationship. And some others would tell you I'm arrogant and ruthless. I'll leave it to you to figure out which category I belong in, if either. I guess I want you to understand that I enjoy being with you… It doesn't have to get any more complicated than that, if that's what you'd like," he said, looking in her eyes for the first time since he'd spoken.

For a moment, Mykel did nothing but stare at him, eyebrows drawn down. She wasn't sure what kind of commitment he sought, but she knew she felt safe around him and might just be willing to move their friendship to another level. His self-confidence and powerful, independent nature were still a little intimidating. In the past, those traits in a man had been a turn-off for her. But for reasons she didn't understand, she found him charming. It frightened her, but at the same, her empathy overcame her uncertainty. Mykel felt she now perceived his true nature. It came like that flash in the sky seen just after the sun set over the sea.

Kyle had grown comfortable residing on his private, personal island. And now he awkwardly confessed his readiness to step off that island for her. She found herself charmed and felt an urge to learn all she could about this man—not to possess him but to discover his essence, that part of a man that women seldom learned. Each time they were together, the window cracked open a little more. He was a wildly exciting change from any other man she'd known. Now everything about him stirred deep desire in her.

She placed her hand on his arm and searched his eyes. "Thank you, Kyle, for your honesty. It had to be hard for you. I hope this is the start of a lasting friendship with many great adventures in our future." Noticing the twinkle had returned to his eyes, she said, "Well, all right then. I'm ready for a cup of coffee. How about you?" Pausing for a split second, her eyes grew wide with excitement. "And how about a piece of pie? I'm starving!"

He put the car in gear and said, "You got it, ma'am, and I know just the place. But please, don't forget that from now on, you'll lock the doors to your offices after hours."

An eyebrow lifted flirtatiously. "Why, Detective, I declare I'm flattered that you've appointed yourself to be my personal body-guard… How chivalrous of you. Where do you find the time? Let me calm your fears by saying the office doors are normally locked. But tonight, if you hadn't come along when you did, who knows what terrors might have befallen me."

He wondered and worried a little about the truth of it.

They spent the next hour drinking coffee and sharing apple pie à la mode. The conversation flowed lightly, with both smiling a lot, interrupted occasionally with conspiratorial laughter.

Mykel broke the spell by saying, "I hate to end our little party, Kyle, but I should get back to my car. It's late, and I still have an early day tomorrow."

A long slow grin spread across McNally's face. "Funny you should mention that, Mykel., I'm thinking that we're not so far from my place… How'd you like to come home with me tonight? I'd feel better if you waited and went home early tomorrow. I've got steaks in the fridge, and it's a long drive for you on the Eisenhower this late at night." His grin broadened. "And I have an extra toothbrush."

"That's a tempting offer, but I need to get to bed early tonight. You look like you need some sleep too."

He returned a look of innocence and raised both hands in the air. "Doctor, that's all I had in mind—getting to bed early."

Mykel frowned.

He continued, "I'm not merely a self-serving wolf. And it's not like I hope to seduce you every time we're together," he said, feigning shame.

A sigh of mock resignation escaped her lips. He teased her now, and any further parrying on her part would goad him on. She conceded that she did not look forward to the long ride home. "So then, if we hope to get to bed early, don't you think it's time to pay the check?"

CHAPTER 51

A dark figure slipped through the doorway and stood for a moment inside the room. The bright lights hurt his eyes. He licked his lips and flipped the light switch off. Darkness returned to the room. As he gulped short bursts of air, his hands opened and closed at his sides. As if his own weight had become a burden too heavy to carry, he slumped against the door and reached around behind him, snapping the lock in place. He realized these last two were not as simple to dispatch as the others. His quest had become more complicated; unforeseen obstacles were frustrating him, leaving him weak and exhausted. His original mission was nearly complete.

These floozies and gluttonous snakes, by my judgment and action, they will now be delivered into that place where relentless burning winds blow. With the mighty horn of the Minotaur, I've speared all but two so far.

He shivered and convulsed from sudden exhilaration. His eyes glazed and rolled up beneath closed lids. A narrow stream of foaming drool trickled from the corner of his mouth.

So close. I am so close.

Moist heat burned the skin beneath his clothing. These thrashing trash piles of human waste would be dealt with. He held all the power. He would not falter. He would not fail.

When they see me standing before them, they cower and cry for mercy and forgiveness.

His whole body trembled, recalling their yielding flesh and bone giving way beneath his righteous potency as red life flowed from them. He loved the sound of their tortured yelps for release. A thousand ghosts were stirred in them by his presence. His greatest thrill came from taunting and teasing them, just as they dared to taunt and tease all men. He would bait them with a promise of quick death. Never! He intended to purge the evil from them by spilling their poisonous blood and desecrating their dark, vile pockets. He crushed the life from the witches' hearts with his sacred staff. He demonstrated his mercy by allowing these daughters of the damned to glimpse his limitless virile power before he delivered them.

Yes. Oh yes. I may have missed that one, but another one waits for me on the street. The hour of atonement is coming for the hedge whore. She'll have to wait.

The Slugger, with renewed clarity of purpose, left his lair with his hand wrapped around the bat concealed beneath his jacket.

I am the way into the city of woe. I am the way to a forsaken people. I am the way into eternal sorrow.

—Dante Alighieri

CHAPTER 52

He stood across the street from her, crouching, eyes squinting from the steady falling rain.

She stood sheltered beneath the awning of a neighborhood shop. The blinking neon sign announcing the JOB PC Rescue store intermittently bathed her in red light. Though her red hair had fallen from the damp weather, her face had regal lines with high cheekbones and a soft rounded chin beneath full lips showing a deep Cupid's bow. Her green eyes were bloodshot, and she'd covered up most of the dark circles with makeup. She wasn't aware he watched her. She only stopped here to find shelter from the rain. There were no Johns on the street or driving by in this weather. She'd gone out before the rain began and now regretted taking this last shot at making rent money.

He knew she didn't want to be out in this weather, and he knew her mistake would be his boon. He despised his prey. They were common. They stunk of too much cheap perfume. He watched patiently, waiting for the right moment to close in. She scanned up and down the street, and he realized she might get away. He stepped out from the alley where he'd parked his car after first sighting her.

Tessa Breedlove, miserably bored and frustrated, stepped out from under the awning to leave for home, a hot bath, and a change into dry, warm clothing. Giving her quest one last shot, she took one more look to her left and right. Nothing. She was taking her first step toward home when he emerged from the shadows across the street and hailed her.

"Hello, pretty lady," he said with words that surprised her with their dry delivery and sharp edges that broke off on the last letters. That wasn't unusual given the dance she knew was about to begin. He came under the awning, moved in beside her, and continued, "On a miserable night like this, may I offer you a ride? If that's what you'd like." He wore a dark fedora with a broad brim and had the collar of his trench coat turned up, so she couldn't clearly make out his face.

The dance continued. "And is there anything I can offer you in return, mister?" she replied with a coy smile. "I ain't no genie, but I can offer you one wish if that's what you came here looking for."

"Yes, I have a big wish I'd like from you." His voice surprised her with its deep, raspy tone. "So please come over and join me in my car, where we can discuss the nature of your gift and the nature of your reward."

CHAPTER 53

McNally's body jumped at the pulsating sound of his beeper. He reached to the table next to him and clicked it off. Warm memories of the previous night's intimacy put a peaceful smile on his lips. He leaned over and lowered himself to place a light kiss on Mykel's forehead. Propping himself on one elbow, he read the number on the display. His eyebrows drew down. The department had only one reason to page him at this hour. Another victim was found.

Mykel stirred next to him, and he turned to look at her. Even in sleep, her beauty stunned him. She blinked open her eyes and smiled. For a moment, he considered delaying his call. Oh well. He threw his legs over the side of the bed and sat up. He didn't want to leave her here, not now.

"You have to work this morning?"

"Yeah, no rest for us warriors watching over the thin blue line. Sorry, but I don't carry a cell phone. Can I use your phone?"

"Sure."

The duty officer on the other end of the line answered immediately, "Area 1."

"This is McNally. Somebody paged me."

"Yeah, hold on, Mac. I'll patch you through to Ramirez."

Mykel lay beside him with a playful pout on her lips. He hoped he wouldn't have to leave her yet.

"Ramirez."

"Yeah, Roy, this is McNally. What's up?"

"We've got another one. Shit. Worst one yet. Blood's splattered everywhere. Meat's still warm, though. The ME's on the way."

"Okay. What's your location?" McNally said.

Mykel handed him a pencil from her nightstand drawer, and he scratched the address on a scrap of paper.

"Be there in forty-five. Call Petrocelli for me, and tell him to meet me there."

After reaching back across her curled body to hang up the telephone, he lowered his head and kissed her. "Sorry, lady, but I have to go."

"Like some company?"

"Ramirez told me the ME on call is already on his way."

"That'll be Sawyer. He's capable," she said, burying herself deeper beneath the comforter.

"Just capable?"

"Uh-huh," she murmured.

Before leaving, McNally kissed her long and hard. "I'll call you later."

* * *

Thirty-five minutes later, he walked into an alley near the corner of Halsted and West Forty-Seventh Street. He flashed his badge to the officers manning the perimeter as requested by the attending ME. McNally asked the officers to point him out. One of them gestured to a man standing by a small portable table behind a county van—a tall slender black man; six feet, three inches, he guessed. He had prominent cheekbones, leading Kyle to imagine the man might have had one Asian parent. The man's eyes were green, and his hair had a relaxed curl. He stood, one elbow resting on the hand of the other, rubbing his chin, studying the arrayed contents on the table.

Partially uncovered, he studied the victim's head and upper torso. If it weren't for visible shreds of a dress, he wasn't even sure of the gender. Mac could only make out red pulp, splintered bones, torn flesh, and lots of blood splattered around the body.

Kyle walked up to the examiner and introduced himself.

226

"Name's Tom Sawyer, Detective. Quite a mess, this one. Worst I've seen. From what I've determined so far, she took quite a beating before he snuffed her."

"Come to any conclusions yet, Doctor? Cause and time of death? This looks like the murder scene, right?"

"From the body temperature and lividity, my best estimate right now is a time of death near 10:30 p.m., give or take thirty minutes. And yes, this is the location of the crime. Cause appears to be a fatal blow to the face, driving her nasal bone up and into the frontal lobe. That was quick. But from the other damage to her upper body and skull, it occurred only after a brutal assault on the torso and lower extremities. I'd guess a small club or pipe to be the murder weapon, judging from the impressions left. Oh, and as you've proba-bly guessed, I found evidence of severe vaginal trauma, and to answer your next question, a signature baseball card was inserted."

"This one appears more vicious than the previous three. I'd like to see the baseball card. Please tell me you've found some other evidence."

"Nah, not yet. Like the others, he's been meticulous."

"Shit," Kyle said.

"The card is Billy Williams from 1970. It's bagged and tagged. It's over there on my cart," he said, pointing out his staging cart behind the county van. "Did you know he hit three home runs in one game in '68?" Sawyer said, obviously proud of his baseball expertise.

"Do me a favor, Doctor. Tell no one about the card. I'd like to reduce the likelihood of any copycat actors."

"Can do, Detective."

Tony Petrocelli walked up and hailed Kyle. "They're telling me this is another one of Slugger's trophies," he said.

"Yep. Tony, this is Dr. Sawyer. He'll fill you in on the details. Take notes, okay? I'd like to think we can get an ID on her, so stay on it. Assign patrolmen to canvas the neighborhood for witnesses. I'll give the area a quick survey, then I'm heading back to the station."

"Roger that, Mac."

After completing his own walk-through and finding no other evidence, Kyle drove away more frustrated than ever. Damn him to hell.

CHAPTER 54

The sun had set two hours earlier, replaced by the full moon's reflection rippling over the surface of the small lake fronting his manor. Silhouettes of tall pines a half mile beyond formed a natural barrier between his retreat and the rest of civilization. Over the years, the night sounds served as John Marshfield's natural soporific. The soothing sound of the surrounding nature he often relied on to meditate when his burdens became overwhelming.

Today he saw the tree line as more like a gateway to his desolate mood. The solitary screech of a great horned owl served as a doleful reminder of how empty his life had become.

Napoleon, his fat Persian cat, had jumped onto his lap but, sensing his master's tension, leapt back off to find solace in the comfort of an overstuffed chair. He kept an attentive yet casual watch on his owner through half-closed eyes.

The hand-carved mahogany desk sat in front of an immense bank of open bay windows. On his desk lay a red leather-bound book and a thick white envelope bearing the inscription "For My Daughter."

A faint smile touched his lips as he watched the gentle moonlit water lapping against the shore and thought back to the long-ago sounds of a child's laughter. He recalled a beautiful garden abounding with a wide variety of bright and colorful flowers, now choked and smothered with weeds in the years since his daughter left.

He struggled to relax his old, aging body. Unable to shake a nagging sense of helplessness from recent events, an avalanche of pain and remorse broke over him. He could not—and *would not*— restrain this need for vengeance pulling and tearing at his heart. Tonight would be a night for account collections.

His housekeeper knocked at the door, which interrupted his uneasy reverie. "Forgive me, Mr. Marshfield, but I'm all packed and ready to go. Is there anything I may do for you before leaving?"

"No, thank you, Mrs. Clancy."

"I wanted to thank you again, sir, for your generosity in giving me time off to visit my daughter and her children." She prayed he wouldn't change his mind and ask her to stay.

"Please don't concern yourself. I'll be fine," he said without turning from the window. "I plan on being away most of the time, so this will be a fine time for you to visit your family. And you'll be back in a few days."

"Well, sir, thank you again." Before closing the study door, she noted with surprise how tidy the top of her employer's desk appeared. She'd noticed his recent strange behavior. She bit down on her lower lip and then said, "Sir, forgive me, but I have to ask… Is everything all right?"

"Everything is fine, Mrs. Clancy. Please enjoy your visit."

Mrs. Clancy nodded. "Yes, sir. Fine, sir. Well then, I'll be off." She closed the door and left the house.

Marshfield turned in his chair to face the desk and ran the palm of his hand over the soft leather of the book lying there. Only someone who knew John Marshfield well would recognize warning signs from the muscles that jutted from his jaw. He walked to a bookcase and retrieved a flat leather-covered box. He put it on his desk and snapped open the lock to inspect its contents. Satisfied, he closed the cover. With a sigh, he walked across the room to where his cat relaxed, balled up like a large roll of raveled yarn left on the chair.

"I'll be back, Napoleon," he said, pausing to pet his drowsy companion.

As he left, Napoleon lowered his ears and hissed in displeasure at the invading gust of cool night air that blew past his master and swirled about the room.

CHAPTER 55

Impatient and in a foul mood, Senator Wayne Reynolds reached across the width of his car and drew a silver flask from the glove compartment. He had endured yet another stressful day completing the plans for his departure. No one would suspect a thing. After years of laying the financial groundwork, he'd spent the past few months completing plans and preparation, every detail considered. He'd made no mistakes. He told everyone he'd be preparing for a speech he scheduled with John Marshfield before an audience at Northwestern University—that was, after a weekend trip to his Colorado retreat to fine-tune his presentation.

He'd left his vineyard purchase contracts in his desk at the office—reckless but not catastrophic, nothing more than an annoyance at having to leave the comfort of his home and his carafe of Johnny Walker to return to the office. Yet the irritation festered, caused by his own carelessness at getting all the way home before he remembered it. A momentary panic had seized him, but it abated when he realized he still had plenty of time. His flight in the morning wasn't until eight o'clock. That gave him more than enough time to drive the forty-five minutes back to the city, grab the packet, and head back home.

When he got home later, he'd call his patsy, Marshfield, pretending excitement over the last-minute details. Maybe he'd even have one last grudge fuck with the hag. It'd piss her off royally, but that made it even more attractive. The way he'd set it up, nobody would miss him until the moment the introductory applause ended and he didn't walk onto the stage to take the podium. Marshfield would explode, but he'd soon calm down when he heard the cops were dragging the Colorado River for the poor senator's body.

Evelyn would never think to call anyone in the middle of the night when he didn't arrive home on schedule. She'd relish the extra time alone, relieved that he wasn't there to force himself on her again. It would be like an answer to prayers she'd whispered many nights. By the time all the searchers determined his body might never float to the surface, he'd be basking in the warm spring sun on the right side of the Atlantic, celebrating his brand-new life.

He'd ordered his useless "other half" to confirm his round-trip reservation to Denver for him. She'd also confirm his arrival at O'Hare since he'd asked her to drive him there. And to complete the ruse, he'd also ask her to accompany him as far as the security checkpoint "as a special favor." One last tender kiss, and he'd be waving to her for the last time. She didn't have a clue he kept the one-way ticket to Paris' Orly Airport along with his new passport and various identity papers in his locked briefcase. It contained property papers for his estate, plenty of euros, and several Swiss bankbooks.

Reynolds ticked off the items he'd take along. He double-checked the time on the dashboard clock. The hour approached when he'd pack it all together and whisper, "Au revoir." He'd arranged a clever trap for his lone adversary. His overseas connections believed him to be Robert Walker Manning, successful retired Canadian architect.

After swallowing another hearty mouthful of the booze, he laughed and hiccupped, spraying the liquor in a fine mist across the dashboard. *Damn, Wayne, this is really happening!* He felt a sudden surge of electric excitement coursing through his body, something he hadn't experienced in a long, long time… *Though I'd give my left nut to be there to see that asshole's face when the police pound on his door. Frank Butler holds the keys to my demise, but thanks to me, he'll be busy trying to weasel his way out of the surprise I've left for him.* Admittedly, he'd miss DC, with its excitement and all those hot-lipped hedge whores. *Oh, well, sleazy women are easy to find no matter where I go.*

The allure and attraction of the Washington pace provided a sweet distraction from his whiny, insufferable wife and the dull duties of his Chicago office. He derived immense satisfaction from traveling back and forth to the capitol and the international junkets with his colleagues, which he'd milked at every opportunity. He'd miss those times of drinking champagne and rubbing elbows with the rich and famous DC elites. He might also miss the movie-star popularity he'd earned as a man of the people, seeing his picture on the cover of *Time*, and shaking hands with the POTUS, waving the American flag like a true Uncle Sam patriot.

Well, truth be told, he'd miss those days only a little more than the first girl he'd romanced, bedded, and then broken up with—deeply mourned but quickly forgotten.

Reynolds watched the streetlights flash past him like streamers of yellow ribbons as he picked up speed on Lakeshore Drive. He'd run in, grab the envelope, and be home in time for the evening news.

Reynolds stretched his neck and unbuttoned the collar under his tie. *I wouldn't be in this mess today if Frank Butler Sr. hadn't dropped dead on the corner of State and Adams.* He shrugged his shoulders, realizing that from another view, his death might have been a blessing. *One less witness to testify against me.*

He pulled into the Grant Park lot. So he croaked, and his kid swooped in like a vulture to a fresh carcass, didn't even wait for his father's body to go cold before he rifled his personal safe. The old man had always kept his brooding offspring on a tight rein. After his death, the brat went nuclear on Reynolds. That was when the blackmail began...

Reynolds maneuvered the car into his parking slot and cut the engine. He sat in the deserted lot, enjoying the contentment that washed over him, savoring the notion of Butler behind bars. He hurried to the elevator, anxious to get back home and finish preparing.

His mood had brightened considerably since he'd left his house. Revenge would be a sweet reward for his suffering.

CHAPTER 56

Frank Butler's swollen bloodshot eyes scanned the lines on a single page from the thick brief before him. He struggled to concentrate, but his vision blurred, and words were moving around the page like caterpillars. Frustrated, he slumped against his chair back. Spent from working long hours on this pathetic civil rights case, he cursed the legal system's stringent pro bono demands. This client, incarcerated in the county lockup, had lodged his fourth suit against the state and once more claimed to be the victim—framed, fucked, and found guilty by shadowy actors at the behest of an overreaching government agency.

What a waste of oxygen!

The Palumbo trial was his primary concern now. Without having to dig too deeply into his bag of legal tricks, he'd reconnected with the jury by manipulating their sympathy for his client. But he feared any further delays would just give the state more time to uncover new evidence. Once the ASA's cross-examination finished tomorrow, he'd relax until closing arguments next Tuesday. Though it'd never been a strength of his, Frank Butler could feign patience when necessary. He had other strengths.

Frank always saw his father as a weakling, satisfied with crumbs as he stood before the banquet table of success. He suspected the partners laughed behind his father's back and only patronized him because of his role as the firm's founder and the man who signed their checks. It wasn't from true respect. He knew they thought he'd be no different when he joined the firm several years ago. Against their best judgments, the senior partners approved. As she loved to remind him, Auntie had done some arm twisting to assure his junior partner position. But he fooled them all. He felt the time was fast approaching to make his move.

Soon, very soon.

In the meantime, the Palumbo case would raise his image in the legal community, allowing him the freedom to kick start his real plan. He wanted to show them all how mistaken they were.

Knock, knock.

His body convulsed and lurched forward over his desk. He'd nodded off, and the knocking woke him. Sweating profusely, he grabbed his handkerchief and swabbed his face.

He switched on his desk lamp, "Yes. Who is it?"

Judy Fuchs, the dark-haired beauty he'd met in the elevator that morning peeked through his doorway. "I didn't mean to disturb you, Mr. Butler. I thought, well, since we both seem to be working late, maybe you'd like to meet for a drink when you're finished here."

"Well, that would be nice, Judy. But I have a couple more things to wrap up here." Like someone cut off on the expressway, he recognized her disappointment while detecting a rising excitement at her obvious attraction for him. "Perhaps you'd like to meet somewhere later? Say, half past ten?" From their first conversation, he recognized her as a shallow young corporate climber; he saw no harm wasting a few hours for a diversion.

"Oh, that would be terrific, sir. How does Scampy's on North Wells sound?"

"Scampy's it is, ten thirty sharp. I guess I need to remind you to call me Frank, Judy," he said with an exaggerated wink.

She giggled behind her hand as she closed the door.

Frank's eyes gleamed with anticipation as he half-heartedly returned his attention to restraighten the papers on his desk. For a time, he tried to study the pages but found it impossible to concentrate. He collected his raincoat and briefcase, laying them on the chair next to his desk. He had one last phone call and an important stop to make before his rendezvous.

A smile that never reached the corners of his eyes spread across his lips as he picked up the phone.

CHAPTER 57

A few streets away beneath Grant Park, Senator Wayne Reynolds shoved a thick envelope into his breast coat pocket and backtracked through the massive underground parking lot. He was eager to pick up his papers and get home. He wasn't even aware of the echoing footsteps keeping pace with his.

He threw his briefcase on top of his car and searched his pockets for the keys before he noticed the unusual silence, not unlike being in a tunnel with both ends sealed shut. No more footsteps, no car door opening, just silence. He paused. Did he just imagine someone nearby? He listened for a moment to the sound of his own breathing. He scanned right and then left for any sign of movement in the shadows of the lot. There were only a few cars near his. Silence. Fear prickled the back of his neck as he fumbled with the keys in shaking hands.

"Is someone there?"

No response.

Instinctively, he sensed he should hurry. In shame, he realized he'd just pissed himself. He cursed as he watched the keys fall from his shaking hand and clatter on the garage floor.

He bent to retrieve them, and as he started to straighten, a blinding, paralyzing pain shot through the back of his head. His head swam in dazed confusion. He attempted to grab the car door for support when the second blow struck.

What the...?

CHAPTER 58

Frank Butler arrived at the Chi-Tech lot and parked in his private space. His key card gained him access through the outer doors, and he walked hurriedly past the night guard. "Just picking up some contracts for the boss to sign, Jimmy," he said. Jimmy wasn't even aware of his presence.

Jimmy Blossom, the night guard, bounced to the rap of Snoop Doggy Dog's "Gin and Juice" blasting through his headphones and wasn't aware that Frank entered the building. Butler walked behind the security desk and was out of sight before Jimmy felt the blast of cold air from the open door. He glanced toward the entranceway and pulled one side of the headphones away from his head. He listened for ten seconds before returning to thumping his pencil on an empty soda can in time with the music.

Frank punched in the security code to the entry door leading to his office and laboratory. He arrived at his private office that no one had access to but him. His aunt had removed the security cameras long ago after deciding they weren't cost effective. He scanned the white-tiled lab, finding everything as he had left it.

He crossed to an antique glass windowed cabinet crowded with dusty bottles. The contents were primarily remnants of lab chemicals, relics of past experiments. He reached in the cabinet and retrieved a bottle from the back labeled copper sulfate. After shaking out a small pile on a nearby glass-topped table, he snorted a quick line of meth and filled a small amber vial with more to take with him. He replaced the bottle into the back of the shelf and relocked the cabinet. No one would guess the contents contained anything other than an old unused chemical leftover from a laboratory shut down years earlier.

He sorely missed those days of watching the scientists in their crisp white lab coats using their shiny surgical instruments to perform tests and experiments on animals. These cold rooms with the bare white walls became his sanctuary in the years since. As a boy, he'd spent many happy days here, pursuing his own version of animal experiments.

He flicked off the overhead lights and left the room. A night filled with promise awaited him. He had a fresh supply of crank in his pocket and a warm body waiting for him. His night had come up all aces. Feeling the surge of exciting energy from the drug coursing through his bloodstream, he said, "Damn! I feel good!" and left the offices grinning and snapping his fingers.

Out in the parking lot, he noticed a car near his he hadn't seen when he drove in. He hurried over to his car, clicking the key fob to unlock the doors. Steps away, he thought he caught a dark shadow in his peripheral vision, off to his right. He tensed and attempted to take the last ten feet to his car door in several long hurried strides. At that moment, he realized he should have pressed the panic button on his fob. He never got the chance; he only made it to his second step when a crashing blow to the side of his head knocked him to the pavement. In his drug-induced state, it occurred to him that he'd be late meeting Judy Fuchs. All went black when the second strike caught him on the top of the head.

CHAPTER 59

By early afternoon, Commander Ed Rouse had dug a trench pacing back and forth between his office at the south end of Property Crimes and McNally's unoccupied space at the north end of the floor. He would get some answers if it meant handcuffing him to his desk. They had differing views on how to run an investigation, but if McNally thought it gave him carte blanche to do whatever he damn well wanted, then Rouse would be there to knock him back down.

But his latest gambit involving McNally's attempt to schedule an interview with an Illinois state senator became the final straw that had his sphincter squeezed tighter than the gap in a Delco spark plug. Rouse thought he'd made it clear Senator Reynolds wasn't his target. He belonged to the Feds.

Rouse circled McNally's desk two times before drifting over to the desk once occupied by Sam Weller. Idly, he slid the top drawer open, ignoring the notion that the other dicks might resent his snooping. What did he care? As their commander, he'd do anything he damn well pleased. To his delight, they'd left a single long thick Jamaican cigar.

Rouse shoved the cigar in his pocket. "Any of you ladies seen or heard from McNally this week?"

McNally—in his usual midcase, head-under-the-radar fashion—had remained elusive, avoiding the commander, and seeing him only when ordered. But Rouse would not stand for it this time. He felt a desperate need to get something to hand the brass, even

"I'm talking to you misfits!" he said, cheeks glowing red, barking louder than he'd intended.

"We've paged him, sir. He should call anytime now," Ramirez replied without lifting his eyes and followed by a roll of his eyes. The overall indifference from the department gnawed at Rouse's gut, but that was a different issue. He'd deal with that later.

He growled out a flood of obscenities as eleven sets of eyes looked away from their ranting commander. Rouse pushed himself off the desk and stood with his fists balled, ready to explode. He would tackle the first one who dared stand in his path when an insistent ring from McNally's desk phone interrupted him.

"Well, what the hell? I wonder if that's my AWOL detective," he said, turning his back to the room. "We'll finish this another time." He grabbed the receiver on the third ring. "Yeah!"

Everyone enjoyed watching Rouse's face inflate and contort into various stages of distemper.

"Where the hell have you been?" Rouse demanded. He listened a few seconds longer before screaming, "I don't give a damn if you're interviewing the president. Get your butt in here. Now!" Rouse slammed the phone back in its cradle and stormed back to his office. Moments later, his door swung open, and an angry but controlled voice bellowed, "Petrocelli, in my office. Now."

Twenty minutes later, Petrocelli returned to his desk. He did a poor job of hiding the grin on his face.

"We thought the next time we saw you, you'd be covered in mud, blood, or spit," Ramirez said. "Yet here you stand with no sign of any wounds and a stupid, pasty-faced grin."

Petrocelli plopped down and stretched like a lazy cat awakened from a nap. "I'm not sure what just happened, but I've been assigned to replace Weller as McNally's new partner."

Ramirez and a few others began to chuckle.

"What's so funny?" Petrocelli asked.

239

"McNally's good, but being assigned to him is the same as painting a target on your back that's all one big center ring. Rouse must have a major hard-on for you."

"Huh? Why's that?"

"No offense, Petrocelli," Ramirez said, "but McNally's now being stuck with an inexperienced partner, and you're stuck with a guy who's never been accused of being mister warmth."

"He's a good cop," Petrocelli said, trying his best to sound positive.

Within five minutes, only the dispatcher and Petrocelli were still on the floor. Everyone else pretended they had somewhere to go. No one wanted to be nearby when McNally returned. He arrived soon after everyone had left.

"Where the hell is everybody?" McNally asked. "Did I walk into the wrong squad room?"

"No, and I don't know. But Rouse wants to see you in his office. Pronto—his word, not mine."

McNally glared at Rouse's office. "Right."

He knocked on the door and entered. Petrocelli listened intently for the expected string of obscenities but heard nothing, only silence. Ten minutes later, McNally left Rouse's office, his expression unreadable.

He'd lost his longtime partner and friend, made too little progress on the most baffling case of his career, and had his commander accuse him of gross incompetence. He came out shaking his head and spewing the word *fuck* repeatedly.

Tony sat still and averted his eyes, waiting to see if a hammer would fall on him too. But McNally simply walked to his desk and stood idly shuffling through a stack of papers. He wanted to say something to break the silence but decided against it.

Mac's problems took a back seat when Nancy Jankowitz, the squad secretary, handed him a computer printout.

"I'm getting some responses on your inquiries. This first one's from Philadelphia," she said.

"Thanks, Nanc," McNally said as she handed him the printouts.

He busied himself reading the first one when dispatch called over the intercom that Detective Webb from the Philadelphia Police Department was holding on line 2.

McNally motioned for Petrocelli to come over. "Look, kid, since we're working together, I'll tell you what I've done. I placed Slugger's MO over the National Crime Information Center with a few of the larger PDs in the country. Seemed like a long shot, but responses are coming in."

Petrocelli stood next to McNally's desk, waiting to hear about the Philadelphia PD conversation. The dispatch stated that the Philly case dealt with an unsolved murder from early May. After a mix-up with the dental records, they just got an ID on the victim.

McNally began jotting notes down and wrote: "Female. Late twenties. Beaten and raped with club. White Sox baseball card inserted in victim's vagina. Found in suburban Philly. Local PD questioned an interstate trucker with a record of female assaults. No arrests. Producer, Philly radio station. From Hinsdale, in suburban Chicago. Will fax picture." He copied the parents' address and sat back in his chair. "Thanks, Detective. I'll call you if I get any more on this end. With any luck, these will tie together."

Then a slow grin spread across McNally's face. "Tony, this is the break I've been waiting for. This sounds like our connection. It's likely they contacted the local suburban PDs, and we never got the word."

"How so?"

Just as the last word left his mouth, Jankowitz brought over another hit on their query. This one came from Staten Island, New York. The victim discovered on the rocks beneath the Verrazano Bridge in late April, her battered and broken body looked like a suicide until the coroner's autopsy. They found extensive damage to her external and internal genital organs. The killer dumped the body there after committing the crime elsewhere. A wooden object had been inserted and repeatedly pounded invasively, causing severe internal damage. There was a White Sox baseball card inserted in her vagina—no witnesses and no suspects yet.

McNally called Central Booking at the NYC Police Department and asked for the detective working the case. Although still an active investigation, the trail had gone cold. Victim number 2. Ava Haas. Local girl living in Staten Island. Law firm paralegal. No leads, no suspects. Family—local—live in Western Springs on Western Avenue (just east of Hinsdale).

He stared at his notes and began thinking out loud. "Two victims. Same MO. Both from western Cook County. This is no coincidence. The detective reports the parents of the Philly vic said she came from neighboring Hinsdale and moved there after college."

"So what's our next move?"

His eyebrows drew up, and a wry grin formed on his lips. Petrocelli hadn't seen this look from him before. These were the puzzle pieces he needed to complete the picture. Petrocelli reread the notes over McNally's shoulder, hoping to see what McNally had written.

"I'll get their addresses and interview the families of these new vics. I'll need you to fill in some blanks. Get me all the information we've got on the hookers murdered here since this began back in February. I've got a hunch we're going to find a connection. If this latest perp is our guy, he would have flown in and out of those two cities within a day or two of the murders. There are three New York airports that service Chicago—JFK, La Guardia, and Newark. And check with the car rental agencies for those same dates. Maybe he screwed up and used a credit card. It's a long shot, but I'm feeling lucky right now. And do the same for Philly, okay? Closest are the international airport and the two smaller nearby ones, Wilmington New Castle and Trenton-Mercer. I believe they all have Chicago connections."

He dropped his pencil and reached for his coat. "The guy is smart and may have used cash, but that's a good place to start, Tony. Time's not our friend here, and the clock's counting down fast before he strikes again."

Petrocelli felt a rush from these latest developments. They were on to something—something leading to the collar of this animal. And Santino Petrocelli's son would be there to nab him. "I'll get moving on this right away. So how'd it go with Rouse? He looked to be a split second from crazy before you came in."

"There's a few teeth marks on my ass. Nothing unusual. Keep checking with the squad secretary too. I'll be out interviewing the parents of those two girls. Tell Nancy that if I'm not at my desk, she's to give all incoming information to you and no one else. You stay on the travel leads. I don't want Rouse spilling any of this until we've got more facts."

"Roger."

McNally double-checked his notes. If the Philadelphia and New York murders were related to the latest victims in Chicago, that would make their killer a methodical monster, a vengeance-seeking woman hater who knew his vics and stalked them. But now it looked like Kyle had found the thread to link them. He also believed he'd made a connection between one or more of the hookers. He still hadn't discovered the connection to the Clayton girl, but he knew there had to be one.

This guy is a crazed sociopath with a bagful of bats and a baseball card in his belfry. It looks like the first few hooker kills may have been batting practice for him. And now it appears the sick fuck's left his signature kills outside the state. How many more kills were on his list? If it was only revenge, would these murders satisfy him? Could it end there? If so, he might disappear for months, even years before he circled back to again satisfy the manic urges that must drive him.

His gut churned, but he felt so close he could almost smell the Slugger.

CHAPTER 60

Later that evening, Kyle's interviews of the Guthrie and Haas families were complete. He reviewed his notes; he'd learned these out-of-town vics had two significant things in common. They were close friends at a suburban Catholic high school, and they were both involved in an incident in their senior year where their boyfriends assaulted a classmate. The girls asked for help when another boy, described as an "odd" loner, began harassing the group. No police report turned up on file. They handled the incident discreetly. The young man, severely assaulted by the boys, subsequently withdrew from school. They suspended the boys for five days, even though there were no criminal charges filed.

The parents of Cassandra Guthrie, the Philadelphia vic, said there were four girls in the group that were close to one another during their last couple years in high school. After graduation, the girls had lost touch with one another.

"They all went off to different colleges except one, an orphaned girl. I think her name could be Tamara or Tracy, something like that. And if I can remember, her last name might have been Breeden. She grew up in the Masonic Children's Home in LaGrange. I don't believe she went to college, at least not from anything Cassie told us," recalled Mrs. Guthrie.

Neither the Guthrie family nor Mrs. Haas, mother of the New York vic, Ava Haas, knew what had become of the Breeden girl after high school, but Mrs. Haas remembered the girl's last name was Breedlove.

Mrs. Haas also remembered a little about the fourth girl. "I believe her last name was Hartman. I heard she lost her parents shortly after graduation. Poor thing. She remembered the Hartman girl as the introverted one of the group. I never heard that she returned to the area after college. I also heard some gossip that one of the girls was either attacked or raped after. I can't recall which one. It's a shame the girls lost touch with one another. They were such close friends those days. On reflection, that whole difficult situation drove a wedge between the girls."

David Haas, Ava's brother, said it couldn't be her, most likely the Breen or Hartman girl.

McNally contacted the Downers Grove Academy of the Holy Family to request the students' records and a copy of the yearbook from their senior year. Planning to pick these items up the next morning, he asked the families to meet him at the local police station to look through the old yearbooks together. He hoped they'd be able to confirm the identity of the remaining two girlfriends and the student accused of stalking them. Both families agreed to cooperate, but neither said they remembered hearing who the boy was. They kept it quiet around the school, and the girls had been told not to speak about it with anyone. They believed he'd come from an influential family.

Although he'd made progress today, Kyle sat, shaking his head. A significant piece of the puzzle still eluded him. At least now, he had some small semblance of control. He decided to call it a wrap for the day and headed home for a stiff drink, some quiet time, and much-needed sleep.

CHAPTER 61

Petrocelli had spent all night scanning through both the airline passenger lists and auto car rentals. He'd grabbed a couch in the break room earlier that morning to catch a few hours' sleep before returning to the reports.

Kyle stopped by his desk and picked up two messages from Ramirez, noting that Mykel had called twice. She wanted to talk with him ASAP.

Petrocelli was walking back onto the floor when Kyle ran into him.

"Hey, Tony. You get some shut-eye?"

"Yeah, enough to clear out the cobwebs."

McNally liked this kid. He wasn't an idiot like so many of the other Twinkie-eating rooks that came through the department. Two points in his favor were that he wasn't afraid to speak his mind and he wasn't in the least bit intimidated by the older "junkyard dogs" in the department. Petrocelli showed ambition and drive. Petrocelli had the right instincts, motivation, and guts to get the job done. It was far better to have Tony Petrocelli than that doorstop Peterson.

With his starched collars, silk ties, and spit-polished Florsheims, Tony didn't have a clue how out of place he looked standing in the center of a group of tobacco-chewing, cigar-smoking, hard-case cops. But none of that mattered to Kyle if his new partner got the job done. Independence of thought and some fresh ideas were what counted. Petrocelli had both.

"Tell me you found something in those passenger and rental lists."

"Well, so far I've gone through about six inches of an eight-inch-thick printout. And I've made it halfway through my crosscheck of the car rentals now. Been taking notes and highlighting interesting-looking names and dates. Nothing that jumped out at me yet, but I can finish by the end of shift."

"Good. I appreciate your hard work on this. Any more hits from the NCIC?"

"Not yet, but the fax's been click-clackin' away all night. Mostly nays. I'm keeping an eye on it."

"Thanks. The interviews yesterday took longer than I expected. Some interesting developments turned up but I've got another stop to make this morning."

"What's that?" Petrocelli asked.

"I'll drive to the girls' high school to pick up their student records and a copy of the yearbook. I heard of an incident involving all four in their last year that may provide some further details about their connections. So stick around. I may need your help."

"Roger that. I'll be here," Petrocelli said, doing a poor job of containing his enthusiasm.

"I'll check in when I get back, so be ready to go if I find anything. By then let's hope you have something solid from those reports."

"10-4."

This is why he'd suffered through all those ass-kickings during his police training. "And thanks, Mac." *Thanks, man.*

McNally shook his head. *This kid is something—whipcrack smart but with a shade too much of the annoying enthusiasm and energy of a kindergartener.*

He'd tried to reach Mykel at both her office and her home numbers. No answer. He figured she was already busy at work. As soon as he'd finished this case, he decided he'd take the first step and ask her to take a long weekend with him—somewhere with a beach and a never-ending supply of those coconut-flavored rum drinks with cherries and the funny umbrellas in them. He thought she'd like that, and it would be a way to see if they were the right fit for each other.

He'd try her again before leaving the high school. Right now, his immediate concern centered on getting the school records.

The school staff helped him dig through the archives. They'd found the records on the incident between the four girls and their boyfriends but learned next to nothing on the boy who'd been harassing them. Someone had removed almost every document about the incident and the student. McNally realized the family must have had a box car load of clout to pull that off in his first year at the school. He'd transferred in from another school. He may have gotten in trouble there before transferring to the academy. And because he left school early in the year, there were no pictures of him in the yearbook.

By midafternoon, he left the high school. He was heading east on the Eisenhower, back to the city, when it began to rain. Pleased at the progress they'd made on the case in the past two days, he now had named vics with documented backgrounds. He listened to Vivaldi's *Four Seasons*, "Spring" concerto playing on the radio. That always inspired him, took him back to a quieter time in Ireland when he used to idle warm afternoons by the side of a river near his home.

He took a break and grabbed a cup of coffee before returning to HQ. He needed time to pull his notes together. He still couldn't reach Mykel, but he'd catch up with her later.

Entering the sleepy coffee shop, he shook the rain from his jacket. He grabbed the first quiet booth and spread his notes in front of him. The waitress came over as he looked over the names of the students involved in the altercation. He would track down every one of those accused of the assault to pick their brains. Who was the boy they hazed? He fanned through the yearbook and glanced at the photos of the girls—pictures of innocents, all now either dead or in jeopardy. He only hoped he wasn't too late to save the remaining two women.

He reviewed what he had uncovered so far. A couple of the faculty said they knew of that clique of girls but said that they weren't athletes or club members and so hadn't left particularly remarkable impressions on them. They dug up pictures and relevant records of the last two girls—Tessa Breedlove and Faith Hartman. No one recalled any information about the Breedlove girl after she graduated. The dean of girls wasn't on campus. He hoped she'd remember more since she kept in touch with the Hartman girl for a time after graduation. McNally asked them to please have her contact him when they reached her.

"Help you?" asked the tall, rail-thin woman standing over him that could be the twin sister of Popeye's girlfriend, Olive Oyl.

He lowered his eyes back to his notes. "Coffee, black."

The waitress returned and slid the coffee in front of him, a few drops splashing from the cup onto the papers. "That be it?" she asked, already completing the green guest check stub.

Stunned by her rudeness, he glared up at her. "I'm not sure right now. Check back with me when you're ready to spill me another cup."

She jammed the check deep in her pocket before snorting and returning to her bored position behind the counter. He glanced at the scowling waitress hunched over her newspaper and decided he'd forego that slice of pie he earlier considered. Their eyes met, and she glowered. Half-grinning back at her, he pondered how agonizingly dull her childhood must have been to have turned her into this public shrew, whose assigned occupation seemed to be to unearth the worst of her patrons' day.

McNally finished his coffee and got up to leave when his pager buzzed. He used the pay phone to call headquarters.

"Detective Shaughnessy."

"This is McNally. Somebody page me?"

"Yeah, I took two phone calls for you. First one came from some dean at that academy you went to today, second one from the ME's office."

As Shaughnessy read the messages, McNally's eyes narrowed to catlike slits, and his muscles grew taut. His knuckles turned white as his large fist tightened into a ball at his side.

"Let me talk to Petrocelli."

* * *

Outside, the wind began to howl, rattling the windows of the coffee shop. The narrow-shouldered waitress shuffled over and peered through the glass. With her shift coming to an end, she cursed the return of the storm as just another one of her life's ongoing slaps to her face. In a weary daze, she watched the gathering pitch-black clouds roll together and collide. Moments later, the sky opened and thousands of shimmering droplets smashed against the windows.

Worst summer I can recall.

Moments earlier, the tall angry man had made a phone call and stormed out of her cafe without so much as a "Have a nice day" or even a "Kiss my ass." It didn't bother her much, though. He'd scared the pantyhose right off her, so she said good riddance to his departing backside.

Probably an axe murderer or worse. She shivered from the gust of cold air that sneaked by him as he left. They come here in all shapes and sizes these days. *You can't trust anyone anymore.*

She cleared away the empty coffee cup and half-heartedly wiped the table where he'd been. She completed this miserable chore, returned the cup to a bus pan, and then slouched back to her spot behind the counter to finish reading the *Enquirer* story about the telescope sighting of a colony of geckos spotted on the surface of Mars.

CHAPTER 62

Absorbed in completing the paperwork for the chief examiner, Mykel didn't even notice lunch had come and gone until her stomach began complaining. She'd also been ignoring the dull throbbing in her head for some time. She reached her hands up to massage the back of her neck, realizing she still had hours of work left. With the chaotic activity of the day behind her, the halls were quiet now. She looked forward to relaxing with a glass of wine and dinner. Deep in concentration, she jumped when the phone rang, surprising her. It jolted her like touching a wire plugged into an electric outlet. She grimaced as it rang once more before she answered it.

"Dr. Hartley," she said.

Silence. She couldn't make out muffled sounds.

"Hello. Is anyone there?"

More silence. Someone was on the other end, listening. It wasn't her imagination that conjured up a faint clicking noise in the caller's breathing. Common sense commanded that she slam the receiver back into its cradle, yet she didn't move. Could it be a wrong number? Or a prank?

"Who's there?"

This must be a prank, right?

She continued to listen. The raspy breathing came heavier, still more ominous, suffocating. Who would do this?

A low, guttural noise broke the deafening silence. In a whisper, distorted and foreboding, she heard, "Mykel, my lovely… Remember

251

me? I can recall how much fear excites you. I remember how you thrill to it. Do *you*? Close your eyes. Can you feel my touch? Do you remember? I've been patient, haven't I? It's almost your turn. You'll look for me, won't you? Watch for me, sweet Mykel."

Click.

Mykel held the receiver to her ear until the rapid beep of a disconnected line startled her back to reality. Tears of rage spilled down her cheeks. She shuddered, letting the telephone fall to the floor. She leaned forward, hugging her knees, rocking back and forth. As she struggled to breathe, she became dizzy and nauseous, trying to swallow the acidic bile in her throat.

Nooooo, this can't be happening again!

Trapped like a caged animal, her eyes darted around the room as the walls transformed into invisible bars. Overwhelmed with the need to escape, she wiped perspiration from her face with her sleeve. Self-preservation prevented her from collapsing into a weeping mass. She ripped her purse from the drawer and spilled its contents on her desktop. Driven by a desperate need to flee, she grabbed her keys and ran. In her confused and fearful state, she thought back twenty years to the incident under the lilac hedges by her home.

Home. She had to go home, to safety. She remembered her mother holding her as a child, folding her within the warmth and protection of her loving arms and promising her that everything would be all right. She needed reassurance that the hideous visions and phantoms would disappear now, those heart-stopping nightmares of him! He had violated her in ways she had forced herself to block from memory. But the fiend wasn't real; everybody had said so.

Oh God. Mama, please heeeeelp me!

A torrent of emotions overwhelmed her as she fought with this door opening to her past. Monstrous silhouettes tore at the tendons of her memory, mocking and taunting her, reminders of what she had fought so hard to forget. Her nightmares came flooding back like the shattering blast of a train whistle screaming through her mind. This monster was real, hot, and covered in a sticky ooze. It reached out to touch her.

Oh, please, don't touch me there! Pleeeeese don't hurt me. I can't see. Somebody help me... Pain... Can't breathe... I don't want to die.

She tried to scream, but no sound escaped her fear-constricted throat to validate her torment. Eyes unfocused, she fought to insert the key into the ignition of her car, though not knowing how she'd even gotten there. The dull throbbing in her head became sharp little daggers slicing into her brain. Just one thought now grabbed hold of her conscious mind: something evil out there was watching her.

CHAPTER 63

Afraid to leave the safety of her car, Mykel drove around her neighborhood for almost an hour as a steady rain began to pound on her windshield. She'd left messages for Kyle at his office. Bracing against her fears, she pulled into her driveway and dashed from her car to the house.

She stopped on the porch to look around and caught sight of a man standing beside a tree half a block down. He wore a dark Fedora with a broad brim turned down over his forehead. The moment she noticed him moving closer to a tree as if trying to hide, she stopped cold. By this time, her chest-high yard shrubs were obscuring all of him but his head. He looked straight at her. She bolted into her house in time to hear the last ring from a phone call she'd missed. Sensing imminent danger from the stranger, she reacted with defensive instinct.

Is this the bogeyman from my past? Could he be the same one who just called me?

Her legs felt like they were moving through quicksand as she moved from room to room, locking windows and bolting her doors...

Faster Mykel... Faster...

Her heart pounded out of her chest, and her body convulsed. With trembling fingers, she pushed aside the lace curtains and fumbled with the locks on the windows. Her ears perked at the sounds of the storm outside; lightning flashed and thunder cracked, rattling her windows. She stopped, feet glued to the floor, when she heard breaking glass from an upstairs window. Her chest rose and fell as she began to hyperventilate. She tried but couldn't swallow. A rush of tears streamed down her face. So this was it? Her nightmare had returned. She felt like a marionette with half the strings missing and this visage from hell tugging on them.

She traced her steps back to the kitchen and tore open the utensil drawer, spilling its contents on the floor. *Damn! Why did I leave my revolver upstairs?* She fumbled in her attempt to grab a butcher knife. *Hurry, Mykel!* Now, near panic, she clutched the thick wooden handle. *I'm not ready!* She saw her reflection in the twelve-inch gleaming steel blade and shivered, seeing the paper-white face staring back at her. *Not me!* She saw dark swollen eyes, recessed in a disfigured porcelain face.

Then she heard it—a creak in a wooden floorboard above her. Every muscle in her body wound tight, a coiled spring threatening to break loose as her body bent down into a crouching position, afraid to run, afraid to stay. A bolt of lightning flashed in the window followed by a tremendous detonation of thunder. The overhead light in the kitchen shook for a moment, then blinked out.

Near blackness enveloped her as her eyes tried to adjust to the dark. Realizing she needed to hide, she looked for a safer place to mount her defense from. She tiptoed to the next room. Moving shadows began playing tricks with her vision as the room began to spin around her like the swirling vortex in the movie *Vertigo*.

Tightly clutching the bannister, she refused to look up the stairs. Her heart leaped to her throat, but she would not succumb without a fight. She'd battle this beast with her last breath and try her best to hurt it as it had hurt her twenty years before. It had stalked her subconsciously for years, the chaos that churned beneath the surface like a cauldron full of spiders crawling around in the basement of her mind. And though she'd never seen its face, it was here in her house now.

Mykel backed to a small closet beneath the staircase and lifted the latch. The door squeaked as she eased herself into the tiny crowded space. She closed the door behind her and crouched within, listening for telltale signs of her intruder's location. The stairs above her began to give and squeak.

He's on his way down.

She pushed herself farther into the closet, wiping sweat from her face, struggling vainly to corral her fear. He'd reached the bottom of the stairs now. Blackness surrounded her, but the knife clutched in her hand helped bolster her faint courage.

Get ready, Mykel! She heard a shuffling noise coming closer to her... *Shish-wish... Shish-wish... Slap!*

Though blind in the dark, she heard the latch to the door jiggle and lift. Her mind screamed as she pushed her quaking body back, deeper into the closet. Her spine pressed painfully against shoes hung from the back wall.

Then the latch dropped back into place, and she heard footsteps receding down the hallway toward the kitchen. She realized she'd been holding her breath and gasped for air. She retightened her grip on the wooden handle of the knife.

Pleeeeease make it quick!

She heard a crash at the front door and the pounding of shoes running past the closet toward the kitchen. Before she processed what had happened outside, the latch rattled, and the door flew open. Her eyes widened as she saw the enormous silhouette of a monster towering within feet of her cringing body. She couldn't take any more. A scream tore loose from her paralyzed lungs. Her eyes blurred with tears, distorting the specter looming before her and ripping its way through the clothes hung on the rod over her head. The demon's giant hand almost touched her.

Now! Kill it now!

She brought the shining blade high above her head, now slashing it left and right in front of her as hoarse animal noises issued from her mouth. She jabbed the blade up and down in front of her, trying to sink it in the monster's flesh.

"Die, damn you!"

Her eyes closed and wouldn't reopen. She refused to face the nightmare, this specter of all things feared. *Coward!* With her arms pinned to her side, she cried as the knife first slipped and then fell from her trembling fingers. Feeling like she had a kick to the chest, she gagged and panicked. He would suck the life from her. *Don't open your mouth!*

This would be her final act on earth. She would first die and then shrivel into nothingness. Strong, vice-like fingers were pulling her closer…closer toward the hollow mouth of the demon. She felt his breath on her face. It lifted her up and pulled her in toward it. She refused to look at the demon.

Mykel would have crumbled to the floor had it not been for its inhuman strength holding her erect. Her moan came from the depth of her being, an animal dying while still struggling for freedom and survival. A sweet blanket of darkness enveloped her as she drifted into unconsciousness. In the recesses of her mind, she thought she heard it calling her name, though not at first. It had a deep, persuasive voice, beckoning her.

"Let me die," she whispered.

CHAPTER 64

"Mykel… Mykel! It's me… Open your eyes!"

Why wasn't it tearing her limbs off? Its hold on her was stronger than anything she imagined. In an instant, her adrenaline overcame her fear, and she knew she would fight against her attacker, even if it killed her!

"I'm here, Mykel. You're safe now."

Muscular arms encircled her, rocking her gently. Convulsively sobbing, she forced her eyes to open upon the face of her attacker.

"Kyle?"

"Yes, Mykel," he whispered, wiping the tears from her cheeks.

"That bastard wants to kill me, Kyle," she blurted as anger pushed through her fear. "He tried once, but I knew he would be back." Her body molded itself deeper into Kyle's arms.

"No one is going to hurt you, Mykel. I won't let that happen."

"You can't stop it. He's not human."

"Oh, he's human, Mykel, and I'll make sure you're safe until I have him."

She jerked her head off his damp chest and dug her fingernails into his arms. "Kyle…"

Anticipating her worry, he pulled her back against his chest. "I checked everywhere. He's left the house. When he heard us breaking through the front door, he ran out through the kitchen and over the railing on the back porch. Tony and three patrolmen are after him now."

"I'm a coward," she whispered.

McNally kissed her on the forehead then held her at arm's length, looking into her eyes. "Coward? Not by a mile in my book."

Putting his arm around her shoulders, he walked her into the living room. He sat her in a chair next to the fireplace and seated himself on the hassock beside her. He wrapped his hands protectively around her cold, trembling fingers.

"Mykel, your monster is real. I'm not certain this guy is the Slugger, but I've found out he knows these victims. He knows them, stalks them, and murders them." He watched as doubt rose in Mykel's blue eyes and realized he had to tell her everything now.

"But except for the Clayton girl, I thought all his victims were prostitutes," Mykel said.

"Several early ones were...but the last one has a link to two others. All three went to the same high school."

"My god."

"I believe those first prostitutes' killings were where he honed his MO. The sick bastard fine-tuned his technique before turning his attention to the ones he was ultimately after. They were easy marks for him—setups, kind of. But I now believe he planned the recent ones years ago. Up until yesterday, he'd been smart enough to get away with it, enjoying the view as he watched us spin our wheels. Every sign pointed toward a pattern of random hate-driven crimes. We'd still be treating them that way if it weren't for these latest ones."

"What latest ones?"

"I've found two more of his victims who were living out of state, and then I learned they went to the same school as the latest murdered prostitute. They were all friends. These last three killings appear to have been revenge for something they all allegedly did to him in high school."

He waited for any sign of recognition from Mykel, some small signal she understood what he said. He read nothing in her eyes. A moment more passed before Mykel comprehended exactly what Kyle had said. Her eyes opened wide as she began digging her fingernails into his hands, fighting to stay calm.

"I don't believe this!" She tightened her grip on his hands and continued, "At seventeen years old, I was attacked. My god, Kyle, this must be the same person," she said in a halting voice.

"Were you raped?"

She sighed and stared into his searching eyes. "The textbook definition following the doctor's examination and put on the police record was aggravated sexual assault."

Kyle wanted to take her in his arms and soothe her. She pushed her lower lip out and stared at a spot down on the floor beside him, averting her eyes as she spoke. Only her mother and her psychiatrist knew the truth surrounding the events of that day.

"Only a week past my seventeenth birthday and I had finished my senior year of high school, I went to the library a few blocks from home that night to finish my research of colleges I wanted to attend. I'd promised my mother I'd be home before it closed. While there, I felt sure someone watched me. But every time I looked around, I saw no one. When I'd finished, I headed home. I still had the sense that someone might be watching me. I passed it off as only my imagination. The streets were empty that night, and since the weather had cooled, no one sat out on their porches.

"At one point, I heard footsteps behind me, in step with my own, yet when I turned, again, I saw no one. I should have run. I don't know why I didn't. My neighbors on the corner had a row of lilac bushes bordering their yard. I thought if I cut through the hedge, I'd get home that much faster."

I bent over to walk through the lilacs and got halfway through when something struck me on the back of my head, knocking me to my knees. He pulled me backward, and things became blurry. He stuffed something in my mouth and slipped a cloth sack over my head. Then he began tearing at my clothes. He made sounds like an animal. He alternately clawed and fondled me. I felt sure he would kill me. I remember clammy fingers clawing against my skin as he dragged me farther back into the hedge." Her voice cracked, and she bit down on her lower lip, drawing a small drop of blood. Kyle listened empathetically as she shared her painful story. A protective instinct he'd never experienced before flooded over him as he held her tighter.

"He ripped at my clothes until he'd torn them almost completely off. I tried to kick him, but he sat on the back of my legs. My hands were bound behind me with the strap from my purse. He rolled me over. I tried to scream, but with the rag in my mouth, no one heard me. He laid on top of me while his hot tongue licked my body. Then he lifted his shirt, and I felt his wet skin against me. He was fat and sweaty, so heavy. I thought I'd suffocate from his weight..."

Mykel paused and looked into Kyle's eyes for reassurance. He clasped her hands tighter. "Kyle...he wasn't human. He called me horrible names and kept telling me he knew what I wanted. After he finished licking me with his wet tongue, he rolled off my body. I prayed he'd finished and would let me go. With the rag stuffed in my mouth, I fought for breath. He made soft, high-pitched gruff noises, and that's when I knew he planned to kill me. He forced my legs open until I thought they would rip apart. Then he sat between them and pinned them under his knees."

A small whimper escaped from her, and McNally leaned closer to listen. She felt humiliated and still refused to look him in the eye. If she had, she would have seen nothing but empathy etched on his face. What she couldn't have seen, hidden behind his sharp green eyes, was his deadly, blazing fury. McNally's protective instinct had focused on finding this fat, scum kid and blowing his goddamn head off.

"Sweaty hands were on the inside of my thighs. I realized he would rape me and then kill me—or much worse than that. Oh god, the fear!" she cried. "I wanted to die."

Her voice cracked again. He knew how hard this must be for Mykel. Tears traced a path down her soft cheeks and fell on his hands. He stretched his strong protective arms around her and held her as a father would hold and comfort a child. Her body heaved with sobs, so he continued to hold her for several minutes, offering quiet words, reassuring her she'd be safe now.

"I must have passed out. The next thing I remembered, I woke up in the hospital with our priest standing at the end of the bed. My first thoughts were that I had died. Then I felt the pain and knew I hadn't. My mother counted beads on her rosary and prayed at my bedside. My father wasn't there… He never did come to see me. He was convinced it had been my fault." Mykel paused for several seconds.

"He died from a heart attack a month later. We hadn't spoken. I'm certain he never forgave me. Two weeks after the attack, when I left the hospital, the surgeon told me what my attacker had done to my body. My organs were so badly damaged they performed an emergency hysterectomy. They told my mother to find a therapist to help with my recovery. And then a month later, only two weeks after my father died, my mother died in a car accident." She paused and straightened her posture. "Bad year, huh?" she said with a slight raising of her eyes, accompanied by a brave smile.

Kyle nodded with a reassuring nod.

"I'd already begun seeing Dr. Fielding, my psychiatrist, just before my mother's death. He'd been a family friend for years before my assault, so I knew and trusted him. He and his wife invited me to move in with them. They insisted I start college as a part of my recuperation. The doctor became my counselor, mentor, and surrogate parent for the next six or seven years. I honestly don't think I'd have survived if it wasn't for him.

"With his counseling, I moved past the trauma and nightmares mostly. When he died several years ago, it devastated me. He represented the last link to both my parents and my past. I'd left those few close friends I had from high school behind. They only reminded me of all the pain I'd suffered back then.

"By my third year in college, I believed I'd never have a normal relationship with a man, so I buried myself in my studies. Forensic medicine seemed like a good place for me to hide, and it's served me well."

Kyle's smile reflected both tenderness and understanding. She wiped more tears from her eyes and continued, "By that time, I thought of myself as an oddity, a freak, not quite a woman and still uneasy around men. For years thereafter, I denied allowing myself the usual preoccupation with the boys my age and, later, with men.

I wasn't afraid of them, but I guess I didn't want to give them that much power over me." A soft, hesitant smile touched her lips. "Until you walked into my examining room that day and leaned against my wall. Do you realize that your slow smile and easygoing arrogance are sexy?"

Kyle's eyebrows lifted, and he stared into her deep blue pools. "Lucky for me you like those attributes."

A wide smile broke across her face. To him, that was the most welcome thing he'd seen since finding her in the closet. Trust radiated in her eyes as she reached her slender arms around his chest and hugged him.

His expression grew stern as he cupped her face with his hands. "Mykel, I want you to listen. If this guy is the attacker from your past, he was scared away this time, but I'm certain he'll be back. I want you to pack a few things and come stay at my apartment until we can get a fix on him. I'll feel more comfortable when you're away from here. And I'll arrange for a patrolman to be posted outside my apartment just to be sure."

He saw no surprise in her eyes. She said, "All right, I'll pack. But what makes you think he'd come back? I mean, he knows the police will be watching for him."

Kyle hesitated, considering what she had been through. He searched for the right words. "As I told you, we're sure he's not murdering women randomly..."

Her lips drew together, and her eyes grew larger as his words froze her to silence.

"What I haven't told you is that three of the latest victims were your classmates from high school. He's found them and is likely looking for you now. I wasn't aware of your relationship to them until an hour ago. Nobody remembered your right name, not until the dean of the school called, your former history teacher. She remembered you as one of the group of friends and located your transcripts. I didn't realize you'd attended school under a different name—Faith Hartman. When I looked her up in the yearbook, I didn't recognize you. Mykel, you're the last of your group of friends involved in the incident at school. You were his first intended victim."

Mykel sat stunned for a moment, blinking her eyes and swallowing hard as she tried to take in what he'd told her. "Well, yes, I told Dr. Fielding after my mother died that I wanted to start over fresh, brush away all the dirt, grime, and pain from my past. Hartley was my mother's maiden name, and Mykel is my middle name. And now you're telling me all my high school friends are…gone?" She fell limp against Kyle. "Why didn't he kill me when he had the chance back then? Why is he doing this now?"

He held her close and shook his head. "Mykel, we'll need your help. You are the last person who can identify this guy. We haven't found a link yet between the Clayton woman and all of you, but we better not rule anything out. There may still be a connection."

Her distress returned. "They were my fr—Did you say I'm the only one left?"

"Listen." He gripped her shoulders. "I got back a little while ago from interviewing the family of one of the murder victims, the Guthries. Their daughter, Cassandra, moved to Philadelphia after college for her career."

"Cassie?" she whispered.

"Yes. Her parents said their daughter was one of four friends that hung out together through high school. The school gave me a picture of her posed with two other vic—" He halted in midsentence when he saw the color drain from Mykel's face. He thought she might pass out. "Mykel, I need you to stay with me."

She nodded.

"I understand this is hard for you, but you must listen."

"Go ahead."

"We've discovered that three of the dead women were friends of yours from high school."

"So you think this madman is killing us for something that occurred in high school?"

"Everything we've put together so far points in that direction— an incident surrounding a group of friends, your friends, and a student who apparently stalked all of you. It was bad enough for the parents to get the school dean involved. We're taking every precaution, but we need to know if there were more."

"Kyle, there were no others that I am aware of. From everything you've said, it's likely I'm the last."

His eyes hardened. "As I say, you'll be under twenty-four-hour police protection until we can nail this guy."

She shook her head. "He will get me, Kyle. Eventually. Somehow that creature will find me. It won't end!" *Not until I'm dead!*

"Mykel, listen now!" He shook her to get her attention. "Nobody will get you. I'll get this misogynist before he can hurt anyone else. You've got to trust me."

Her forehead furrowed with concern as she considered his reassurances. In a moment and despite her fears, she straightened up. "Then I'd better go pack." She left the room and climbed the stairs, with Kyle watching her. Her bravery impressed him.

Outside, the rain had ceased, but the sky had turned black, and the wind kicked up. The front door slammed shut.

CHAPTER 65

Moments later, Detective Petrocelli came bursting through the front door. "We got him, Mac! Found him hiding under a porch three houses over. I sent the uniforms back to headquarters with him to finish the booking. When you get there, we'll begin the interrogation."

"Thanks, Tony," Kyle said, smiling. "Hopefully, this is the one we're looking for. I'd love to think we've got a wrap on this. I'm taking Dr. Hartley back to my place, where she'll be staying until I can confirm this is our bad guy. And hey, do me a favor. Arrange for uniform protection while I'm getting her settled, okay?"

"I'll call for it right away. What tipped you that Dr. Hartley might be in danger today?"

"Two messages from Shaughnessy. First one came from the school's dean at the academy. She said that Dr. Hartley attended school with a different name. Turns out, Faith Hartman is her given name. She's the last of the missing girls from a group that had trouble with a guy I now believe is our Slugger. Second was the message from the ME's office that gave me the name of the latest Slugger vic. Identified her as Tessa May Breedlove, making her the third victim of the Slugger's from that same group of high school friends. Dr. Hartley is the fourth. I found all four in the yearbook from the academy. That's when I knew she was squarely in his sights.

"And, Tony, you may have surmised by now that the doctor and I are seeing each other. Tell you what. She's fragile now after what I told her, and I want to make damn sure this creep never gets to her again—ever."

"No worries. This guy will be my personal mission from now until we get him in front of a judge."

CHAPTER 66

The entire department had heard of the incident at Dr. Hartley's home. Detective Petrocelli made sure they all knew how McNally connected the hooker murders and the Catholic schoolgirls. The overall mood in the squad room was one of anticipation and cautious excitement. Even Rouse had a "Look who just ate the jelly doughnut" stuck on his face. The detectives had been speaking about the collar, a couple even conceding regret at labeling her the Iron Maiden. Now they all knew that McNally and she were an item. That fact moved her up a few pegs in their esteem. When McNally returned to the squad room two hours later, there were high fives and congratulations all around, with the commander leading the chorus.

"Thanks, folks, but we're still too far from closing this case. I've got a suspect in interrogation that may or may not be our serial bad guy. Let's not get ahead of ourselves just yet."

Tony approached Kyle and told him the perp, Randall James Donovan, waited in interrogation.

"Good. Let's not keep him waiting any longer."

* * *

"Hello, Mr. Donovan," Mac said as he sat down across from the collar in the interrogation room. "First name's Randall; middle, James; but they call you RJ, correct?"

"Yeah, you got that right. And who might you be?"

"I'm Detective McNally, and this is Detective Petrocelli, whom you met earlier," he said, nodding to Tony. "You understand why you're in here, right? So how about if we start by you telling us how you ended up inside that house you broke into, RJ."

Holding up widespread hands, he said, "Just a minute, Detective, that's not how it went. I knocked on the front door several times before I busted a window upstairs, trying to get in. A friend of mine used to live there back a few years ago. I didn't know he wasn't living there anymore. Truth is, I been out of town since '95 and he'd always put me up when I came to the area. We were army buddies overseas together in Desert Storm," Donovan said, emphasizing the words *army buddies*, like it was a passkey.

Tony jumped in, "Mind explaining why the victim stated she saw you down the street from her house, watching her, before you broke in?"

"It wasn't me! I've had trouble with PTSD since I got back in the world."

In a challenging tone, Petrocelli barked, "Do you remember where you slept last night?"

Kyle cut in, "Pay attention, RJ. I don't think you want to play games with us now, do you? We've run your prints and should have any priors back on the wire in a moment. So why don't you tell us what you were doing there, stalking the lady and breaking into an occupied residence. If you impress me with your honesty, it'll look better in front of the judge later."

RJ was shaking his head, staring into McNally's eyes.

Then, Kyle said, "Listen, RJ, how about a cup of coffee or a glass of water?"

"Yeah, a cup of coffee—black—and a water would be nice," RJ replied, uncrossing his arms. He slumped backward, clasping his hands together on his stomach.

"Detective Petrocelli, please arrange for RJ to get a coffee and a glass of water."

Tony nodded and left the room.

"Okay, RJ. Tell me. You ever been arrested before? Got any priors you'd like to tell me about? Where have you lived the past few years?"

"I'm not sure what you're thinking, Detective, but you've got it all wrong. I'm telling the truth about my buddy living there before. His parents owned the home before retiring to Florida. At the time, they left it to him. I've moved around a lot since I got out of the service. Never settled on one place or job. Took a few college classes in computers, but I couldn't make any good job connections. Yeah, I got into trouble once or twice—once for royally kicking some guy's ass. He deserved it. And I got pinched for a smash and grab at a convenience store. Nothing that ever bought me a golden ticket, if you take my meaning," he said with a heavy sigh. "But I did catch a year in jail for that."

McNally nodded and encouraged him to continue.

"But you won't find any weapons charges against me. I was done and done for good with those after the service. And now with my record, chances of finding a decent job have gone from slim to next to none. I've been moving from shelter to shelter, picking up meals where I could and odd jobs when I found them. But I'm in a bad streak now and needed some cash in my pocket. It's a nice neighborhood. I remembered it from when my friend lived there. So I'm walking down the street, this lady drives up in a nice car, and I thought..."

"Go on."

"Well, I figured she'd have some cash on her or around her house. I wouldn't hurt her, not for nothing. I swear! You gotta understand, I grew up with sisters. I ran out of options," he concluded with an embarrassed smile, hoping the detective understood.

Tony came back in the room with the drinks and a folder tucked under his arm. He put the drinks down in front of Donovan and placed the open folder in front of Kyle, who studied the first page and then flipped through three more pages before standing up, causing his chair to tip over backward.

Kyle reached into his shirt pocket and pulled out a single 2.5" × 3.5" card with Bill "Moose" Skowron's picture on the front and flipped it face up across the table to Donovan. "You a collector, RJ?" he said.

"Baseball cards? Nah, they're a waste of time and money," he said with a puzzled look.

"Detective Petrocelli, meet me back at my desk," Kyle said curtly and left the room.

Back at Kyle's desk, Tony said, "What's up, Mac?"

"He's not our guy, Tony."

"Huh? What makes you think that?" Tony said, blinking in surprise.

"His rap sheet's all wrong. No history of violence against women. Served in the military and came home with a few medals for bravery. He's made some dumb mistakes and has been beat down some, but this isn't our guy. The baseball card was a tell also. Did you notice he didn't even blink when he saw it? His body language didn't fit either. This is a tough one to swallow Goddamn it, but he's not Slugger. Have Peterson verify that his friend did live there previously. If so, we've got Donovan on B&E of an occupied dwelling, assault, and leaving the scene, but that's it. I won't even go after the stalking."

Two hours later, Kyle returned from finishing and filing his report on Donovan and the break-in at Mykel's. Petrocelli spent the time working on his search of the names from the airline and car rental lists.

"Hey, Tony, you look exhausted. I'm not unhappy with our progress today, even without collaring Slugger. Let's knock off for the night and come back tomorrow morning with a fresh set of eyes. I'm going home and check on Dr. Hartley. You should get out of here and get some shut-eye."

"No need to ask twice, partner," Tony said, already rising from his desk. "And I've got a helluva good feeling we're right around the corner from snagging our scumbag."

CHAPTER 67

The next morning, they'd been back at the area for an hour when Tony looked up with an "I just won the lottery" look on his face. "Well, kiss my dago ass, Mac. Come here. There is a Santa-fricking-Claus. You're not gonna believe who showed up in both cities with flights and car rentals on our dates."

With one look at the names Tony had highlighted from both lists, Kyle said, "Son of a bitch."

"Okay, Tony, here we go. Start by getting a search warrant for Butler's apartment and vehicle. List everything. I'll also need warrants to cover his offices in the Loop and the Chi-Tech labs. After you've got those, I'll send two men to search his offices. You and I will take his apartment and the labs, and I want these to be clean searches. No fuck-ups that this creep can use to slither through at trial. Remember, he's a lawyer."

"Ten-Four."

"His aunt said he works for her at Chi-Tech for a couple of days a month. I want access to every locked door in that building, understood?"

"Understood."

He hollered across the room to Ramirez, "Roy, when the warrants clear, I want you and Shaughnessy to meet me downstairs before heading to Butler's downtown law offices. I want to look them over before you leave. Plan to interview everyone who works with him—secretaries, partners, lawyers, and paralegals. Got it?"

"Roger."

"I'll have the warrants ready in a couple of hours," Petrocelli said above the growing din of the now-bustling squad room.

"Good. Buzz my beeper the moment you've got them. And, Tony, we need them quick. I want to check on Dr. Hartley before we head to Butler's apartment. This'll be a huge relief for her. I want you, Ramirez, and Shaughnessy to meet me downstairs with the warrants when I get back."

CHAPTER 68

"My god, Kyle! He stood right in front of me the day they brought Karen Clayton's body in, and I didn't recognize him."

"How could you? It was over ten years ago, and he'd lost a ton of weight. He's a coldhearted scrap of humanity—that's for certain. His emotional wrapper must be thick to put on that show with Karen's mother beside him and then go back to the streets, searching for his next victim. He may have recognized you that day. If not while he was there, he made the connection later. And don't forget, you had a different name on your ID badge.

"I remember he followed us around at school. First, it just annoyed us. He'd come to the library and watch us study, then to the assemblies, where he would always try to sit near us. It got creepier when he started showing up at the Big Boy hamburger shack after school. He'd be there with his White Sox cap on, sitting alone and always wearing a pathetic look on his face. My friends got angry and started to tease him. One of them ridiculed him so much she made him cry. At the time, I regretted that I did nothing. I wanted him to stop stalking us too!

"Two of my friends, Ava and Cassie, were dating boys who played on the baseball team. They offered to shake him up a little for us. I never thought they'd hurt him so bad. The boys told us they only pushed him around a little to scare him. Later, we heard they forced him into their car, stole his clothes, and left him naked in the middle of the mall parking lot.

"The next day, at school one of the boys who went with them told my friends what had happened. He said that when they made him take off his clothes, they saw his genitals were tiny, underdeveloped. They called him a freak and said he wasn't human. One of them had a souvenir baseball bat in his car, and they molested him with it. God, how awful. I'd completely forgotten before now. I never realized boys could be so cruel.

"We thought they were only boasting and didn't do anything terrible to Frank, but he never returned to school. God, they were so cruel. The counselors and administrators called us all into the dean's office and warned us never to discuss it with anyone," she said, tears welling in her eyes.

Kyle said, "That fits with what his aunt told me about sending him to several private schools at seventeen. He never forgave you and your friends for that shaming. A couple of months later, on your way home from the library, he attacked you. From your description about your assault, I'm certain Butler did it."

Mykel's shoulder's shook as the full effect of his words sank in.

Kyle reached for her trembling hands. "You're safe, Mykel. I'll see to it this bastard never gets another chance to hurt you."

She nodded. "I believe you, Kyle. It's the shock of seeing him and knowing how close I stood to him… For so long, I thought of him as a demon conjured by the devil. I never imagined I'd see him as flesh and blood. I couldn't put it all together because I consciously wiped it from my memory." A sudden, stabbing anger consumed her; she would never be a victim again.

CHAPTER 69

Just before noon, McNally sat in his car holding a steaming cup of coffee. He waited for detectives Petrocelli, Ramirez and Shaughnessy to come down. They brought the warrants. Petrocelli climbed in the passenger side, while Ramirez and Shaughnessy walked to the driver's side window for their final instructions.

He scanned the warrants and found the information he needed. "Roy, you and Shaughnessy know what we're looking for. Grab two uniforms to bring with you, and check back with me before you wrap up there."

Tony reached over and said, "Roy, you've got my number and can reach me on my mobile phone, okay?"

"Roger. Where are you going first?" Ramirez asked.

"Tony and I are meeting the lab tech crew at Butler's apartment before heading to the Chi-Tech offices. I've put an APB on him. It's only a matter of time before he turns up. With any luck, his office will tell us where he is."

"Ten-four." Ramirez turned his back to walk away, then stopped and turned around. He came back to the car and motioned for McNally to roll down his window.

"Yeah."

"Before you go, there's something I need to tell you. Rouse cornered me when you were out before." At that moment, Ramirez felt like someone who threw a dead cat in the middle of the dance floor.

McNally's features hardened to granite. "Go ahead."

"He demanded I tell him everything I knew about the investigation and where it stood. I gave him a few hints about the murders in Philly and New York but skimmed over the details about Butler's connection to Clayton and Dr. Hartley. And I spread the manure real thin so he's got enough to drool over when he calls the superintendent. He reminded me he's gonna be wearin' his mobile phone all day and expects a call when we make the collar."

"Prick," McNally whispered under his breath. "If the press so much as catches a whisper of this, Butler will be a ghost by morning."

Roy stuffed both hands into his jacket pockets. "Sorry, Mac. Thought you should hear it from me. For what it's worth, he didn't say anything about needing to talk to you. He must have figured I'd tell him more than you."

McNally raised one eyebrow. "And did you?"

"Not a chance. He's still scratching his head, wondering how much he can tell the superintendent without taking a chance of gettin' caught in a lie later. There's no telling what Peterson might tell him though. He's been sniffing around the shop all morning."

"Don't worry about that. Peterson won't cross me again," Kyle said, starting his car. "Go, do your search. But buzz me immediately if you find anything."

They headed for Butler's apartment. Tony saw, by Mac's flared nostrils, that he was furious at what Ramirez told the commander.

"Rouse wouldn't jeopardize everything we've worked so hard for…" *Would he?* "Everything's been done by the book. We're clean," Kyle said. "But if Rouse blows this one, I'll beat him to death myself."

At one o'clock, they reached Butler's apartment building on south Indiana Avenue. A squad car pulled to the curb behind McNally.

McNally gave instructions to the uniformed officers. "One of you wait in the back. We're only here to search the place and take Butler in for questioning if he's home. The tech unit should be here in thirty minutes or so. No mistakes and by the book, okay? No pistol whipping," he said, grinning.

Petrocelli pressed the buzzer to Butler's apartment. There was no response after a second try.

"Looks like our boy's out," Kyle said. "Buzz another apartment."

"Who is it?" a woman's husky voice crackled through the intercom.

"Chicago Police, ma'am. Sorry to bother you, but we are here with a search warrant for the tenant in 6-West. No one answers, and we need you to buzz us in," McNally said.

"Oh…" The woman sounded frightened and a little confused. "I'm sorry. Are you sure it's all right? With him not being home and all… Should I be doing something?"

"This is an urgent matter, or I'd wait for the super. Buzz us in, please. And keep your door locked if you would while we check the apartment."

"Yes, yes, of course. The apartment is two floors up from me and at the back of the building."

"You think she's too young to remember how the Boston Strangler gained access to his vics?" Kyle said, pushing open the security door when the buzzer sounded.

"Who?" Tony replied. Mac let it go.

When they reached Frank Butler's front door, McNally knocked. The door swung open a few inches. Both detectives drew their weapons and assumed positions on either side of the door. Petrocelli touched the door and pushed it wide open. He nodded at Mac, who then stepped into the apartment. The lights were on, but he didn't appear to be home.

Kyle called out, "Anybody here? Mr. Butler, are you home?"

Then with pistols drawn, they split the door. Tony tried the knob, and the swung open. Petrocelli waited a moment, then Kyle pointed toward the hallway leading to the bedrooms. Petrocelli nodded and headed in that direction. Kyle's muscles remained tense as he checked the other rooms in the apartment. No sign of Butler.

"Anything?" Kyle asked when they met back in the living room.

"No. Nothing out of place back there."

"Okay, I'm going to check his office. You give the bedrooms a once-over while we're waiting for the evidence techs boys."

"Roger that, Mac. So what are we looking for?" Petrocelli asked.

"A souvenir bat, ladies' panties, and a baseball card collection would be nice."

Tony's face reddened. "Stupid question. I'll get going."

Kyle searched the office bookcases and magazine rack before sitting down behind the large desk. The next thing he heard was a deep voice commanding him to raise his hands and turn to face him. McNally lifted his hands, turned, and found himself looking into the barrel of a 9 mm Magnum. The man holding the gun stood medium height, with hazel eyes behind tortoise shell frames and wide lips that didn't conceal his uneven overbite. He had thick blond hair, which was parted in the center and gelled in place. Stubby fingers held the grip of the gun so tightly McNally could see the whites of the man's knuckles.

"Now!" demanded the stranger.

McNally's eyes narrowed to feral slits, and his facial muscles constricted into a dark scowl. His body hunched imperceptibly into a tight coil. He realized that the man standing across from him had come for the same reason—to find Frank Butler. But this guy posed a threat. He was sweating a river and taking deep breaths, while his finger shook on the trigger. Then it hit him. The starched white shirt, dark gray pinstripe suit, and a wide red tie in a Windsor knot with small black geometric squares gave him away. This man was a cop. FBI, most likely.

McNally proceeded cautiously. The man made an understandable mistake, assuming McNally was Butler.

Even though the agent held a tactical advantage, he showed obvious discomfort under McNally's stare. Kyle made two quick assessments. One, this man had to be new on the job, and two, he didn't want to shoot anyone. His discomfort rose as Kyle began grinning at him.

The agent lifted his gun higher while taking a small step backward, an unconscious attempt to increase the distance from the disingenuously smiling man now seated in front of him. Kyle felt confident he wouldn't challenge him, not unless he pressed hard.

Seconds passed when McNally's ironic look morphed into a sneer as he read his challenger's mind. "FBI's finest I presume." He knew the FBI tried to hijack his investigation early on. Now here they were again, trying to insert themselves into his case. Seconds later, two additional suits entered the room and stood behind their point man.

The detective looked at each of them with mock awe. "Impressive. Pinstripe suits and black wingtips are still the fashion, huh, guys?"

With his buddies behind him, the man with the gun puffed up, and he assumed a poorly rehearsed cocky look. He tilted his head up and looked down his nose. "Seems we've got a real smart-ass here, boys. Think he'll still be smiling when we cuff him to his chair and kick some shit out of him?"

Like quicksilver, McNally's feigned indifference turned to rage behind a tight smile. "Go ahead and try, boys. But then again, you might try another tack and cool your jets. Detective McNally, CPD, Area 5, Violent Crimes. If you loosen your finger on that pea shooter"—he nodded toward the gun—"I'll show you an ID."

The man registered surprise and relaxed his grip, motioning with the gun for McNally to produce his badge. With slow movements, he reached in his pocket and withdrew his credentials as the agent approached.

Pale eyes and face both registered disappointment as he threw McNally's badge back on the desk. He wanted this guy to be Butler in the worst way. "You took a big chance, Detective. It could have gotten messy."

McNally leaned back in the chair, cupping his hands behind his head. "I don't think so." He nodded and fixed his eyes on a point behind the gathering. They all turned at the same time to see Detective Petrocelli leaning against the doorframe across the room, holding his 9 mm semiautomatic across his chest.

"Mine's bigger'n yours," Tony said, waving his weapon at them.

Rising to stand, McNally stood half a head taller than the agent. "Now, gentlemen, I have been gracious enough to identify myself. That is Detective Petrocelli. Suppose you all make nice and show us your badges, and you can tell us who you are and what you're doing here."

The man holstered his gun and reached in his pocket for a hand-kerchief. He wiped his face and licked his dry lips before presenting his badge to McNally. McNally noticed the small muscle beneath one eye was twitching.

"I'm Special Agent Walker. We're here to follow up on a lead concerning Wayne Reynolds, a missing United States senator."

Now McNally displayed surprise. "What has a missing senator got to do with Frank Butler?"

"Our department is treating the senator's disappearance as a kidnapping. We've come across information that leads us to believe Frank Butler may have been blackmailing the senator. We came here to escort him back to the bureau for questioning."

McNally spread his arms and scanned the room. "The Bureau of Engraving? Sorry, no one here but us good guys. What else you got on Butler besides a little extortion?"

"Cut the bullshit, Detective," Walker said, his confidence grow-ing. "We've been building our case for weeks. If you have any idea where he is and refuse to tell us, I swear, cop or not, I'll slap your ass in the Metropolitan Correctional for interfering with a federal investigation. I don't give a shit what *your* reason is for being here!"

Agent Walker attempted to parade his newfound swagger. "What, did he neglect to pay his parking tickets?" The group snick-ered behind him. "Just stay the hell out of *our* way. Do I make myself clear, Detective?"

"Oh shit," Petrocelli whispered under his breath as he recog-nized the familiar tightening of McNally's jaw. He'd seen that look before.

McNally bared his teeth into a half snarl. "Agent Walker, let me caution you. You're over your head here. I suppose we could sit and spit at each other until the sun sets over the Sears Tower, but right now I'm short on time and even shorter on patience. My partner and I are here bearing a legal search warrant." Petrocelli, still standing behind them, coughed and rattled the paperwork.

"And we also have an APB out for Butler. He's wanted for ques-tioning for his involvement in at least one murder. Your interest in this man comes in just this side of a pile of dog shit on my department's priority list. I don't need to remind you, do I, that professional courtesy between law enforcement agencies dictates you take a number and get in line? To put it bluntly, Walker, you're standing squarely in my jurisdiction, and you're not invited to this party. We have a lawful warrant issued by a Cook County Judge office, which makes us all nice and legal. And so far, I haven't seen you pull anything from your pocket but your snot rag. So why don't you take yourself and that fuck-you-Freddie attitude right out that door so we can get back to *our* work."

Agent Walker didn't move. All those in the room saw that Mac was close to losing it, and Walker didn't look like he was holding a winning hand. Mac had the legal papers. He had the right to be there. Agent Walker cursed his squad leader for sending them out unprepared.

McNally took a step closer to the agent. "Oh, and since you don't seem to have anything to add, I must ask you fuck off and leave the neighborhood in case *our* man comes back. And"—McNally's face came within inches of Walker's—"do not get in my way again. Do *you* understand *me*, Special Agent Walker?"

Walker understood the detective was threatening a federal law enforcement officer, but he chose not to push that button any harder. What he wanted, more than anything, was to smash his fist into the cop, but a warning light blinked in his head, informing him that would not be a good move. He didn't want the heat from the bureau over an incident involving the local detective bureau.

Instead he turned, dismissing McNally with a wave of his hand. "We'll come back after you've completed your search." About to close the door, he leaned back in. "Touché, Detective, this one goes on your side of the scoreboard. I look forward to our next meeting. So finish up your business before we return. And don't forget to leave the warrant with an inventory of any items you remove." The agent's insult did not get past McNally.

After they left, Petrocelli snorted. "FBI's finest? What the fuck! Should we have known something about the deal between Butler and the senator?"

"Exactly. That's why I'd like to know everything they do. I have a friend at the bureau. I'll call him later. If they have anything that bears on our case, he'll tell me. And I'd better not find out that Rouse knew anything about this."

"Now let's get back to work, Tony."

CHAPTER 70

Kyle could see Butler had a compulsive personality. His office resembled a law library with everything organized by subject, author, and date—even down to several monogrammed Aurora fountain pens meticulously arranged on a leather-bound blotter. Not one sheet of paper was out of place. He had a variety of certificates, licenses, and awards displayed on the walls.

With gloved hands, McNally found and opened a checkbook register in one of the desk drawers that revealed several deposits spanning a six-month period in amounts of $5,000 and $10,000 per deposit. There were no written memos indicating their sources. He reasoned that if what the Feds said had any truth, they were likely from Wayne Reynolds. And within six months, he had written two checks of more than a thousand dollars each with memos to "CAITA, contribution." McNally recognized that the donations occurred during the time he knew Karen Clayton. There were none since her death. He dropped the register into a clear plastic baggie.

A lock on the last desk drawer popped with a twist of the letter opener. An autographed baseball in a plastic case and a lone manila folder lay at the bottom of the drawer. Half a dozen former Chicago White Sox players signed the baseball. He recognized a few of the names from the midsixties, including Tommy John, Juan Pizarro, Johnny Romano, and Tommie Agee.

When he opened the folder, he found a few newspaper clippings. He flipped through them, reading the headlines. They all concerned the CAITA organization and their efforts in the Chicago area and beyond. A few mentioned the founder, John Marshfield, and his PAC, Concerned Citizens United, designated in support of Senator Reynolds. One of the articles, eight months old, showed a picture of Marshfield and the senator together. Helen Butler was there, mentioned as a key fundraiser. He'd drawn a red circle around Senator Reynolds's face in the picture. Kyle scanned the article describing CAITA and its goals along with a few lines about Reynolds and his commitment to the organization. Karen Clayton wasn't in the picture but was mentioned as CAITA's newest researcher and Marshfield's protégé. Butler had underlined her name. Though the expression on Marshfield's face appeared parade-worthy, Reynolds looked uncomfortable. That triggered an idea for McNally.

He realized now that Karen Clayton, John Marshfield, Wayne Reynolds, and the Academy of the Holy Family High School victims all had either direct or indirect links to Butler. With Reynolds, the connection looked to be financial (extortion); with Clayton, personal. So where did that leave Marshfield? With no obvious personal ties to either Clayton or Butler, was he even a player in this four-act drama or simply a piece of useful art hanging in the gallery of Helen Butler?

He'd already confirmed the direct connections between Butler, Mykel, and her high school friends. And he now had a theory concerning Clayton's connection to him and her demise. Could simple unrequited love have spawned her slaying, or had she discovered something about him, perhaps his murderous proclivities? She worked as an investigator for CAITA. Maybe she'd found something that threatened him. But now that Butler was missing, Kyle wondered if these new connections might expose a larger separate conspiracy. He didn't have all the pieces in place yet, but the circles were tightening.

He needed answers from his friend at the FBI. Since he'd learned Butler could have been blackmailing Reynolds, he'd have information about Marshfield and his relationship with the senator. As McNally began to close the folder on his lap, a byline caught his eye. Reynolds had scheduled a speaking engagement on animal rights at Northwestern University for students and faculty the following Monday.

"What'd you find?" Tony said, walking into the office.

"Butler saved articles about Karen Clayton, Senator Reynolds, and CAITA's founder, John Marshfield. Butler appears to be the lynchpin tying them all together."

"What do you make of it?"

"I'm beginning to get a clearer picture about why Clayton may have been murdered. And I'm certain Frank, the Slugger, did it and not a copycat killer."

"What makes you think so now?"

"He'd underlined her name in the article I saw. Funny thing is, the article was eight months old. He told us when we spoke with him that he'd only known her for three or four months. I'd bet my retirement he saw or even met her well before he first showed an interest in her romantically. And that leads me to speculate that he may have even stalked her first."

"So why on earth would he target her? That's a long ball, Mac, even for a guy with a bat."

"Don't forget that although he pursued her, she never returned his attentions. Simple unrequited love? He'd tried impressing her with gifts, even went to the trouble of developing a relationship with her mother. He'd done everything a suitor does to win the favor of someone he cares about. Even so, her friends suggested he creeped them out. No, he wasn't getting what he wanted from her. Given when her murder occurred, I'd wager she told him the night he killed her. That and something else may have convinced him to off her. Remember, she worked as an investigator at CAITA, a place where he worked periodically. It's possible she uncovered something incriminating about Frank's extracurricular appetites. I'm hopeful we'll find more in the labs where he worked there."

"So why the dramatic staged crime scene? Angry at her lack of attention? Or the discovery of his night work? So first, he beats her to death ruthlessly. Then he stages the body. And finally, he puts the baseball card in her mouth. That's two details shy of his normal MO. Something triggered her murder. Something she said to him or something she did. That was when he decided to kill her. In either case, Clayton pushed the wrong button with a man she never knew was a psychotic killer." He shrugged his shoulders. "But in the end, she became another moth caught too close to his flame."

"Are we talking about a genius here or a fucking animal with multiple personalities?"

"Maybe a little of both. I'll leave that to the shrinks."

"What's next?" Petrocelli asked.

"You find anything?"

"Nothing incriminating—an old baseball team picture hanging on the wall in the back bedroom, most of them autographed. And one souvenir picture taken at Comiskey Park. Probably him and his father. It had been signed, 'For my son, on his birthday.' But that's about it. The place is clean."

"No bats lying around?" McNally asked, smiling.

"No, no bats." Petrocelli replied, frowning.

McNally reached in the desk drawer and threw a baseball to Petrocelli. "Now we know he liked baseball, let's hope we find the bat that goes with this. Time to get over to Chi-Tech."

"You spoke with his aunt?" Tony asked.

"Yeah, she's pissed off about the search warrant and threatened something about calling her attorney, but she agreed to meet us there. She wants to make sure we don't wreck the place."

"Shit. Butler's aunt!"

"Is there a problem?" McNally said, curious over Petrocelli's outburst.

"Yeah, she called Rouse earlier, demanding they tell her where Frank was. I forgot to tell you."

"Why would she think we knew?"

"Guess because we're looking for him."

"He say why?"

"No, but after seeing his bankbook, I get what Shaughnessy told me. Seems the IRS audited her, and Butler intended to meet the agents downtown with five years' worth of receipts and ledgers. He never showed up, and now they're banging on her door."

Tony laughed again. "Maybe we should tell her that at the same time he shuffled her money around, he was a little distracted with pounding women into hamburger."

"Terrific. This means we now have both a missing senator and a serial-murdering lawyer. Oh, fucking well, doesn't change our case. With the APB out, we'll find our scumbag."

Petrocelli laughed. "So Colonel Mustard did it in the kitchen with the pipe."

McNally pressed the down button on the elevator. "Huh? You care to share that?"

"Never mind. It's an old board game I remember playing as a kid."

McNally stared at Petrocelli and shook his head. "Anybody else, I might recommend a few days off. In your case, Petrocelli, your empty stomach is making you goofy. We'll stop for a Satay Chicken at the Chinatown Café on Wentworth before you pass out."

CHAPTER 71

By the time they arrived at Chi-Tech, Helen Butler was waiting for them. Her driver stepped out and opened the passenger door. She got out, a little bent over at first before straightening with discomfort and glowering as two squad cars arrived, following the detectives into the lot.

"Hello, Mrs. Butler. My apologies for this inconvenience. I promise we'll be brief and disrupt as little as possible," Kyle said.

"What exactly do you expect to find here, Detective? Francis only works one day a week when he doesn't have a trial—that is, when he can find the time…" she added dryly. "My deceased brother's firm handles most of my business. I sometimes allow my nephew to perform minor bookkeeping work for me. You are here with a search warrant, which grants you permission to rifle through my nephew's offices. It won't bother me at all."

After waving a threatening finger at the sleepy-looking security guard, she led them past an empty reception desk, then down a long carpeted hallway. Along each side of the blue carpet runner were modular walls separating small office cubicles. Farther down, there were windowed doors on either side of the hallway. Kyle saw these were the laboratories, the heart of Chi-Tech's former research center. There were dozens of glass door cabinets filled with labeled chemical bottles. Larger pieces of lab equipment sat on top of stainless-steel rollaway tables, and the floor-to-ceiling shelf units were crammed with microscopes, index drawers, utensils, and scientific glassware.

They arrived at the end and stood before a second large shiny steel door. Helen Butler retrieved a small plastic blue card from her pocket and slid it down through the security lock scanner. "Francis thinks he is the only one with access to these rear labs. I never told him differently. He can be, shall we say, petulant at times. When he asked about offices for his own use, well, I never allowed him that level of autonomy."

"Is it possible he came in to work at night?" Petrocelli asked.

Helen Butler's eyes flashed angrily. "Pardon me, Detective Vermicelli, but are you suggesting that I don't know my nephew?"

Tony reddened. "Petrocelli, ma'am. My name is Petrocelli."

"Yes. Whenever Francis came here at night, my security team informed me. No matter what time, day or night, I received regular reports of his comings and goings, I assure you," she finished with a frozen smile.

"How many access doors are there to the building?" McNally said with renewed authority. He had tired of her complaints about a nephew she clearly held in low regard, and by now, his patience was thinner than onion skin.

She glared at McNally and continued as if she'd never heard his question, "We keep logs documenting the use of each key card— which reminds me. You haven't told me why you are looking for him."

"He's wanted for questioning."

"For what? Jaywalking or a speeding ticket he couldn't buy his way out of? What?"

"It's concerning a homicide," McNally said.

All the blood drained from Helen Butler's face. She looked as though she would pass out. McNally reached out to grab her arm when she swayed back a step.

She stiffened and raised her hand. "No, I'm all right. But are you telling me he's involved in a murder?"

"No, ma'am, I'm telling you I want him for questioning."

"Why on earth?" She appeared to find the idea somewhat amusing. "No, not Francis. He suffers from various immature appetites, but you are mistaken if you assume he's involved in anything like that. I've known him his whole life, and I tell you, he's a coward. Cats maybe or gerbils, but nothing on two legs. Nothing that fought back."

Petrocelli interjected, "Pardon me? Cats?"

Helen Butler's expression changed. She elaborated, "When he was a teenager, my researchers caught Francis conducting peculiar experiments in our laboratories."

"Did you attempt to get him help?"

"No. Initially, his father refused to believe it when I told him, and he rejected any notion that Francis needed therapy. At first, I enrolled him in a strict military school. Later, I registered him in a series of private schools. One after another, they demanded I remove him for behavioral reasons. I arranged for counseling at several of the schools, but I also insisted he undergo psychotherapy."

"And would one of those private schools be the Downers Grove Academy of the Holy Family?"

"Yes, what a repugnant affair for me," she said, scrunching her nose like she'd smelled rancid meat.

Kyle nodded. "I see."

"After he started at the university, his visits were rare. There were occasional holidays and short breaks until his graduation from Yale Law School. It quickly became clear how much he despised me. I heard he told some people his father died when he was a child."

"Do you think he blamed you for his problems?"

"Yes, I do. Our relationship is only slightly better now. But I will never forget the cold defiance I saw in those eyes the day he left for military school." She pushed open the final door leading to Francis's private labs. "A bad seed—that's what I came to believe. Too much like his mother. He never shed a tear when I would take the riding crop to him. At times, I pondered if he may have been born bad, with deviant blood running through his veins."

"Deviant?"

She flipped on the overhead fluorescents and entered the room ahead of the detectives. "Doesn't matter now. What's done is done. Whatever he did, he'll have to take responsibility for it." She turned on her heels to leave. "I must insist that you leave the place as you find it during your search. Of course, I'll expect a full inventory of any items you decide to remove. And turn off the lights when you leave. The doors lock automatically behind you."

"Where can we reach you if needed?"

"I'm out today, but I should be home most of the day tomorrow. You have that number."

CHAPTER 72

Before entering the laboratory, both detectives put on latex gloves. The stark white walls smelled of fresh paint, and the room had a recently waxed linoleum floor. There wasn't much furniture, and it felt much cooler than the other areas. They saw a bookcase and dark metal desk against one wall. A large six-foot glass door cabinet stood against another with a folding cot on either side. The cabinet shelves held a variety of dust-covered brown chemical bottles bearing faded yellow handwritten labels. Three smaller white metal cabinets supported a seven-foot-long stainless-steel operating table in the center of the room. The overhead lighting was the high wattage kind found in hospital operating rooms.

"Crusty old broad, huh?" Tony snorted. "No wonder Butler's got squirrels in his attic."

"Well, there aren't many kids growing up these days, living in the Cleaver household. Fortunately, for most of them, they get past that and move along to become semirespectable citizens. My guess is, tops, 1 percent end up like Butler." He walked to the center of the room. "But that's not our problem, Tony. We have to make a case for the state's attorney."

"What's a Cleaver house?"

Kyle lifted his eyes to the ceiling. "It'd get lost in the explanation. I should have said *The Cosby Show*. Better?"

"Oh, okay, now I get it. So you're telling me we're kind of like city janitors… We're left to clean up the 1 percent's messes."

McNally had already begun searching the chemical cabinet. With deliberate care, he removed one of the dusty bottles and read the label. After sniffing the contents, he winced. "Jesus, this stuff smells like battery acid." He worked his way down, shelf by shelf, lifting and turning each dust covered bottle, examining it before placing it back. On the last shelf, he noticed one of the large brown bottles pushed toward the back that appeared dust free.

"Hello. What have we here?" He picked up the half-filled container and loosened the top. He licked the end of his gloved finger and dipped it into the powder, putting a small bit on the tip of his tongue. "Well, well, Frank Butler, there's enough shit here to keep you high for a long time." McNally handed the bottle to Petrocelli. "Add a little meth to someone who's already playing with a poorly shuffled deck, and you've got a psychological profile with a flashing neon arrow pointing at our serial killer's front door."

Tony examined the contents of the bottle. "A psycho lawyer with a nasty drug habit. Who'da thought?"

A loud scraping sound echoed through the room as McNally tried pushing the metal cabinet away from the wall.

"What are you doing? You find something?"

"His aunt referred to Butler's *offices*, meaning there's more than one. There are some scrape marks by the wheels in front of this cabinet. And since there's no door leading to another office, I'm guessing this might be our missing room."

Petrocelli scanned the room. "Why not? Those secret rooms are always hidden behind the party cabinet, aren't they?"

Mac wheeled the cabinet away from the wall.

"I'll be double-damned," Petrocelli said, shamed. He had overlooked the reference. He'd learned more in three days with Kyle than he picked up after a year in the department. Though the door didn't have a card scanner like the others, it had a lock that required a key.

"So how do we get in?" Tony asked, dismayed by the new snag.

McNally smiled and reached in the inside pocket of his jacket. "Not a problem." He pulled out a small black case and waved it in the air. "It's a gift I got from Weller." He cast a warning look to Petrocelli. "You never saw this."

"Saw what?"

Within thirty seconds, the door swung wide. He left Petrocelli to finish checking the first room and flipped on the overhead lights and studied his surroundings. This room was smaller than the first and contained a metal chest supporting a gurney with leather straps hanging to the floor. A four-foot-high, three-drawer file cabinet on casters stood against the far wall. To the left, it had a narrow door that looked to be a closet.

The air smelled stale yet vaguely familiar. Kyle didn't immediately recognize the scent. He walked to the gurney. This table had leather straps intended to restrain its occupant.

He opened one of the drawers in the small metal chest, and his eyes hardened and saw shiny surgical utensils neatly arranged by size. He held one of the scalpels in his gloved fingers as his anger rose. That sensation mingled with a surge of compassion for whatever or whoever had suffered on the cold table. Now he identified the odor that eluded him earlier: death—cold, ugly death.

He searched the remaining drawers in the chest under the gurney. Nothing incriminating. He went to the file cabinet. While examining the top drawer, his eyebrows rose. There were nine labeled file folders, each one containing a photo and several having an accompanying newspaper clippings. Three of the pictures were of Mykel's friends in high school. They were all shot revealing the full-bloody horror of each victim, and two of the articles contained obits. Only a couple of the earlier hooker photos had obits with them. Early on, Kyle, suspecting the start of serial crimes, had insisted that Rouse withhold them from the press.

Christ, there's several here we didn't even make for this guy. The first three bore some slight similarity to what became his evolving MO. But there'd been enough differences to make it difficult for initial reviews to tie them together, not until Kyle connected them. Likely they were early morbid rehearsals. With each new murder, he'd become bolder, more brutal, and wanted the cops to know who did it. That was when the White Sox signatures started showing up. He found an old newspaper article discussing Dante's Virgil stapled to a picture of the serpent, Minos, said to be responsible for judging sinners before they entered the second circle of hell.

He held up the picture for Tony. "Looks like this might have been his role model. And he documented every unsuspecting victim as he judged and delivered them to their final destination. I'd say we can add demon worship to his list of psychoses."

"Good God! How on earth did this man function as a high-class lawyer with all this baggage between his ears?" Tony said.

Kyle emptied the rest of the drawers and spread the contents on top of the gurney. He recognized several of the women by name on the folders. Among those were Mykel's high school friends, Cassandra Guthrie, Ava Haas, and Tessa Breedlove. Mykel was much younger in the picture cut from the high school yearbook. Kyle's jaw muscles tensed, and his eyebrows drew down.

You were to be the last of his revenge trophies.

There were Topps baseball cards in collector's boxes in the second drawer. All were former Chicago White Sox from the '60s, '70s, and '80s. Mac recognized that the only cards used thus far were from midsixties players.

Could he be planning to employ the later cards in the future?

When Petrocelli joined him, he'd methodically searched the remaining drawers and placed everything on the gurney. The items included the vic's opened folders, the boxes of baseball cards, several pairs of women's panties, and various pieces of jewelry.

"Good Lord!" Tony said, staring wide-eyed at the table.

"Yeah, we've got this prick cold now. You find anything else?"

"No. It's clean."

"Check the closet for me."

Petrocelli opened the door, half expecting it to be empty. "You ready for this?" he said, lifting a black raincoat off the hook. He handed the coat to McNally and dug further into the closet. "Come on, baby... Bless my dago ass with a little more luck, wont'cha?"

McNally searched the coat pockets while Petrocelli disappeared among the hanging lab coats. From an inside pocket, he retrieved a pair of woman's pink lace panties and placed them on the evidence pile.

His latest kill?

"Gotcha!" Petrocelli's muffled words drifted out. He backed out of the closet. He clutched a small wooden T-ball bat stained with telltale smudges of what resembled dried blood.

"I think we hit the trifecta, Mac," he said.

McNally took the bat from Tony and turned his eyes to the table holding the evidence. "Call the lab team, Tony. We've got everything we need."

Tony sighed as he picked up a gold filigree cross lying on a picture of Ava Haas, the New York victim. His eyes were moist and red. The picture showed her mutilated corpse, but around the girl's neck, he saw a small gold cross matching the one he held in his hand.

"When I interviewed her brother, he mentioned this necklace," Kyle said. "She got it for her confirmation and never took it off. That's why they didn't find it with her body."

He placed the cross back with the woman's folder. "Goddamn, this is the sickest shit I hope to ever see."

"Get those uniforms in here to cordon off the area."

"My guess is he's halfway to South America by now," Tony said.

"I seriously doubt it. Right from the beginning, I've suspected the Slugger watched us. No, he may have gone to ground, but he's not gone. It's cat and mouse for him, and I suspect he's still enjoying the game. And he's not aware we've found his lair. We'll find him. We've got a wide net out. And state's got extra bodies posted in the airports, train stations, bus depots, and highways. Even if he wanted to disappear, he wouldn't get far."

CHAPTER 73

Back at headquarters, they documented the evidence list for the state's attorney's office. At Butler's office, Ramirez and Shaughnessy had found files documenting his extortion of Senator Reynolds. By the time they finished their reports, it was twelve thirty in the morning. They notified Commander Rouse, who made a brief appearance to superficially congratulate the team. He glanced at the reports before leaving.

"Okay, Tony, I'm gonna cut out of here for a while. Will you be sticking around?"

"Yeah, I'm too hyped to leave. I'll stay here. I'll beep you if we find Butler, okay?"

"Right. I'm going back to my place and check on Mykel. Maybe get some sleep. I'll be back in the a.m."

* * *

Kyle stood in the dim light of his bedroom and watched the curled sleeping woman on his bed. Her features reflected the peaceful innocence of a child. The long, thick lashes fluttered before she opened them, revealing sleep-filled eyes. Her smile was beguiling and sensuous.

It's good to be home.

"Hi," she said sleepily. "I tried to wait up for you."

He bent and placed a gentle kiss on her lips. "Sorry, lady, I didn't mean to disturb you. I came home to grab a little sleep before heading back in a few hours."

She stretched her supple body toward him and wound her slender arms around his neck. "I missed you, Kyle. I miss your warmth next to me. I'm sure you've spoiled me forever."

His heart raced, more than just his blood was rising. "Ah, there you go again, making me regret any time spent away, Mykel." They both laughed. "As you can see, I'm happy to see you too."

Mykel pulled the sheets back, revealing her charmingly naked figure. She slid away from the edge of the bed, inviting him to join her.

"Mykel, you sure this is what you want?"

"I'm the doctor, Detective, not a shy virgin, and I'm old enough to know what's good for me and what's not." She lowered her eyes and added mischievously, "And it's obvious what you'd like."

Kyle undressed and crawled into bed next to her. In only a moment, he found himself lost in the subtle fragrance of her perfume and the butterfly touch of her exploring fingers.

Mykel's arms wrapped around his neck. "Kyle…" she whispered.

He kissed the tip of her nose. "Mykel, it feels so good with you beside me."

He inhaled and pressed his mouth against her neck. It transported him to a shady oasis in the middle of a desert. And with that image weaving through his mind, he fell sound asleep.

CHAPTER 74

A week later, the APB still hadn't turned up either Butler or Reynolds. The FBI had continued their reluctant cooperation with the Chicago PD. Their case against Reynolds was rock solid given the evidence they'd found at his home office and the false trail he'd left about a fishing trip. They'd also traced his criminal activities to the assumed name, airline ticket to France, and the property he'd bought there.

McNally's team executed all search warrants for Butler by the book, so Rouse had been treating them like war heroes. But he didn't fool anyone into believing his changed attitude would be permanent. It had everything to do with Area 5 Violent Crimes Division saving his worthless ass. Again. Nevertheless, the former tension eased some, and Rouse settled back into his usual state of benign apathy.

McNally understood the Feds difficulty in discovering or sharing information that would have helped him to track Butler across state lines. Their National Crime Information Center (NCIC) still suffered from a shortage of complete data. And he figured they might still feel the sting of rejection from when Rouse, in a moment of righteous bluster, told them to "butt out." Rouse took full credit for solving the Slugger case, and now that the superintendent backed him, he'd begun parading around the offices like a peacock.

McNally was leaving when Rouse called him into his office.

Petrocelli smiled. "Oh boy, good time for me to get a cup of coffee." He spun on his heels and whistled all the way to the break room.

"Chicken shit," McNally grumbled under his breath. He entered the shuttered office, expecting the worst.

"Close the door, McNally," Rouse ordered without lifting his eyes.

The familiar curtain of nonchalance settled in on McNally's face as he sat down facing Rouse. "You wanted to see me, Commander? Here I am."

Rouse appeared agitated, fidgeting in his chair. "Yeah, I wanted to say I read your report and liked the job you and your team did on the Butler searches. By the book. The way I like it. I also finished reading the report covering all the evidence you collected. This guy's a major loony tune, and goddamn it, we've got to get him before he kills again... You understand? I won't tolerate any letup until you make the collar."

McNally noticed a rising red tide crawling up Rouse's neck. If this was one of his backhanded compliments, it would be the hardest thing he did all week.

McNally smiled. "So am I right in assuming the superintendent is passing out favors and we may be in line for a special 'attaboy'?" He slid farther down in the commander's wooden victims' chair. "I mean, because you look uncomfortable right now." He didn't wait for an answer. "So let's stow the bullshit, shall we? We haven't made the collar yet, which makes this slap on the back a tad premature."

McNally dropped his usual calm demeanor as a rush of angry words tumbled from his mouth. "No disrespect intended, sir, but you've been riding our backs and throwing road blocks in our way since this investigation started. Now you expect us to perform back-flips and thank *you* for saving *your* ass? So you throw us a bone and expect us to give you a sincere and hearty hail to the chief? Ed, I think it's way past time you woke up and noticed the steam rising off that pile of dung. We did what we did because it's our job. That's all. Like it? Don't like it? I don't give two shits. But please don't pretend you're someone else now, and we'll reciprocate. Trust me, it's better for you, better for me, better for the entire department."

The blood had drained from Rouse's face. "The...the mayor's office has leaned on the superintendent, and his assistant followed orders and leaned on me. You're the last person I need to tell about shit rolling downhill!"

McNally sensed it was time to make his exit. "Nope, haven't got the time. But now I've got more important things to take care of, such as finding Butler before he kills again. Anything else, sir?"

"Yeah. I'm to advise you that our little problem in Chinatown, officially now, never happened. You're exonerated. There'll be nothing in your file about it. Let me add that I hope we can put all that behind us now—wipe the slate so to speak." Blue veins bulged on his forehead. He leaned across his desk, staring fixedly at McNally, and continued, "Well, *they* may forget what went down, but after this little show of yours, I can see you're still the same prick you always were. Nothing's changed. But I'm done with you for now. Keep me advised, McNally, or I'll bring a hammer down on your head so fast you'll think it's Tuesday for a week. You got that? Now get the fuck out of my office!"

After McNally left, Rouse retrieved his pint of single malt scotch from his desk drawer. He downed a healthy gulp of the burning liquid.

Cocky son of a bitch! Ungrateful bastard. He took a deep pull on the bottle.

The moment McNally left Rouse's office, he took a deep breath and refocused his attention back onto the case.

Petrocelli walked over to McNally. "Kyle, I've been thinking, if this guy's that far off the reservation, he may not quit until he gets to Dr. Hartley."

"I've thought of that."

"How's she holding up?"

"She's not."

While Butler's whereabouts remained unknown, Mykel was in danger. Her normal routine, along with their love life, was history now. The constant police protection during her days and nights spent sequestered in Kyle's apartment took a severe toll on their relationship. Former nights filled with excitement and ardor gave way to the realities of fear and pressure. They became uncommunicative and increasingly short with each other by night.

Mykel continued to believe that somehow, some way, Butler would get to her. She snapped at Kyle and began to develop a compulsive habit of rubbing her jaw and wringing her hands. She complained about the futility of having her every move watched. With twenty-four-hour surveillance, the protection made her feel more like a criminal than a victim. Her loss of independence and freedom magnified the tension between them.

Kyle's concern for her ballooned into his own version of compulsion. He'd begun obsessing on her daily routines and the level of protection provided by the department. They both realized it must end. Something had to give.

CHAPTER 75

A lush pine forest surrounded the estate, six miles from the nearest town in Kane County. Untended bushes and ground cover now concealed the narrow stone path that twisted this way and that through the privately owned woods. Once an equestrian trail, the long-neglected path peeked from the dense undergrowth that grew wild between the trees. It reached for miles from the manicured grounds of the estate through the tall towering pines, leaving only shadows and darkness in the densest part of the forest. It ran along the property line perimeter, then wound its way back toward the estate. At one point, the path paralleled an old service road that ran through the south end of the property and branched east toward two small shuttered buildings, the only remaining remnants of the original mink slaughter houses.

Where it could, bright sun radiated an early season warmth on this balmy day. Each day, the forest came to life with its own characteristic sounds. The songbirds had finished building their nests among the maples and tall oaks that edged the property. The squirrels chattered as they foraged for food, and a vigilant red fox stalked a wary rabbit that hopped between the shadows. A dove called for his mate, his cooing melody rising above the tranquility of the forest. The plush moss carpet that covered the ground quenched its insatiable thirst from a recent rainfall and stretched broadly among the clusters of red and yellow *Russula* mushrooms. There were a myriad of caps with their tiny umbrellas scattered along the path, increasing numbers among the rotting trunks of the giant fallen trees.

A distant sound interrupted the natural serenity of the woodland, barely audible yet distinctively incongruous with the usual buzz of forest sounds. A mournful, hollow wail of despair unfurled into the still air. It was a human cry of inconsolable misery and desolation coming from one suffering through the final stages of hopelessness. Its echo carried with it the awful portend of imminent death.

CHAPTER 76

Mykel caught herself, recalling the time of their first romantic encounter with each other. Three days later, she was at home, frustrated and even a little angry that she hadn't heard from Kyle since. He'd promised to call, and she'd begun to fear she was falling into that most hated category—the one-night stand. She remembered being ready to start a knife-throwing competition in her kitchen when she heard a knock at her front door.

She'd ordered Chinese food delivered, and when the knock came, that was whom she expected. She opened the door with a slight scowl on her face. However, it morphed into a combined look of surprise and pleasure. Kyle stood in front of her, holding a bottle of Courvoisier with his eyebrows arched and a half-smile of contrition on his face.

He explained that his preoccupation with the Slugger case was the reason for his neglect, but he offered repeated apologies for his tardiness. She forgave him and welcomed him into her home. They spent the rest of the evening relaxing and enjoying each other's company. It began with them sitting on the floor, eating the Chinese food and laughing together with Patricia Barber's soft, sultry jazz playing on the radio, and concluded with hours of passionate and playful lovemaking.

She was sequestered in his apartment now, and that memory seemed years ago.

* * *

Kyle poured himself a long shot of Maker's Mark over ice and collapsed in the chair next to the fireplace. It had been eight days since Butler and Reynolds went missing. He'd arrived home after hours of interviews, compiling reports, and satisfying the absurd whims of Rouse. He closed his eyes and laid his head back when he heard Mykel enter the room.

Unconsciously, his muscles tensed, and he winced at the litany of complaints he felt sure was coming his way. It had become a diffi-cult task over the past few days to remain patient with her. Though he did everything possible to alleviate her fears, she was confident Butler would find and kill her. He'd run out of any new reassurances to offer her. And at this moment, he didn't have the energy to try.

He didn't need to open his eyes to recognize she stood in front of him.

"We've got to talk."

Her voice was gentle and beseeching. He opened his eyes. The soft yellow glow from the table lamp was behind her, and he saw her exquisite form beneath her sheer silk robe. As she stood before him, he recalled how warm and sweet his life had been only days ago. A rift had crept into their relationship and stood between them both now.

Damn Butler.

He watched her teeth bite into her lower lip. Her eyes were soft and vulnerable, but they'd begun to show light shadows beneath. A familiar stab of guilt struck him. Butler should be behind bars by now. That was what it would take to ease her fears.

"Kyle, this can't continue. I'm getting stir-crazy, and I can tell you're starting to feel more like a prison guard than my lover. I can see this leading to our ruin, and that would be devastating to me. So now I've got to insist, for both our sakes, that you arrange for a return to my home and to work without an armed detail. I've got to claim some normalcy back in my life. At least with that piece of normal back, I can breathe again. So please do whatever it takes, okay? My fears are a distant second to my claustrophobia right now. I hope you understand. But regardless, I've got to have my day-to-day freedom of movement back." She heaved a heavy sigh, tears tumbling down her cheeks now as she cast her eyes downward, wringing her hands.

Kyle stood, wrapping his arms around her trembling body.

"Mykel, I understand. And although it chafes against my best instincts, I'll arrange tomorrow for a limited team to get you back and forth from your place to your office. I'd prefer to secure you here. Nevertheless, I'll do what you ask. But try not to worry about Butler. I know we haven't found him yet, but we'll get him before he can hurt you. I swear it."

CHAPTER 77

Detective Peterson collided with Petrocelli in the doorway. "Sorry, man. I'm on my way to give McNally a message."

"I'll give it to him," Petrocelli snapped impatiently.

"What message?" McNally asked, walking up behind them.

"Some lady's been calling for you since early this morning. Wouldn't leave a name but said it was important and that she'd call back."

"Dr. Hartley?"

"No, sir. I'd recognize her voice."

"Hey, McNally, call on line two," Roy Ramirez yelled through the open door.

McNally went over to his desk, picked up the receiver, and punched the flashing button. He listened in silence to the caller. "Yes, thank you. Can we come over to pick it up now?" He nodded at Petrocelli and looked at his watch. "We can be there in thirty minutes."

"That was Marian Clayton, Tony. She has Karen's diary."

"What? How?" Tony asked.

"She didn't say. Grab your coat. She has a story to tell."

CHAPTER 78

Petrocelli knocked on the front door of Marian Clayton's home. When she answered, McNally had difficulty concealing his surprise at how much thinner she appeared even in the few weeks since he'd met her. She appeared pale with deep purple shadows beneath dull, lifeless eyes.

She offered them a frail smile. "Please, gentlemen, come in and sit."

"When you called earlier, you said that you had Karen's diary," McNally said.

She lowered her head. "Yes, I do." She motioned for them to sit in the chairs across from her. A large padded envelope lay on the coffee table between them.

She drew in a deep breath and picked up a white envelope next to the package. As he waited for her to begin, Kyle listened to the mechanical ticking of the grandfather clock in the entry hall. Here in this house as we watched her slow, deliberate movements, time seemed to have slowed perceptibly.

"Is that the diary, Mrs. Clayton? This must be difficult for you, but if you'll give us the book, we can—"

She raised her palms up, waving her arms. "No, please." She straightened an imaginary wrinkle in her wool skirt and lifted her eyes to them. "You, gentlemen, are busy, but there are a few things I must explain to you. There were details of Karen's life I did not share with you before. I withheld them because I couldn't imagine they would have any bearing on your search for her killer." She paused and began daubing her cheeks with a handkerchief.

To bring her back to her story, McNally interjected, "But now you feel it might?"

"Yes." Her eyes darted between the two detectives. "I must tell you everything I can—for Karen and for myself. So please bear with me."

She expelled a deep sigh, and her strength seemed renewed as she folded her hands primly on her lap. "A messenger delivered this large package and letter several days ago. It was to be hand-delivered, unopened, to the detectives investigating my daughter's murder. Under no circumstances should anyone else read its contents. By its size, I recognized that it must be Karen's diary. It came from my father.

"Per his instructions, I am delivering the package to you. I apologize for the delay in contacting you, but these past several days, I've been dealing with a great deal of pain and remorse. The letter disturbed me tremendously. Most of its contents are personal, being of little interest to anyone but myself. However, there is something I must tell you. John Marshfield sent the letter and package."

"CAITA's John Marshfield, the philanthropist?" Tony asked, confused.

"Yes. CAITA is one of his many achievements I wasn't aware of. Also, he is my father and Karen's grandfather."

This revelation took both detectives by surprise. McNally had tried to connect Karen Clayton and Marshfield, but he never believed it to be more than an employer-employee relationship. They'd learned from the FBI that Senator Reynolds had been siphoning donation money from Marshfield's contributors, but they were unaware of any deeper connection. This was a significant new twist.

Kyle scanned the room, feeling sorry for Marian Clayton. She lived well but was not well-off. Her furniture, though comfortable, was threadbare, and her small home seemed hardly big enough for herself, much less for she and Karen—hardly the way he expected the daughter and granddaughter of a wealthy financier to live.

"Please go on."

She read the questions in their eyes and smiled. "You must understand, my father and I are both stubborn people. For reasons he explained in his letter, he kept his relationship with Karen from me." She laughed softly. "Imagine that. All these years, and he thought I would be the one unable to forgive him." She shook her head. "So much time. All wasted."

She held her handkerchief to her nose and sighed before continuing. "I was young, nineteen, a sophomore at Valparaiso University. Being away from my father for the first time, I was immature but had no idea just how naive I was. I worked hard to keep my grades up so I wouldn't have to return home. You understand, I loved my father, but after my mother died, I became his whole reason for living. He smothered me with his protection, and I waited for that day I'd break free. College became my first chance for independence."

She hesitated and offered them something to drink. When they declined, she continued, "I read in the newspaper about Senator Reynolds's disappearance. Is it possible that there may be a connection between the senator's disappearance and Karen's death? That's the impression I've gotten."

"May we please see the letter?" McNally asked.

"Please believe me when I tell you there is nothing in the letter but a short paragraph referring to Senator Reynolds, which I will read to you in a moment. Karen told me that the senator had been CAITA's most powerful political advocate. I never...my father, the founder of CAITA." She wiped a stray tear from her cheek. "I never realized it. Karen's grandfather and I had a horrible rift before she was born, and since then, I knew nothing about his life, and I thought, he didn't care about mine."

"I'm so sorry, Mrs. Clayton, but I must insist on taking the letter with me. I'll make a copy of it and return it to you."

"In all those years, neither one of you spoke to the other?" Petrocelli asked.

"Please let me explain. Then I think you'll understand why. During my second semester at college, I met a young man, and we fell in love. We had discussed marriage, and he begged me to tell my father, to secure his blessing. I knew my father would never approve of such a marriage. Karen's father did not have a background worthy of a Marshfield.

"I lied to my fiancé and said that my father had given his blessings but couldn't attend the ceremony. We married in the campus chapel with a few friends. At two months pregnant with Karen, I realized I had to tell my father I'd married and that he'd be a grandfather. Two months later, I told my husband I had to go home to sign some insurance papers for my father's lawyer. I had decided not to wait any longer to tell him.

"There was a horrible scene. My father demanded that we annul our marriage. I refused. He promised to cut me from his will and leave me penniless." She smiled at the detectives. "I thought I was so brave, heroic. I stood before my father and dared him to break up my marriage. After I returned from that weekend with my father, I received a letter from him. He had not only removed my entitlement to the inheritance, but he also blocked my trust fund and took the jewelry my mother had left for me and told me he'd sell it at auction.

"It devastated me. During that weekend, I not only deceived my new husband but also destroyed the relationship and the life I had with my father. I refused to tell my husband the truth for some time. When I did, he supported me and assured me that my father would forgive me when we brought him his grandchild. I lived for that moment. I missed my father and wished for nothing more than to share the joy of sharing his grandchild with him."

She looked away as she began to cry and her lower lip trembled. "But it never happened. He refused to speak with me when I called about the birth of his granddaughter. I left word with the housekeeper. I'd heard no word from him again until yesterday, when I received this letter.

"Back then, I wanted to call my father but was frightened. Regrettably, I never did. Six months later, my husband died from a sudden heart attack. I thought the insurance policy he left paid for our subsistence—that is, until now. You see, my husband stopped making payments to the insurance company, and they dropped our policy. It has been my father who has been supporting Karen and me all these years. He provided his money to us, using what I believed to be an insurance trust fund. Those same monthly checks allowed me to buy this home, get Karen through college, and put food on our table. Karen knew and never told me. My father explained in the letter that one of the conditions of his continued support was that Karen never divulge the source of our income," she said barely above a whisper.

"It must have been difficult," McNally said.

She nodded. "That brings me back to the reason I called you. As I said, my father requested that I contact the investigating officers and hand them this package with the stipulation I not open it. I've honored his request and am giving it to you." She handed the padded envelope to McNally. "I wanted to speak with him before delivering this to you, but I can't reach him."

She refolded the letter and handed it to Kyle. "I'm extremely worried about him and what he might have done. I fear for his safety and pray that you can help him. He implies that he knows who killed Karen, though I don't see how that's possible." She rose from her seat. "Please help him, Detectives. It would be terrible if he was..." The tears rolled freely down her cheeks now and fell like liquid crystals onto her handkerchief.

The detectives rose at the same time. McNally picked up the package. "I'll have someone check on him for you. I'm sure he'll be contacting you soon. Thank you so much for your help, Mrs. Clayton."

As soon as they returned to the car, Petrocelli tore open the taped end of the package. He pulled out a red book and read the inscription, "Diary of Karen Ann Clayton. So Marshfield's the grandfather. That one caught me off guard."

"Not only that. He's connected to Reynolds, who's connected to Butler, who's the antagonist and key villain in this four-act play. And now three of our leading actors are MIA. We've still got work to do. Start at the back. Scan the last days before her murder. We'll find some answers there."

CHAPTER 79

Tony began reading aloud from Karen's diary.

May 17
Chi-Tech investigation completed. Relieved to find no clear signs of animal research. Had dinner with Grandpa last night. Tried to convince him to contact Mother. He refused. Keeps telling me it's in her best interest. It makes him so sad. Promised to keep his secret, but it's difficult for me because I love them both. Hate this deception. Won't give up. They're both so stubborn... and so miserable.

May 18
Had dinner with Frank. Told him I gave my notice at Chi-Tech. Told him my studies were suffering and I couldn't handle both the job and school. Will continue my work for CAITA, however. He asked me to marry him. What! Never even slept with him, never loved him. Told him we were friends, nothing more. He cried and told me he loved me and I'd been leading him on. Wouldn't do that. Then his voice changed. Weird and threatening.

May 19
Didn't go out or answer my phone today. Frank called several times, crying into the machine, begging me to see him. It's bad. Not sure what to do. For the past couple of days, I've had a sense that someone's watching me. Sure of it now! Phone hang-ups all night. Tried to call Grandpa.

May 20
Someone keeps calling. They just breathe on the line, scaring the shit out of me! And that feeling someone's watching me won't go away. Called police. They said they can't help until someone commits a crime. What about the stalking law? Who is stalking me? Frank? Would he hurt me? Whom do I tell? Mother's not strong enough. Grandpa hasn't returned my calls. Sense someone is close. Afraid to be alone. I will stay with Mother tonight. Am I being paranoid?

May 21
Frank continues to call and harass me. Sense anger beneath his whining, and it frightens me. Mother said he calls her and tells her how much he loves me. He told her our relationship is serious. I'm pissed about that. Get a life, Frank! Fuck it, we can't even be friends now. He says I'm the only one that calms the demons in his head. What demons? Hope he doesn't find out about CAITA job or ties to the investigation at Chi-Tech.

May 22
Time to cut ties with Frank. Fuckin' weirdo! I'm at my wit's end. He called again. Told him let's talk. Gonna tell him can't see him again. Don't

even want to be friends with him. Want my life back! Frank begged to come over and talk. Said no! He'd never leave. Too much a creeper! Hoped to end this, and so I relented and told him I would come by his place tomorrow.

May 23
Went to Frank's apartment today—biggest mistake of my life! Now he thinks I love him because I came over. Wouldn't listen. Fuckin' freak! Didn't want to stay. Tried again to make him understand. Said he had something important to tell me. The phone rang, and he went to the other room to answer it. He began screaming angrily, so I picked up the extension. The other man was mad as hell and yelling too. Frank threatened him. Kept calling him senator and laughing. Horrible laughing. Senator Reynolds? Grandpa's senator? Threatened to expose this "senator." Tell everyone about some scheme with the CAITA money. At first, couldn't put the phone down. Scared shitless! Frank sounded crazy with rage. Said he would kill the senator. I hung up the phone and ran out, fearing for my life!

May 23 (evening)
Writing this entry from the school library. Too afraid to stay in class. Need time to think and too afraid to go home. Can't go home! I'm giving my diary to the librarian and have asked her to mail it to Grandpa. He will know what to do. Will stay at Mother's tonight and move to Grandpa's tomorrow. I'm certain Frank doesn't know about Grandpa. I'll be safe at Cedarwood. Got to get away from crazy, weird Frank!

CHAPTER 80

Kyle sat in stony silence, considering the diary. The muscles in his jaw were tight as he imagined the last few terrifying hours of Karen Clayton's life.

Tony interrupted him, "Kyle, she made that final entry the day of her murder—"

Kyle interjected, "That proves his motive for killing her. He loved her, and she posed a threat to him. She was the only person who knew his secret about blackmailing Reynolds and might tell. That also explains the different MO used with her.

"And now we've got evidence that Butler extorted money from the senator. On the same day, Marshfield discovered Butler murdered his granddaughter, he found out Reynolds had been skimming from the CAITA accounts for years. What a shit storm of lies, deceptions, and betrayals."

"But was Butler involved in Reynolds' disappearance? That's what the Feebs thought," Tony said.

"There's a problem with that, Tony. I suspect after Marshfield realized that both men were responsible for the two biggest losses in his life, he did something about it. And I don't think it's a coincidence that both men disappeared on the same day.

"It's time to talk to Marshfield. Radio dispatch, and ask them for an address and directions to his estate. And tell them to contact the Kane County sheriff's office and have them meet us there.

Don't tell them anything more than it involves an ongoing homicide investigation."

He stomped on the gas pedal and headed west on the Interstate 88. It would take almost an hour to get to Marshfield's estate outside Sugar Grove.

"So Marshfield found out that Reynolds was scamming him?"

"I think so… I believe after reading Karen's diary, he went back over CAITA's financial records and discovered how Reynolds did it. The more I think about it, the more I'm convinced that Marshfield is involved in the disappearances of both men."

"Now we've learned Reynolds tapped Marshfield and Butler tapped Reynolds. And now Marshfield likely kidnapped both Butler *and* Reynolds." Petrocelli laughed abruptly. "Assuming they're all still alive, why don't we put the three of them in a room and give 'em Glocks? Damn, sometimes I crack me up."

"Yeah, yeah, you're a riot. I don't want the county cops to do anything stupid before we get there," McNally grumbled. "I just hope they wait until we get there."

McNally, following the curve of the expressway, was always amazed how the scenery morphed from urban dust-gray neighborhoods to pastoral green countryside within a few miles.

"What's eating you, Mac?" Petrocelli said, staring wide-eyed at the road as he fumbled with his seat belt when they passed eighty-five miles per hour. "Looks like we've identified the bad guys, right? Now all we got to do is turn over the rocks and watch 'em slither out."

"What's eating at me is that Butler's not behind bars yet." McNally noticed the smell in the closed car for the first time. "Christ. I still smell fucking cigars. It stinks in here. Crack your window."

"Okay, I get it. This is about Dr. Hartley, isn't it?"

"No, this is about the fact that my last partner was a pig and always ran his mouth, asking too many questions."

Petrocelli cracked his window and slunk deeper into his seat. He'd been around McNally enough to recognize when to act invisible, and this was that time.

CHAPTER 81

They turned onto the long gravel road leading into the estate. Tony viewed the overhanging tree branches of the shaded woods on either side of the road and shivered. He had a sudden sense of foreboding that this day would end badly. "This is a goddamn forest preserve, and I think you're on the bike path. You sure we're heading the right way?"

"These are the directions dispatch relayed. North on Woodgrove off Plano Road. This is Woodgrove, and this is north."

They passed three "Private Property" signs as they drove down the winding road through the woods. The gravel road turned into a cement drive leading to a sprawling brick-and-cedar house.

"Nice little cottage, huh?" Tony said, amazed by the enormous size of the house and surrounding grounds. "What did he do for a living?"

"Good. The county boys aren't here yet. Go around back and check for cars in the garage. I'll see if anyone's home."

"Aren't we waiting for backup?" Tony asked.

"They'll be along. It was professional courtesy. Somehow, some way, things always seem to go south when another agency gets involved. Don't worry. I promise I won't step on any toes unless they try to walk in front of me."

"Who's worried? I didn't want to see you get hosed by Rouse again, that's all," Tony quipped.

"Thanks, but I'm not the one on the losing end of those skirmishes."

Petrocelli headed for the back of the house, leaving McNally knocking on the front door. Nobody answered. He tried the doorknob to see if it would open. It did not. For a moment, he toyed with the idea of picking the lock but, thinking about Commander Rouse's reaction, decided against it. Instead he raised the large brass lion head knocker and let it drop.

"Come on, Marshfield, be home," McNally said. He turned, hearing two county sheriff's squads pulling up behind his on the immense circular drive. McNally didn't have much experience with rural county police, but he was inclined to regard them as a bunch of cowboys. Experience taught him to be skeptical of any interlopers, invited or not. Fortunately, in this case, jurisdiction didn't matter because it involved a murder. This group of uniformed sheriff's deputies would be welcome to tag along, nothing more. He put on his best take-charge expression and walked to the first waiting squad.

He leaned into the window of the white and orange squad. "Who's in charge here?"

A square-jawed black man wearing dark sunglasses hidden beneath the wide brim of his hat smiled at McNally. "I'm Sergeant Hoover. What's this all about?"

McNally relaxed a little and identified himself, explaining the reasons for his being at the Marshfield estate. He needed to question John Marshfield regarding Frank Butler's disappearance, a suspect in several interstate homicides. He also recounted the probable connection between Marshfield, Reynolds, and Butler. He ended by asking the sergeant, though not optimistically, for his full cooperation.

Though it surprised McNally, Sergeant Hoover nodded and asked what he needed his men to do. McNally decided he might have to rethink his earlier opinion of these county cops. Then he asked that Sergeant Hoover send his men to search the immediate vicinity. Sergeant Hoover complied by dispatching another one of the deputies from a squad car. The older one grumbled, but after Sergeant Hoover shot him a stern glance, he shrugged and turned to leave.

McNally and the sergeant had knocked again when they heard another car approach. A battered and neglected Ford Torino station wagon sputtered and groaned to a squealing stop. Black smoke belched from the tailpipe and filled the air with a putrid stench. McNally and the sergeant coughed as they approached the car.

An elderly gray-haired woman with a round face and worried blue eyes slid out of the passenger side of the wagon. The driver remained behind the wheel. McNally watched her slow approach, wondering who she was and if she knew Marshfield. If she was family, they wouldn't need to break down the front door. She shuffled her short thick legs toward him. She had gray hair pulled to the back of her head in a tight bun emphasizing her plump face. The soft blue eyes and a small turned-up nose softened her aged features. With a frown of disdain, she eyed the sheriff's deputies first and then McNally.

"What's happened?" she asked as she scanned McNally's credentials. "Has something happened to Mr. Marshfield?"

McNally raised a hand to calm her down. "Please, ma'am, I need to ask your name and what your business is here." He softened his voice. "Are you a member of the family?"

The woman's face reddened to a deep scarlet hue, and her cheeks puffed up like balloons. She sputtered, "Oh, gracious, no! I'm Agnes Clancy, young man. I have been Mr. Marshfield's housekeeper since before you were born, would be my guess. Mr. Marshfield doesn't like visitors who arrive unannounced, so you'd better tell me why you're here, or I must ask you to leave."

McNally was opening his mouth to speak to the flustered woman when she interrupted, "If you're soliciting for a donation to the County Police Association, I can save you time by saying that my employer is generous with those charities but never allows solicitors at his door. The 'Private Road' sign is quite clear!"

McNally heard background snickers, and the sergeant cast a warning look toward his waiting deputy. "I apologize for the intrusion, Mrs. Clancy, but we are here to ask your employer a few questions about an investigation. We shouldn't need much of his time."

"Well, why didn't you say so instead of giving me such a fright? I can't be straining my old heart this way." She cast a wary eye toward the two deputies as she fumbled in her purse for the keys to the house. "Oh dear, I hope this has nothing to do with the death of his granddaughter. Bless her soul. He took it hard. She was the light of his life, poor man. He hasn't been the same since. Brooding is all he does. He doesn't go out much and never accepts calls. With all his sorrow, he still thought of me and insisted that I go ahead with a long weekend visit to my family. I told him I would only go if he promised to get back to his work while I traveled."

"How long have you been away?" McNally asked.

She began to clasp and unclasp her hands. "Only a few days. I never should have left. I wouldn't have considered going if my daughter wasn't ill. Oh my, I hope nothing has happened to him since I left."

As Agnes Clancy worked the key into the lock, Petrocelli returned from the rear of the house. He glanced curiously at the stocky woman taking up the whole space of the doorway and whispered to McNally that there were two cars in the garage.

Surprised, she said, "Two cars? Mr. Marshfield has three cars. Oh, what a relief. Mr. Marshfield must be out. Please, you must come back later."

"Forgive me, Mrs. Clancy, but we can't leave until we are sure your employer isn't home. It will only take another moment of your time and save us from making another trip back here in an hour."

She grumbled something in Gaelic under her breath. McNally understood what she said. She knew Mr. Marshfield would be angry at the intrusion when she turned the knob to the front door. She blocked the entire doorway and sternly instructed the officers to wait outside until she announced them.

After several minutes had passed, he began to pace. "What in God's name is taking her so long?"

A high-pitched scream pierced the air. McNally and Petrocelli pulled out their guns and bolted through the front door, racing across the foyer and through the wide double doors, where the screams grew louder. Two deputies followed close on their heels.

They found Mrs. Clancy crumpled on the floor, sobbing into her hands. Behind her, slumped over the top of the large desk, John Marshfield's head lay in a pool of dark blood. One arm had fallen to his side, and the other hand lay on the desk next to his head, clutching a long-barrel pistol. Detective Petrocelli immediately escorted the hysterical Mrs. Clancy out of the room as McNally slipped on his black crime scene gloves and stood looking down at the body and the surrounding scene. He asked Sergeant Hoover if a couple of his deputies could assist Detective Petrocelli in searching the house. Though the body was cold, he placed two fingers at the pulse point on Marshfield's neck.

As soon as the body was found, Sergeant Hoover followed crime scene protocol and told McNally that he had notified his watch commander. The commander reported back that their crime scene unit and the county medical examiner were en route to the scene. McNally guessed that Marshfield hadn't been dead over thirty-six hours. The placement of the body and gun at the scene suggested suicide, but he'd wait for the examiner's call. On a second look, he realized that this had been the same man he'd seen at Karen Clayton's funeral.

He inspected the pistol without touching it and identified it to be an antique Colt revolver, from the turn of the century. An open letter was next to his bloodied hand, and he read the message, no doubt left for Marian Clayton. There were only two words on the page: "Forgive me." Marshfield's blood stained the bottom half, but McNally knew those two were the only words written.

Tony walked over to the bookcase and found a brown leather box. "Looks like this is where the gun came from."

On the front of the open case, there was a gold engraved plate with the inscription "For my son, John." The soft red folds of the velvet lining had indents formed to accommodate two long barrel pistols. They examined the gun in Marshfield's hand and identified it as the missing gun that matched its twin in the case.

While they waited for the ME to arrive, McNally went to speak with Agnes Clancy. He found her weeping in a large adjoining room.

"Mrs. Clancy. I'm sorry to bother you, but I need to ask you a few questions."

"That's all right, Detective," she said, blowing her nose in her hankie.

"Did Mr. Marshfield give you any hint he might want to take his own life? Did he say or do anything that might have led you to believe he might have been considering suicide?"

"Certainly not!" she wailed. "Mr. Marshfield is a kind man without an enemy in the world. He'd lost his granddaughter and suffered since then. I never should have left him. Oh! This is all my fault."

"You are not to blame," McNally said to console her and quiet her hysteria. "I need you to try to remember what happened the last few days before you left."

She lifted her head and dabbed her eyes. Instantly her hands flew to her mouth. "I remember one thing. He received a package in the mail a few days before I left, and it seemed to upset him terribly."

McNally knew the package she spoke of was Karen Clayton's diary.

"I shouldn't have left him," Agnes Clancy cried renewed tears, "but he insisted that I go. He told me he would be all right. He said he needed some time alone." Her eyes begged the detective to understand. "People need time to mourn."

"Yes, yes, Mrs. Clancy." McNally helped her off the couch and asked one of the waiting deputies to take her back to her car.

As she departed through the door, the detectives heard her repeat over and over, "I should have been here."

Forty-five minutes later, the county examiner arrived with the sheriff's Crime Scene Unit and began his preliminary examination of the body. When Kyle returned to Marshfield's office, he found a small Asian man bent over the body, taking fingernail scrapings and placing them in a clear plastic bag. He chattered like a squirrel into the small hand recorder he had set on the desk. Small fingers zipped the evidence bag shut, and he placed it in his medical case. When McNally approached, the examiner straightened and turned to speak with him. The top of his head came to Kyle's chin.

His eyes closed and almost disappeared into his face when he smiled. "Dr. Kurosuchi. Nice to meet you. And you are the Chicago PD officer, correct?"

"Yes, Doctor. Detective McNally. Anything you can share with me yet, Doctor? Do we call this a suicide?"

He flashed a toothy smile. "Yep, the melon's gone. Death was instantaneous. Suicide. No question. I'll complete the autopsy as soon as I get the body back on my examining table, but I can tell you this man ended his own life."

"Please explain."

The doctor bobbed his head and, in quick puppet-like movements, gestured with his arm. "Be happy to. Please step closer." He positioned himself behind Marshfield and on the right side of the body. He plucked a pencil off the desk to use as a pointer. "The gun in the right hand. See here?" Kurosuchi asked.

"Yes."

"It was a contact shot, meaning he held the barrel to the side of his head against his temple. The bullet entered here, right at the temple, and exited here." He pointed the pencil tip close to the exit hole left on the forehead. "The blood sprays correspond with the way the bullet entered and exited the head." He smiled slyly at McNally. "I found powder traces on the hand, and there are burns at the point of entry in the head from the hot gas that left the barrel. Well, you can see where it broke the skin open to form the starlike pattern." His finger traced the burn ring. "This shows he shot himself at point-blank range."

The doctor pointed to the blood on the left side of the desk and carpet and continued, "The trajectory of the blood splatter pattern is consistent with my findings." He lifted the right hand on the body and put the barrel of the gun to the open wound. "And there you have it."

"Thank you, Doctor."

"Blood sprays, trajectory, position of body, and a dozen other things tell us this was done by his own hand. That's what you'll read in my report," Kurosuchi declared with confidence.

"Right," McNally replied.

A tall thin CSU tech stepped in front of the desk, holding a camera. "Sir, we need to finish taking the pictures."

"Please, go ahead," McNally said, moving away from the desk.

Dr. Kurosuchi followed McNally. "It's a messy way to die, but almost always effective." He left the detectives and returned to instruct the cameraman on the pictures he needed for his report.

"So where are we now?" Petrocelli asked.

"We still have a missing senator and lawyer. I think we can assume Marshfield discovered he had two rotten apples floating in his barrel. Let's walk it one step further. I'm now convinced he took matters into his own hands with both Butler and Reynolds. It's a little surprising, but not beyond the bounds of behavior from a grieving, despondent grandfather who'd found out he'd been scammed by a politician he trusted. We need to comb the house and the grounds for evidence confirming I'm right. Lots of places around here to bury the bodies if that's what he did."

"Agnes Clancy said Marshfield owned three cars. Where's the third?" Petrocelli asked.

"Get the make and model, and put out an APB on it."

CHAPTER 82

"Detective McNally!"

He turned as one of the sheriff's deputies made his way through the group of crime scene technicians. He was panting from running and spoke between gasps for air.

The deputy flung his arm toward the door. "Sergeant Hoover sent me to get you. We found a small building back in the woods. I'm supposed to bring you back with something to pry the door open or cut the lock off. It looks like a new lock."

"Okay, lead the way," McNally said, and to Tony, "Grab the bolt cutters from the car and join us at the building."

The building was the size of a large hunting cabin built from rock and mortar. There were several windows with iron mesh screens covering the openings. It had a solid oak door with a large padlock barring access into the structure. Six empty rusted wire mesh cages were in front of the building.

McNally stood next to one of the empty cages and turned to Tony. "Marshfield's daughter said this used to be a mink ranch. This must be the place where they skinned the animals and cured their pelts. Tony, hand me the bolt cutters."

The wood on the door was dry and rotted, though the padlock securing it was new. With a quick snap of the cutters, he removed the lock. McNally pushed aside thick cobwebs before entering the room with a flashlight he'd borrowed from one of the deputies. The detectives stepped into the darkened room with damp, noxious, stale air.

Several years of cobwebs and dust clung and settled along the walls and ceiling. Old lawn mowers, shovels, crates of various shapes and sizes, and even a bedspring and frame were leaning against one wall.

McNally searched the room for another door. He used the flashlight to scan every corner. He was about to tell Petrocelli to head back out when he noticed a blocked stairwell leading down to a doorway below ground level. Four stone steps led down to a smaller door that stood open a crack. The odor in the stairwell was fetid and sour. McNally pushed on the door. It groaned and creaked, scraping the floor as it swung into the room. As soon as they stepped over the threshold, their nostrils filled with the stench of decay and mold.

Petrocelli's hand flew up to cover his nose. "Jesus, what the fuck is that smell?"

"Ignore it, kid. They used to cage minks here. In Swedish, the word *mink* means 'stinking animal.' Give it a moment. You'll get used to it."

The room was long and narrow. A slop sink and long wooden counter spanned the length of one wall. A large brown spider tiptoed across his lace web that stretched from a shelf on the wall above the sink to the faucet.

"Gotta say I'm now creeped out, McNally," Tony moaned. "And you were wrong. I can still smell dead animals."

"It's the smell of something dead, but it's not mink," McNally observed. He aimed the beam above him and saw a string attached to a light bulb in the ceiling. He pulled on it, and string, light bulb, and fixture ripped away from the ceiling, followed by a cloud of dust. *Outstanding.*

"Can we get this over with?" said Tony, who coughed and sneezed at the same time. "There's nothing in here but you, me, and a few man-eating spiders with legs the size of a Christmas turkey. How about I join the others outside?"

"How about you hold your flashlight up for me so I can see where the hell I'm going?"

Petrocelli knew his whining wouldn't get him out of there any faster, but it made him feel a little better to bitch about it. Mac was on his habitual no-stone-unturned mission, and they weren't going anywhere until he had checked every square inch of this dungeon.

Three rows of cages lined the narrow low-ceiling room. These cages were smaller than the ones on the outside of the building. The detectives walked down each narrow aisle, shining the flashlight beam into each empty cage.

"Now can we go? Nothing but you, me and the hairy legged critters in here," Tony said.

"Not so fast. We need to check the cages in the back."

They proceeded down the last row of cages.

Petrocelli began gagging from the worsening smell. "Good Christ! This is really disgusting." He covered his nose and mouth with his handkerchief. "So much for that theory of yours. Mac, this stink's likely to stick to me for a week."

"Just zip it and shine your light on the cages. We're close to the end."

They walked a few steps farther.

"Christ! Can't you smell that?" Tony stopped and began dry-heaving.

Kyle said, "Yeah, we must be close."

Tony groaned, "Close to what? The gateway to hell? You sure you don't want to get the counties to finish up? I'm ready to blow chunks."

"I can tell you I prefer this to that male magnet aftershave you use... Hold it," McNally snapped. He stopped midstep, forcing Tony to run into his back.

"What the hell!" Petrocelli groaned.

"There's something here."

"What? What the fuck is that?"

"Tony, may I introduce you to the formerly illustrious Senator Wayne Reynolds."

The naked body of Reynolds, twisted and misshapen, stared back at them. Sunken eyes bulged from a lifeless gray distorted face. Bruised fingers curled around holes in the wire mesh cage told a tale of his final struggle for freedom before dying. His wrists and ankles, shackled with iron bracelets and chains, were locked to the floor of the cage. Next to the body were several heaps of dried human excrement. His wrists, bloodied and swollen to twice their size, had turned black below the elbow and appeared broken.

"Jesus! What a fucked-up way to die," Petrocelli said from behind his handkerchief. "I'd say Marshfield had the better exit strategy."

McNally kneeled and inspected the cage next to the one holding the senator. "This one had an occupant too. That broken chain held the shackle. Its occupant pried a bar out and used it to get free. There's fresh blood on the floor of the cage." He held up the lock from the broken cage door. Then with an ironic tone, he said, "I assume the former tenant was Mr. Frank Butler, Esquire. The old man had an ironic idea of justice for them. Looks like the senator hasn't been dead long. If Butler saw it, he didn't need more motivation to break the chain on his shackles and kick his way out of here."

"Yeah, and he's likely the one who stole one of Marshfield's cars. He's got to be holed up somewhere, licking his wounds right now." Petrocelli stole another glance at the body and shivered. "He knows by now we're after him. He can't go home. But where's a bloodied, half-crazed serial killer gonna go?"

"Christ! Tony, I know where he's headed. Notify dispatch, and have them contact the officer parked on the street to go to Mykel's door and stand guard until we get there."

Cave! Cave! Deus videt.
Beware! Beware! God is watching.
—Hieronymus Bosch

CHAPTER 83

Mykel slipped her tired, aching body into the steaming water and sank deep into it and reached for the glass of wine on the edge of the bathtub. She'd been so busy over the last few days at work that there hadn't been time to relax. Squeezing the large sponge in her hand, she recalled the last time she'd seen Kyle. She'd been a total bitch, but she hoped he understood her feelings of being a prisoner in a cage.

Mykel understood that his stress was in maximum overdrive with Frank Butler still missing. She'd felt a lot of it too. She picked up the bar of soap, appreciating the soothing fragrance of vanilla, and idly began to lather her long legs.

She resigned herself to the fact that the nagging pain in her gut came from missing him.

Mykel, you've been a total idiot!

She hoped he understood, and she prayed their new relationship could weather this storm. She hadn't expected him to chase after her when she moved out of his apartment, but it hurt and disappointed her when he didn't call.

The police protection provided small comfort, but it didn't replace the safety she felt when he was by her side. More than ever, she missed his kisses and the soft touch of his hands on her body. The music heard now on her radio was no longer soft jazz but the sounds of their lovemaking. She began feeling better.

Mykel was descending into a world of semiconscious daydreaming when her instincts alerted her that she wasn't alone. A soft sound, almost imperceptible, snatched her out of her reverie. She froze and strained to hear over the music. Even though it now seemed quiet in the next room, she rose and stepped out of the tub, turned off the radio, and reached for her bathrobe. She crept toward the door.

"Is someone out there…? Kyle, is that you?"

Silence.

"If anyone is out there, answer me!"

A small sound broke the silence. Had she heard a shuffling, or was it just her imagination? Her heart pounded with shadows of nightmares bursting from her memory. Hands shaking, she tied the cord of her bathrobe around her waist. With two long strides, she reached the bathroom door and flicked the lock.

Someone was out there, just beyond the door, and was playing with her. Backing into a corner of the bathroom, she stared at the knob, looking for a sign, any sign to tell her she might just be imagining it. Her unblinking eyes watered as she stared at the knob. For an instant, she began to think her eyes and ears might have been deceiving her when she saw it turn.

Panic set in, and she searched for a way out. The glass blocks in the window above the tub were unbreakable. "Go away!" she screamed, praying one of her neighbors would alert the policeman sitting in his car on the street.

Deep within her soul, she sensed who waited on the other side of the door. When he spoke with a hoarse raspy whisper, it felt like ice water flung in her face.

"Mykel. My sweet Mykel, I've waited so long."

Her memory spun her back in time to an ugly place from her youth.

She found no solace in knowing the name of the monster scratching at her door. Her nostrils inhaled the heavy, suffocating essence of lilacs again. Mykel remembered the sickening sensation of sweaty hands on her body, and she cried, begging him to go away, "Please…leave me alone!" her voice croaked.

He began to whisper through the door, the only thing standing between her and certain death. "You're the last, my lovely Faith."

Her eyes grew wide, and her hand flew to her mouth. Bile rose in her throat, and the vision of her attacker from long ago slashed through her memory as the nightmare resurfaced.

"I've saved you for last. Soon you'll be joining your filthy, stinking girlfriends in Hades. You should be joyful to see me. I am delivering you. This is your salvation and my long-overdue gift to you." Then almost screeching, he continued, "Oh yes, I am! Yes, I will."

Her thoughts suddenly transported back to the attack that changed her life. As she sank to her knees on the floor and whimpered, her eyes swollen and shut tight, a feeling washed over her, and she realized her paralyzing fear was replaced by rage. Seconds ticked by while she listened to her attacker's fist pounding, then battering the door rhythmically until it started to splinter inch by inch, board by board. The intensity of his anger grew more violent with each crash on the door. Though her body flinched with each new onslaught, she was determined to face the monster.

He growled now, the sounds from his throat mimicking a wounded, starving animal. It was only moments before the solid wood would crack under his charge, and he would be there in the room with her, reaching and groping for her. She sensed his frustration mounting as the crashing increased in frequency and intensity. Her lungs filled with air, and she screamed, "Goooo away!"

Where had her protection gone?

Help yourself! The words echoed in her mind as the door shivered and separated from the hinges.

"No!" she screamed, realizing that only precious seconds separated her from her tormenter. But then, as the welcome adrenaline pumped through her body, she knew she wouldn't give in now and let him have his way with her, not after all the years of shame, anger, and frustration she'd lived through. She tore through her vanity drawers in search of something to use as a weapon. There would be no giving up. She remembered the hair scissors she kept on the shelf high in the linen closet. As the doorframe buckled, she knew it wouldn't withstand another blast.

Frantically, she ripped towels and cosmetics down from the shelves. Where were they? Her hand flew over the smooth, empty surface of the shelves. Tears flowed down her cheeks as her frustration mounted. Then her hand grazed the cold metal of the long steel blades, and she grabbed them, holding them securely in her palm.

One last kick, and the door would give completely. Her eyes became fixed and dilated as she planted herself deep into the corner of the bathroom. Perspiration ran down her face, and she started panting like a cornered, caged animal.

Lucky, lucky, lucky, she repeated to herself over and over. *Only one chance.*

Boom! The door shattered and fell from its hinges. Years of pent-up fury burst forth like a raging hurricane at the edge of the eye. He would not win. He would not end her. Mykel, without realizing it, had been preparing for this moment, the moment she'd confront this long-repressed menace and exact retribution. It was hers to demand. She lifted the blades high above her head and sprang across the short distance, sending the gleaming steel blades slashing through the air; they found their mark in the soft flesh of the monster's face.

"Ahheee!" he screamed, cupping his hand over the gaping wound.

Blood sprayed in every direction in a fine red mist. She lunged at him again, only to miss her mark when he dodged backward from the room. Oblivious to her fear, her mouth twisted into a threatening sneer as her body coiled itself, ready to spring again.

Eyes wide open and shocked by the level of his pain, Frank Butler emitted a deep moan, stepping farther back into the shadows of the dark bedroom, out of her line of sight.

"Come on, you pig! I'm ready for you," she hissed.

The ensuing silence turned into a deadly calm as minutes ticked by.

Where is he? She scanned the small tile-covered room, knowing the only means of escape was through the bathroom door. She continued holding the scissors high, waiting for the next attack. *Damn it, where is he? Why isn't he charging again?* She glanced down and saw the large stain of blood on the floor. *Did he leave? Or did I kill him?*

With the scissors clutched in her hand, she crept toward the open door, listening for him, praying he'd be dead or mortally wounded. She moved silently, slowly stepping into the dark bedroom. Peering through the doorway, she had to squint as the only light came from the bathroom behind her. Mykel could not see the blood trail past the edges of darkness in the bedroom, but she could see a body sprawled face down on the floor. She detected no immediate movement.

If Frank Butler hadn't died, she hoped he was unconscious. She would try to slip by him. She dared to take another step into the bedroom even when her instincts warning her not to. With only primeval courage to move her, she took a deep breath, waving the blades back and forth in front of her.

But something was wrong! She heard him. She realized the body on the floor was that of the officer guarding her place. The phantom of her nightmares still lived, now only an invisible deadly shadow. Her body froze as she sensed him watching. She tried to run, but her legs balked. She only had enough time to turn around and take one step toward the bathroom when something hard crashed against her neck and shoulder. The power of the blow propelled her with such force she flew against the wall. The pain was excruciating. Her fingers lost their grip on the scissors, and they fell to the floor. Numbness spread through her shoulder and traveled down her arm. It was broken.

Her mind screamed, *Ignore the pain! Find the scissors!*

She twisted her back and rolled over on her stomach, using her legs and her uninjured arm to drag herself along the floor toward the scissors. She pushed herself to her knees. Her trembling fingers reached for the shears. She fought waves of nausea and bit down hard on her lower lip until she tasted blood.

Oh, God! Please, God, don't let me pass out.

It moved into the room behind her. Its shadow stood over her! He sounded like a hungry animal. His broken, uneven breathing clicked in his throat, and the sound was not even remotely human. He began laughing at her as she reached for the scissors. The laughing ceased as he raised the bat over his head.

Thwump!

A burning pain shot through her ribs, and her arms gave way beneath her. She struggled for air but found it impossible because of the pressure on her chest. The force of the strike to her side rolled her over onto her back.

Whoosh! Whoosh! Whoosh!

Three more ferocious blows struck in succession on different places on her body. She felt the pain, but she had no sense of its anatomical location. Mykel felt warm liquid spreading down her side beneath her robe. She flinched and moaned, realizing one of her ribs was poking through her skin. She couldn't survive another blow.

The next sound she heard from behind the attacker was a loud boom that exploded in the air and jarred her pain-numbed brain. There was a desperate cry from her attacker, or was it her own voice? Her body floated, rising with arms spread wide. She vaguely heard voices beckoning and beseeching her. Mykel felt an unbearable, stabbing pain mixed with the cooling tile floor that soothed her hot face.

Rest—she just needed a moment to rest. So tired. Her eyes closed. She was no longer afraid.

CHAPTER 84

McNally grabbed Butler's arm and flung his unconscious body back into the bedroom. His heart raced as he reentered the bathroom and kneeled beside her. She was still alive, but her breathing was shallow, labored. Gently, he wiped a silken wisp of hair away from her face and spoke soothingly in her ear. Before he left the Marshfield estate, he radioed for backup, and now the hallway was filled with uniformed police officers. He heard sirens in the distance. He surveyed the damage to her body and then closed her robe, folding and laying his jacket under her head.

"Mykel, I'm so sorry… Hold on my love, please," he whispered in her ear as he remained kneeling over her. "He will never hurt you again." He tenderly stroked her bruised cheek with his hand.

A uniformed officer entered the room, and McNally overheard him tell Petrocelli that an ambulance was on its way. McNally placed a gentle kiss on Mykel's tearstained cheek and stood. He walked over to where Petrocelli held a gun over Butler's unconscious body and raised his own weapon, pointing it at Butler's head.

"Kyle, don't," Petrocelli said. "That won't help her. He's never going to have a chance to hurt anyone again. Don't do this, man!" Petrocelli stepped in front of Butler and placed his hand on McNally's wrist. "Please, Mac. Think about it."

Conflicting emotions tormented him. His hatred for the man lying on the floor was all-consuming, but it was over now. Finally, over. McNally lowered his gun and held it at his side and returned to Mykel. He would stay with her until the ambulance came.

"How's she doing?" Petrocelli asked.

McNally didn't take his eyes off her face. "I think she'll be all right. I can't tell if all of this blood is hers or some of his, but she's lost a lot of blood."

Petrocelli put his hand on McNally's shoulder. "We got here in time. She'll be okay."

"That bastard almost won."

"Don't even think about it."

"What about him? Still breathing?" McNally asked, nodding toward the other room.

"He'll live," Petrocelli said. "But he ain't gonna be pretty."

"I thought the uniform watching the house would be enough."

"You had no reason to think Butler could get to her," Petrocelli said, trying his best to sound convincing. "The cop watching the place will have one hell of a headache, but he'll live. Nobody figured it. But we got here in time, and that's what matters."

The paramedics arrived and prepped Mykel for transport to the hospital. They lifted her on to the gurney, and she moaned but didn't wake. McNally moved to stand over Butler. He looked at the damage Mykel had done. As he stared at the gaping, bloody hole in Butler's cheek, he thought the bullet wound in his shoulder would heal, but thanks to Mykel, there was no way to fix the disfigurement to his face. The severed muscle and surrounding tissue hung from a jagged three-inch hole in his cheek.

A shadow fell over his eyes as he recalled Mykel's account of the heinous monster she described from her nightmares. Butler's face fit her picture of him now. He was hideous to look at. He resisted the urge to smash his foot into that face in a parting shot.

CHAPTER 85

Kyle arrived at the University Hospital half an hour before visiting hours began. Mykel's wounds were healing well, and the concussion she suffered would cause no long-term damage. For a week, she had clung to life tenaciously. Her first smile lit up the room; her first words filled him with joy. At that moment, he knew the time had come to start living again—and not alone. Quietly reassuring himself, he touched the pocket that held the two plane tickets to Hawaii. He was really going to do this... It was right to do so. He could commit unreservedly to this woman.

During the weeks that followed, Mykel convalesced, and for the first time in his career, he found himself questioning what direction he wanted to take as both a professional and as a man. His life was about to take a new turn, and he knew he wanted Mykel to be there with him. This would be their fresh start. They had talked most of the week, and she told him she wanted the same things he did, starting with spending a lot of time getting to know each other.

On the immediate horizon, they had time to take off, weeks of saved leave. Right now, the only important thing was to get her well and take long walks along deserted beaches, feeling the warm sand beneath their feet and the sun shining on their faces.

EPILOGUE

Dr. Oliver Sharpe, a psychiatrist for the criminally insane, entered the interview room and set down the thick red three-ring binder on the conference-sized table across from his patient. It had become the doctor's habit before any session with a patient to walk across the room and admire the beauty of the view from the windows. It always served to calm him before a session.

Through the wire mesh security gate over the window, he saw that the well-maintained green lawns had lost none of their beauty on this unseasonably hot September afternoon. To his right, giant red maples circled a large koi pond. Benches for sitting and paths for strolling along the grounds provided a serene place for visitors and their family members who'd come to the hospital.

More relaxed now, the doctor seated himself in the chair across from his patient, opened the binder, and wrote "Francis Butler" at the top of the day's calendar. At the opposite end of the table and hidden from direct sunlight, he could barely make out the face of the broken man whose head rested on his hands, which were splayed on the cold Formica table. From beneath distended brows, dead glassy eyes leered back at him.

Dr. Sharpe had memorized the original diagnosis and shook his head in frustration. Klinefelter's syndrome is a genetic condition that affected one in every six hundred births and was predominant in males. The child was born with a second copy of the X chromosome rather than the single normal X and Y only. Small testes, enlarged

343

breasts, and reduced facial and body hair were classic symptoms. After the physical abnormalities appeared anywhere from age five to fifteen, they tested for and often diagnosed with azoospermia, which was a failure of normal sperm production. Even more rare, and further complicating the patient's physiology, was an underdeveloped penis, known medically as a micropenis. It was not uncommon for men with this affliction to suffer from low self-esteem and depression.

If Francis Butler had received proper counseling before the symptoms escalated, it might have averted some of the severe psychological outcomes. The doctor understood the consequences of prepubescent neglect. Untreated, the emotional spillover became far more devastating than the initial diagnosis. A sociopath was the frequent outcome of these collective issues. Butler's history revealed years of abuse and ridicule from his peers, teachers, and even (the doctor had learned) family.

He fanned through the pages of the report, reviewing Francis Butler's early history. The notes from Dr. Michael Cunningham, Butler's pediatrician, were clear and concise. After diagnosing his nine-year-old patient's condition, he recommended professional counseling to help the child overcome his affliction as he matured. Sharpe reread the final entry in Cunningham's file.

"The patient, Francis Butler, has become distant and withdrawn over the past year. I suspect a malady more disturbing than the plethora of physical symptoms themselves. There are telltale signs of neglect or abuse. I have spoken with the father, his sole living parent, to recommend further psychiatric counseling. To date, I've seen no affirmation of any further counseling."

Nothing in the reports told Sharpe that Butler had any counseling until his enrollment into a military academy at age thirteen. After several reported incidents of unexplained erratic behavior, Dr. Ruben Carston, the academy's staff psychiatrist, had evaluated him. He reported, "All attempts at counseling have failed to reveal the source of this patient's hidden rage. In my opinion, he has the capacity for extreme violence but conceals it behind a calm, lucid exterior. I recommended that Francis Butler be removed from the academy and enrolled in an institution that will provide immediate psychotherapy. The guardian, his aunt, has since removed the cadet from our academy."

Camouflaged by the shifting light and shadows in the room, Sharpe couldn't clearly read the expression on his patient's face. Inwardly, he cringed at the evil he knew existed behind that lashless stare. The sound of his patient's raspy, uneven breathing rose and fell, the only sounds in an otherwise silent room.

Butler looked up, showing his deformed face. The plastic surgeon at County Memorial had mended the muscle and torn tissue, but the muscular damage had been extensive and left him with an obscene permanent disfigurement. What used to be a whole face bore a lifeless sag on the left side, below the cheek. His eye drooped, and his mouth curled down, manifesting itself into a permanent, unalterable snarl. The wide puckered scar was thick and rippled, beginning below his eye and extending down the length of his face to the corner of his limp, contorted mouth.

As he sat in the low-lit room, the doctor fidgeted in his chair. "Would you like to talk with me today, Francis?"

Dr. Sharp felt uneasy, his feelings exacerbated by his patient's reticence and his obvious aversion to the light. Since Butler's arrival at the institution three months ago, he hadn't spoken. Under normal conditions, that would have been fine with Sharpe. Once he got past the man's repulsive disfigurement, scientifically he was a marvelous specimen.

Sharpe wanted to find the key to unlocking the door to his twisted psyche. He folded his hands and rested them on the file again. "Perhaps you'd begin by telling me about your aunt."

Silence.

From his first examination, Dr. Sharpe had insisted Butler arrive at his sessions in restraints. Any pretense of normalcy he possessed disappeared after his incarceration on the Marshfield estate. He'd read the police case file and saw the evolutionary stages of a depressed sociopath who'd descended into clinical insanity and had considered diagnostic techniques, including electroshock therapy and psychotropic-assisted hypnosis. He'd have to study its application before testing it with someone as volatile as Francis Butler.

Discouraged by the continuing silence in the room, Sharpe glanced at his watch and reached for the button under the table to order the attendants to take Butler back to his cell. He stopped, detecting a faint sound that disturbed the silence. At first, he thought Butler might be attempting to speak, and Sharpe grew excited. He listened and stared at the shadowy visage at the other end of the table. Slowly, he realized that the sounds he heard were gibberish. They weren't words. Rather, they were disjointed noises mingled with fluctuating vocal pitches. They were brief short spurts, low and grating, from deep within his throat.

A cloud passing outside had blocked the sunlight, obliterating all light in the room.

Dr. Oliver Sharpe's heart beat faster, and he began to experience panic. In another moment, he recognized the sounds that almost seemed to originate from somewhere behind his patient. His whole body shuddered violently. His fingers groped beneath the table for the silent alarm to summon the attendants. Though the hoarse, labored gurgles escaping from Francis Butler's throat had no discernable pattern, there was no mistaking them now. The sounds were undeniably those of morbid, sinister laughter.

ABOUT THE AUTHOR

 M. Brooke McCullough was born in Seattle, Washington, and grew up in LaGrange, Illinois. During her teen years, she developed a love of reading, starting with the Nancy Drew mystery books, and later became an avid fan of the entire detective/crime genre. In preparing to write this story, two things were clear: it would be about a detective, and must take place in Chicago. Early in 1992, she committed to writing her first novel and began putting pen to paper. Her lengthy career with the Secret Service and federal court system afforded her many insights into criminal behavior and motivation, which she relied on to create the Canarytown story. McCullough is currently planning for the next Kyle McNally detective story.

CPSIA information can be obtained
at www.ICGtesting.com
Printed in the USA
FSHW010324170321
79523FS

9 781662 405389